THE ONLY MIND
WORTH HAVING

THE ONLY MIND
WORTH HAVING
Thomas Merton and the Child Mind

Fiona Gardner

Foreword by Rowan Williams

CASCADE *Books* • Eugene, Oregon

THE ONLY MIND WORTH HAVING
Thomas Merton and the Child Mind

Cascade Books
An Imprint of Wipf and Stock Publishers
199 W. 8th Ave., Suite 3
Eugene, OR 97401

www.wipfandstock.com

ISBN 13: 978–1–4982–3022–3

Cataloging-in-Publication data:

Gardner, Fiona

    The only mind worth having : Thomas Merton and the child mind / Fiona
Gardner.

    xiv + 228 p. ; 23 cm. —Includes bibliographical references and index.

    ISBN 13: 978—1—4982—3022-3

    1. Children—Religious life. 2. Merton, Thomas, 1915–1968. 3. Spirituality. I.
Title.

BL625.5 G25 2015

Manufactured in the U.S.A.   11/06/2015

For Lara and Frankie

"Truly I tell you, unless you change and become like children, you will never enter the kingdom of heaven."

—Matthew 18:3

"I . . . ask the Lord to give you every blessing and joy and to keep ever fresh and young your 'child's mind' which is the only one worth having."

—Thomas Merton, *The Hidden Ground of Love*, 614

Contents

Foreword

BY ROWAN WILLIAMS

Becoming a child again: the first reaction may be a feeling that this would be wonderful—no responsibility, no battling with expectations, no long memories of failure and ambiguity. But when Jesus of Nazareth tells us to become like children, and when spiritual masters urge us to connect with the "child mind," they are not being nostalgic or sentimental. They are drawing our attention to something we all instinctively recognise. There is something that our habitual adult consciousness has lost or buried, and it must be found, not as a comforting reinstatement of half-forgotten happiness but as a breakthrough to a new mind. When we were children we did not know we possessed it; now we must drop everything in order to find it.

Talking about this is full of paradoxes. Often when I think about "rediscovering" the child's condition, what I'm really longing for is for me, the present adult me, to have some agreeable experiences of the kind I vaguely remember from my early years. Many people use a wide variety of techniques to attain this goal. But it is not the same, because it is a self-conscious quest for another satisfying experience. The true mind of the child is found in an emptying out of the self that collects nice experiences. The child mind is simply the mind that inhabits where and who and what it is, that lives in the world without the shadows of craving and fear and self-objectifying.

In this humanly accessible and often moving book, we see how one of the great spiritual guides of our age gradually clarifies his understanding of this journey towards the present moment of inhabiting the place where life is happening. Merton does this through his contemplative discipline, but also through his imaginative writing, especially his poems, and in his courageous exploration of other religious frameworks such as Buddhism.

Fiona Gardner shows how he delineates the process of coming to recognise the call to inhabit the moment and the place, and in so doing gently guides us to begin the same journey—without sentimentality or backward-looking yeaning for a golden age. Merton is presented to us in this book as a fierce critic of all the cultural falsehoods that keep the gulf between my treasured ego and my true "place" so deep and apparently impassable. He repeatedly invites us to see the "adult" judgements we make—about politics and society, about religion and psychology—as both childish and hostile to real childlikeness. He invites us to that home which (as St Augustine famously says) does not fall down when we are away, the home that is the simple present actuality where God lives and acts. And Fiona Gardner opens up the demands and promises of this journey with sensitivity, warmth and candour, challenging us to believe that we can after all learn to be where we are and "know the place for the first time."

Acknowledgments

Thank you to Christine M. Bochen for her positive feedback to a conference paper I gave on the subject of the child mind in 2013. I would like to give my appreciation to Robert Hamma for his helpful comments on an earlier version of this book. I am always grateful to Paul Pearson for his advice and support. Thank you very much to Hugh Gee for his invaluable insights and his understanding especially on Jung's thinking on the transcendent function. I am extremely grateful to Rowan Williams for writing the foreword to this book.

Colleagues and friends in the Thomas Merton Society of Great Britain and Ireland and in the International Thomas Merton Society constantly provide inspiration and a sense of community—so thank you.

A huge thank you to my husband Peter Ellis both for his loving support over the writing of this book and for his professional skills in copy editing, proof reading, and compiling the index.

This book is dedicated to my wonderful granddaughters. I hope one day they will find this of some interest and that part of them as they grow up will remain forever young.

Copyright Permissions

Several of the chapters that follow contain material by the author previously pub-lished as lectures or articles; they have been substantially rethought and expanded for this study. I acknowledge permission to quote from the following earlier publications:

"'A Tremendous Experience': The Influence of St. Thérèse of Lisieux on the Spiritu-ality of Thomas Merton." In *The Merton Seasonal* 37.4 (Winter 2012) 11–18.

"Thomas Merton and the Concept of the Child-Mind: 'The Only One Worth Hav-ing.'" In *The Merton Annual* 26 (2013) 157–67.

"Merton and Zilboorg." In *The Merton Journal* 11.1 (2004) 6–12.

I

Introduction to Jesus' Command, to Thomas Merton, and to Ideas about the Spirit of the Child

In three of the four gospels Jesus commands those wanting to follow him to change, to receive his teachings and experience discipleship as a young child:

> Truly I tell you, unless you change and become like children, you will never enter the kingdom of heaven. (Matt 18:3)

> Truly I tell you, whoever does not receive the kingdom of heaven as a little child will never enter it. (Mark 10:15; the exact same words are repeated in Luke 18:17)

What did Jesus mean by his statement to become like children—or the "little children" of Mark and Luke? What does it really mean to become as a small child when you are an adult and now in this secular twenty-first century? Is it only possible to become as a small child and so receive the kingdom of heaven when you are weak, ill, or vulnerable or could we choose to search for it? Is it possible to find a spiritual practice that encourages this without becoming sentimental and mawkish, or regressive and pathological in some way? How can this be understood as part of our contemporary spirituality? Is it just about being immature or is it in some mysterious and paradoxical way the path towards spiritual maturity?

Although the gospel words are regularly read and widely known, certainly amongst Christians, the command is so counter-cultural and so personally challenging that perhaps there is often only a superficial sense of what it might really mean. Most grown-ups feel that they have left childhood far behind and for anyone who has struggled to escape from the long

1

shadow that a difficult childhood can cast over adult life anything that might seem like a form of regression is anticipated as a potential danger zone. Yet all grown-ups, including theologians, carry within them both the child they were and memories of childhood; these can be happy or sad or, as for most people, a bit of a mixture.

Alongside this there can be often also a feeling of shame when childish thoughts or feelings belonging to the past suddenly re-emerge. This may be especially so around belief, or worship and the personal relationship with God. Perhaps it feels we have to be very grown up and reasonable and rational with God, so what is judged as childish emotions have to be suppressed or disowned. However, perhaps when particularly weak and susceptible, the illusion of adulthood seems to melt away and we are left turning to God stripped of our usual defences. In such moments we can feel quite small and vulnerable and this is often an uncomfortable and an unwanted feeling.

"Unless you change and become like children"—Jesus' command in Matthew is quite clearly about a process of disruption and development. None of us like to change as it means breaking up what seems to be familiar and predictable—even if one is stuck in a place that is not particularly helpful or comfortable. There is always a resistance to interrupting what we usually do and who we usually see ourselves as; there is often apprehension of what a change might lead to. "Become" means to begin to be, to come into existence, to change and to grow, to develop into. It is a word that describes movement and a process. It is about potential, it seems to be about moving forward, but in the context of becoming a small child it is also paradoxical. It then seems to be a backward step and a contradiction to become something that we have already once been.

The poet Czeslaw Milosz wrote: "The child who dwells inside us trusts that there are wise men somewhere who know the truth,"[1] and it is here that Thomas Merton can be of real help. The Trappist monk and writer Thomas Merton (1915–1968) has been an inspiration and influence to many. The centenary of his birth—he was born 31 January 1915—has given another opportunity to reconsider his legacy and welcome his often unconventional and penetrating insights. He was born in France and spent part of his youth in England before settling in the United States. He became a monk based in the Abbey of Gethsemani, in Kentucky, North America for twenty-seven years, and was a prolific writer and a poet. He wrote over seventy books including volumes of journals, poetry, and spiritual writing, as well as about 250 essays on all sorts of issues including peace, social justice, and inter-religious dialogue. He also wrote at a conservative estimate at least

1. Heaney, "Door Stands Open," xv.

10,000 letters to around 2,100 correspondents. The probable number is much higher. Correspondents included many who sought spiritual advice and guidance from someone whom they recognized as having struggled to make sense of life and to find God.

Thomas Merton has been called a theologian of experience as he wrote about his own life experiences, his environment, and the world in all its complexities. In that sense he is an experience-near as distinct from an experience-distant writer and thinker. He thought and wrote about what he personally knew and about what had affected him. He carried as an adult the child that he once was and he wrote about his childhood in an early autobiography. This account will be explored in a later chapter. He also wrote about something that he called the child mind. This book is in part an exploration of what he may have meant by that term. In his writings about his life and his spiritual insights he sometimes used the term "child mind"—as in the quote at the start of this book—to describe a way of being with God. Indeed he thought that it was the real way to be with God—it was the only mind worth having.

Both spiritual and psychological insights can be helpful here, and it is possible to use ideas from both as a way to understand what Merton might have meant and beyond that to illuminate that most enigmatic of commands from Jesus: "Unless you change and become like children." It is a command and a direct piece of guidance from Jesus and yet also a concept that becomes cluttered, confused, and resisted by our own experiences of childhood, our ambivalent experiences around children, and the societal views of what and how children are or even should be.

The command is enriching and surprising, and as my understanding of what it might mean has deepened so I appreciate that it is less about the clinging and neediness of an actual infant—though dependency plays a part; nor is it only about accepting a sense of humility, loss of status, and powerlessness—though that is another aspect. It is not about returning or regressing in a pathological way to one's own past, though some elements may be relevant. It is not about sentimentality or a stereotyped view of innocence, and it is not about pretending to be simple or simple-minded. It is not about denying or decrying adulthood. What it is about is the adult mind uncovering, discovering, recognizing, and then integrating the eternal child—the Christ child—who is present and within the psyche of everyone.

The central suggestion in this book is that as he matured spiritually Thomas Merton came to embody the spirit of the child and that he is the ideal spiritual guide who can help to illuminate this process and the command—"Unless you become . . ." There is no specific work in which Merton wrote on this—rather he lived it, and it is the becoming and the living of it that shines through in his writings and that can provide inspiration. It is worth noting that if you look in the index of any of the published volumes of his journal, there is only one reference to the word "child" or "children." This reference though is absolutely central to Merton's life and work; this is about what it might mean to become a child of God.

> To say I am a child of God is to say, before everything else, that I grow. That I begin . . . The idea "Child of God" is therefore one of living growth, becoming, possibility, risk, and joy in the negotiation of risk. In this God is pleased; that His child grows in wisdom and grace.[2]

Thomas Merton's spiritual journey, from the time before he entered the monastery and including his many years there, was a journey to become the person that God intended him to be. He wrote about recovering the promise of childhood spirituality as he described what happened to his sense of self during contemplative prayer. He wrote about a way of being alive, and he thought that as adults this state of mind, when it happened, brought us spiritual wisdom and led to maturity. He understood this as paradox, an apparent contradiction but a contradiction that was worth exploring both from a psychological and spiritual perspective.

For Merton the spirit of the child found in the child mind was above all about a lack of self-consciousness; for him this was a process of letting go of the self or the disguise that we present to the world. He called this the false self, an idea discussed later in the book. It involves a process of renewal, almost a re-emergence of another more genuine part of our selves, which he called the true self. In Merton's experience the child mind also involved a journey towards a simplicity, trust, and openness in the adult relationship with God. Although as an adult Merton was clearly an independent person he was always open to God and Merton's ongoing cycle of conversion and renewal inevitably brought increased closeness to God—what I later refer to as a state of being-in-dependence with God. Thomas Merton understood that this was a state of being-in-dependence with Being. It was not about a sentimental nostalgia for an idealized time in his childhood, nor about psychological collapse into pretend babyhood. Instead it was about recapturing qualities of attentiveness and receptivity. It was about being awake to connections and the life force within all creation. It was therefore about a change of consciousness, or rather a return as an adult to an earlier state

---

2. Merton, *Dancing in the Water,* 334.

of consciousness that is actually known to everyone from infancy. Thomas Merton thought that this restoration essentially came about through contemplation.

As in contemplation, this developing consciousness is about being totally present to the moment and is something that each of us already has experienced when very small. It involves times when thinking is minimized, and when the focus on God excludes some of our usual self-consciousness. It is in other words a state where, even if only for a second, we are preoccupied with and absorbed in God. Many of the other writers, whose thinking and experiences are also included in this book, would agree with Merton that this can be approached through the stilling of the mind in contemplative prayer. For contemplation brings with it a change of consciousness. Gradually in the silence old preconceptions and ways of being can begin to loosen and a different way of relating both to God and to ourselves becomes apparent. This in turn affects how we are with others and how we are towards creation and the environment.

Contemplation can, over time, bring us to an appreciation that all is connected, and all is held in creation by the merciful God. Merton wrote extensively about contemplation and believed that it is the way in which each person can let go of the false self—the mask or disguise that we carry—and come to know the true self. In this book one of the suggestions is that this true self, present in each of us, is the child mind. It is the spirit of the child, where we can recover the promise of a childhood spirituality we have all once known, a spirituality that can be returned to without dismissing what we have become.

It is suggested that within each person is the early mysticism known to every small child—a state of heightened experience and amazement. This amazement is about wonder and can also include fear. It can lead to a remarkable and seemingly firm certainty of oneness and connection within the world. This childhood mysticism becomes buried in the journey to adulthood and the reasons for this are explored in the book. Yet the feelings linger somewhere within the psyche and it is seen as "something that shines into the childhood of all and in which no one has yet been: homeland."[3]

Edward Bouverie Pusey, the nineteenth-century Tractarian, thought that the words of a child spoke greater truth than they (the child) knew; they had a glimmering of the truth though they could not grasp it.

> And yet they hear it will rightly wonder at it, and they who understand it better than the child itself, will yet confess that they could not have uttered it so simply and so forcibly. . . . It comes

3. Bloch, *Principle of Hope*, 1376.

> not from the child itself, but from a power within it; they are in
> truth the words of God, in the mouth of the little one, so lately
> come from its Maker's hand.[4]

As adults there can be such moments of re-experiencing deep connections where we forget our everyday self, and where we return to an earlier
simplicity. It could be seen that we join with the presence of the eternal child
deep within each one of us. It can be a moment of grace through which each
can be renewed, a moment of rebirth. At that moment we reconnect with
the true self and the experience of God. Merton, in a much quoted passage,
wrote about contemplation as the experience of God's life and presence
within us "as the transcendent source of our own subjectivity."[5] In other
words we lose the separation between ourselves and Divinity—the connection that is obscured as we grow older.

It is ironical that the qualities belonging to childhood spirituality can
only be re-experienced once we are grown up, through our adult consciousness. Inevitably this will at some point include thinking about them. This
then leads to the definition about the central idea of this book which is that
an understanding of the promise of the spirit of the child can be interwoven
through adult experience and from this integration a third position becomes possible. This is the synthesis of the two apparently opposite states of
mind and this third position is what Thomas Merton called the child mind.

The book takes the reader on a journey exploring the process of reaching this synthesis—the process of "becoming." The book is divided into
three parts. The first part—chapters 2 to 6—is essentially about understanding. These chapters explore the basic elements involved in the child mind
and the different perspectives used in the book. Thus chapter 2 looks at what
it means to be an infant and what the infant makes of the world. Here and
throughout the book insights from poets have proved illuminating, and so
their reflections on innocence and the lack of self-consciousness found in
small children are included. The mysterious state of childhood, as seen by
such poets, has been fruitfully explored by psychoanalysts and analytical
psychologists in particular Carl Jung. The terminology used by Jung and
others, and the basic ideas, are explained. As the mind of the small child
begins to respond to their environment there is a developing sense of self—
and it is the child's sense of "me" and what that might mean that is particularly important. These insights are then contrasted with those about how the
child's state of mind can effect later religious belief and our relationship with
God. Jesus' command to become as a small child lies at the heart of the book

4. Allchin, *Joy of all Creation*, 151–52.

5. Merton, *New Man*, 19.

and so it is useful to explore again Jesus' interactions both with children and with his adult disciples. In both the psychoanalytic and the religious view of the child mind the theme of the original "me" prior to the formation processes from the society the child is born into is of crucial significance.

Chapter 3 explores the paradoxical idea of God as parent and God as child. Understanding psychoanalytic ideas about the unconscious and the relationship between conscious and unconscious thought has a bearing on our relationship with God especially in our society where negative feelings tend to be repressed. How the infant attaches to the parent early on often dominates the later life of the adult albeit in an unconscious way. Bringing these insights from the unconscious into the light can fundamentally alter conventional views. However it is fascinating to see that in considering God as parent some of the experiences of saints and mystics such as Catherine of Siena and Meister Eckhart are comparable with modern analytical insights. They describe the need to become open, vulnerable, and thereby dependent. The maternal imagery used by Cistercian monastics and the specific visions of Julian of Norwich guide us to thinking of God as mother opening up the whole question of the gender of the person one is dependent on and so the nature of the dependent person's response. But there is also in Christianity a profound relationship with God as a child. Thinking in this way, the incarnation and the fellowship of the crib offer deep connections to the potential spirit of the child within the adult. Of particular importance is the exemplar of Mary. It is possible to think in terms of the eternal child—the Christ child—being already within us as is witnessed by many such insights by saints and mystics.

Having looked at some of this background material, in chapter 4 I bring Thomas Merton more sharply into focus especially looking at the influence on his monastic thinking on the spiritual maturity of the child mind. Bernard of Clairvaux and Guerric of Igny were both twelfth-century Cistercians whose writings Merton studied intensely and whose thinking he shared in his teaching of the novices at the Abbey of Gethsemani. Both Bernard of Clairvaux and Guerric of Igny proposed that childlikeness is linked with simplicity and humility. This was taken further by Nicholas of Cusa who developed the paradoxical view of "learned ignorance," which is a central tenet of this book. Another influence on Thomas Merton was Franciscan spirituality with which Merton was initially directly involved with and later, after becoming a Cistercian, continued to explore. From the recent past Thérèse of Lisieux had a great influence on Merton and his vocation as a monastic. Her "little way" of spiritual childhood is again an important contribution to the ideas of this book. All the material discussed so far can be seen under the rubric of Jesus' command to become as little children. The chapter ends with a brief overview of some of its theological interpretations.

In chapter 5 the perspective widens to move away from Christianity and to look at the contribution of Eastern teachings to Thomas Merton's understanding of the child mind. As elsewhere in Part 1 the approach is informative and intended as an aid to understanding. The idea of the child mind as an authentic experience across spiritual traditions is thus of major importance occurring in Aldous Huxley's perennial philosophy and in other writers outside the Christian tradition. For Merton, and for the purposes of this book, the correspondence between John Wu and Merton is especially illuminating, as is Merton's exploration and comments on Taoist texts. Merton had a deep connection with Zen as a way of "emptying out" the mind and arriving at a state of "spiritual poverty," which has a connection with Zen teachings on the child mind.

Chapter 6, the final chapter in Part 1, discusses the move away from the experience of childhood spirituality into the adult life of care. This process of growing up and taking responsibility can produce a two-dimensional personality. The terms "shadow" and "disguise" are considered from both a spiritual and psychological perspective, thus helping in our understanding of the development of the false self. The adult life of care obscures the image of God within the person but Jesus' command to return to become like a small child goes against all the prejudices that are built in to the adult personality. Thomas Merton was well aware of the numbing of our lives through the life of care as is illustrated by one of his talks as novice master. Merton also addressed the seduction and dangerous limitations of materialism and technology and looking at his views here helps our understanding of how early experiences can become clouded and dulled.

The second part of the book, chapters 7 to 10, is about the process of re-finding the spirit of the child. This section looks at practical ways of orienting the adult mind to re-enter the mind of the child. Informed by the material in Part 1 intended for understanding, Part 2 enters more fully into the voyage of becoming. Chapter 7 is an exploration of the sense of an enchanted world of childhood. This is the world we grow out of as cultural and social norms take over, making us capable of playing designated roles in the world, but, at the same time, carrying a sense of disenchantment. The archetypal memory of enchantment is sometimes deeply buried; we retain traces of the associated sense of mystery somewhere in the adult psyche. This is the thread we need to follow on the path of re-finding. The memory of enchantment is present in myths and legends and also in accounts of personal experiences of revisiting childhood memories of the world's appearance. Thomas Merton suggests that we have a vocation from God to expand these glimpses of enchantment and to choose a different way of looking at things as adults specifically to see them as enchanted images of God's creation. For some this can be a moment of actual willed decision, for others there is a mystical aspect accompanied by a moment of revelation.

Chapter 8 confronts the great obstacle in the way of re-finding aspects of one's childhood: the legacy of a damaged upbringing. All of us carry childhood wounds but in some cases there is major trauma. This can have a negative effect on any possibility of recovering a child-like relationship with God based on simplicity, trust, and dependence. Childhood experiences can be carried by the child and later adult as personal secrets remaining undiscussed. Deep damage can be caused—the term "soul murder" has been used in the darkest cases. It is impossible to discuss the child mind without acknowledging the terrible experiences of some children. Once again Thomas Merton acts as our example and his disturbed upbringing characterized by loss, loneliness, and uncertainty illustrates many of the difficulties in developing a spiritual life from childhood suffering. Despite these difficulties it is apparent that the spirit of the child can still survive, albeit hidden and secret.

Chapter 9 looks at three different but interconnected ways that enable healing of early childhood trauma. One is the idea of grace occurring as an entirely unforeseen divine breakthrough. This is where grace builds on the natural world and on a person's life experiences to allow healing to take place. The numerous scripture stories of this are well known but there are also extraordinary personal accounts of the intervention of grace. A second form of healing can come from spiritual direction. Here a person can be helped to face past pain and begin to reveal their inmost self, using methods derived from longstanding traditions where spiritual exercises and practices have been developed. The third way is the more modern process of psychotherapy. Although this differs from spiritual direction in many aspects both methods share the idea of a personal interaction between two people where the director/therapist role is not judgmental or one of superiority. Thomas Merton experienced psychological healing through the structure of his monastic life as well as through actual encounters with secular therapy.

To complete Part 2, chapter 10 invites us as adults to find again glimpses of paradise. One way of beginning to do this is through the spiritual practice of really looking and minimising conceptual thought. Working on being aware can change one's consciousness and lead to new ways of seeing. The resulting transformation can feel like a rebirth and is indeed a route toward the child mind. People's experiences of a different level of consciousness through such a transformation have been seen as an entry into a golden world following a golden string connecting us with paradise.

This connecting string is not outside ourselves but already lies deep within each person. We are aware of it as a nostalgic longing to return to paradise.

Part 3 comprises chapters 11 to 15 and moves on to the process of becoming. The emphasis shifts away from the person's understanding the child mind concept (Part 1) and re-finding it (Part 2), and turns to centering attention on the enchanted world itself. Chapter 11 looks at our innate attraction to movement as part of the cosmic dance and how we are invited to join in and feel our connection and interdependence as part of all creation. The love of creation and the recognition of the divine spark in nature are part of a heightened consciousness where all can be seen as sacramental. This brings the adult back to the experiences of children and to nature mysticism, aspects that poetry seems to have a special ability to explore. Recapturing that original vision cannot but lead us to ecological compassion and to a deepening of our connection with all living things. Thomas Merton's environmental awareness gradually emerged as he became more attuned with nature and this led to his being an early critic of our destruction of the environment.

Chapter 12 picks up the theme of poetry from the last chapter. In poetry words are refined in simplicity and so can be seen as forming the ideal language of the child mind. The poet as the paradise-hearer can cut through the shadow and the disguise of the reader or listener by reaching to the heart of the subject. Some poets have written directly about innocence and experience, both those who felt that only innocence should prevail and those who understood the importance of adult experience in reaching a synthesis of innocence and experience and hence moving to a different dimension. William Blake is the great example of the latter and his longer poems work out his ideas on what he called "organized innocence." Blake himself came to live a creative life very close to Jesus' command to change and become like a child. Interestingly Merton wrote an MA thesis on Blake before entering the monastery and never left his sphere of influence as is especially notable in his own late "antipoetry"—an expression of the language of infancy by an adult.

Chapter 13 brings us to the core activity of the child: play. The child's playing is fundamentally an exploration of creativity and of the power of the imagination. Yet this is one of the principal areas that alter as childhood is left behind. Analysis of the child at play has revealed an extraordinary process whereby the infant imaginatively endows objects—described by one psychotherapist as transitional objects—with the power to bridge the gap between themselves and the world. There is no great step from this idea to the sense that the adult concept of God occupies this transitional space and that God can be met through play. Creativity is a way of connecting with

God and breaking through to eternity and the connection can happen if we recover the idea of developing a transitional space to allow creativity and the imagination to flourish and where we can play with a playful God.

Chapter 14 explores the internal landscape of the child mind. It looks at the question of how this mind, the one that Merton thought was the only one worth having, might be characterized. Here our notions of who we are begin to deconstruct themselves. Our self, our identity and what we call "I" are all brought into question. When the self becomes problematic and capable of being challenged it is possible to think of positive ways of detaching those parts of our self that obscure our vision of God. The painful process of separating out the false and the true self is at the core of the process of becoming. It is not a process that is undertaken in isolation but one that occurs in relationship and in the world as it is. The movement to the child mind is away from independence—the initial goal of growing up—to dependence on others, on the world and on God. Thomas Merton and other writers offer us models and guidelines of the child mind way of being as lying beyond words and discursive thinking in a realm dominated by the mystery of the return to God.

The last chapter, chapter 15, explores three epiphanies of the child mind in depth. These are all taken from Thomas Merton's own experiences at different stages in his life and are used to help illustrate the central suggestions covered in the book. The first comes from the time of Merton's ordination as priest in the monastery and turned on his experience of the Mass. The second occurred at a street corner in Louisville when Merton saw that everyone was walking around luminous with God's love and so shining like the sun. The last came just over a week before his death and took place at the feet of the great carved Buddhas at Polonnaruwa in Sri Lanka. All three act as a summing up of one person's experience of the child mind that is open to all of us.

The final Afterword in the book concludes this exploration of Jesus' command—"unless you become as a small child"—and what it might mean to experience the child mind as the only mind worth having.

PART ONE

UNDERSTANDING

2

Infancy and Rebirth

What does it mean to be an infant?

See, everything has become new! (2 Cor 5:17b)

For the small child everything is of interest and natural. He or she enters into the world that surrounds them with great energy. In one sense there are few boundaries and so the child imbues everything with equal interest. "He enters into the world of things with all his senses . . . everything is alive, full of eyes and ears . . . the child is initiated into the secret life of ordinary objects, often the most miniscule."[1] The tiny details matter and there can be either a pleasurable rapturous immersion or the opposite—great desolation.

It has been said that the adult is prefigured in the child and for some adults the child is consciously recognized as remaining ever present in them. This experience of intertwined time is often found in poets who tend to keep their inner child alive and so best remember and understand this. For example, the poet Rainer Maria Rilke in his writing made a conscious and assiduous effort to "carry out" or "realize" his childhood once again, though later he was to judge his efforts "abortive" as somehow in his writing his adult creativity took over by creating specific characters that blurred his childhood.[2] Some psychoanalysts and therapists also have much to say that is helpful, both from their observations of babies and from work with regressed adults. When we are small children we lack the self-consciousness to observe our state of mind, but vestiges of our experiences can act as

1. Eiland, "Foreword," xiv.
2. Szondi, "Hope in the Past," 8.

reminders, and, indeed, can return to inspire and comfort, or to haunt and inhibit us, long into adulthood.

The poet William Wordsworth describes infancy as a mysterious state where we are still held by and in divinity. The majesty of God is proclaimed: "Out of the mouths of infants and children" (Ps 8:2a). This is no superficial sentimentality but a deep connection to the source of life. The seventeenth-century poet Henry Vaughan, a poet who really "caught hold of Thomas Merton,"[3] writes in "Childe-hood" of how he longed to reach that state again:

> . . . my striving eye
> Dazzles at it, as at eternity . . .
> Quickly would I make my path ev'n
> And by mere playing go to heaven . . .
> Since all that age doth teach is ill,
> Why should I not love childhood still?[4]

Vaughan realized such a state lasts a very short time as we begin to respond to our environment and react to those who take care of us. One of the characteristics of infants is that they are often seen, especially in the spiritual sense, as innocent. This can carry the weight of later adult projections about sin and judgment. Therefore it is perhaps more helpful to remember that the Latin root of the word "innocent" means "not wounded" in the sense that the world has not yet caused damage.

This move from a state of innocence, as the Franciscan Richard Rohr has points out, has nothing to do with moral right or wrong, it happens to all of us one way or another. In this way it is an archetypal image, in other words a typical pattern, and Rohr sees this as the killing of our holy innocence by power and abuse (as in the killing of the Holy Innocents by Herod (Matt 2:1–23).[5] It has to happen for us to develop and grow up. In other words we have to leave the innocence of the garden of paradise.

In his essay "The Recovery of Paradise" Thomas Merton writes of the Desert Fathers and their search for "lost innocence," which they saw as an emptiness and purity of heart "which had belonged to Adam and Eve in Eden. . . . They sought recovery of that 'unity' which had been shattered by the 'knowledge of good and evil.'"[6] In a letter to the Zen practitioner and writer D. T. Suzuki Merton discusses the simplicity which was "normal" to Adam and Eve in paradise. He quotes a passage from Philoxenus,

---

3. Allchin, "Foreword," 6.

4. Vaughan, *Selected Poems*, 151.

5. Rohr, "Original Innocence."

6. Merton, "Recovery of Paradise," 53.

a Christian philosopher describing how in their simplicity Adam and Eve had no thoughts about the nature of God or why they had been created or placed in paradise. Rather, "Simplicity is completely absorbed in listening to what it hears." Merton sees this state of mind as akin to the "little child, completely absorbed in the person speaking to it." This was a state of unity where "thought is mingled with the word of him who speaks."[7]

This unity that had been lost was, as the Desert Fathers saw it, the unity of being one with Christ. The separation had come about through consciousness of the values and reasoning of the world—through separation, through growing up, and developing self-consciousness. In another essay Merton writes,

> Oblivious of his external self and empty of self, man was originally one with God his creator. So intimate was their union that the creator could live and act with perfect freedom in his created instrument. Having fallen, and been redeemed in Christ, man is once again able to recover this state of innocence and union, in and through Christ.[8]

Here Merton suggests a process of separation and disidentification with the source of life and ground of our being, a lost connection to which we can return through identification with Christ. This sense of oblivion about the external self and lack of self-consciousness can be seen as having much in common with the thinking on infancy of the psychoanalyst Donald Winnicott. Winnicott understands the baby experiences themselves and the mothering person initially as one: in other words the baby has no sense of being separate from the mothering person. There is utter dependency, no sense of ego or indeed of doing what one wants. At this stage there is no separate self.

From a spiritual perspective, what is this lost innocence? And can we understand it by looking at what it means to be an infant? Infants are both vulnerable and dependent, and if a baby's needs are met with love and consistency then the state of paradise lasts longer than for those who have a troubled start to life. However all infants are exposed to strong feelings and impulses basic to human life—hunger, discomfort, loss, and tiredness—which lead to feeling angry, fearful, and upset. Most babies make these strong feelings known and gradually, as infants, we learn, if we are lucky, how to manage fear and feelings of collapse alongside great excitement and

---

7. Merton, *Hidden Ground of Love*, 570.

8 Merton, "Theology of Creativity," 99.

pleasure. When the frustrations are resolved and the baby feels safe and contented then there is a state of bliss. The learning comes from love.

Infancy is really the only time in our lives where we can be loved for just being alive, just being born, just being. The psychoanalyst R. D. Laing describes a patient he saw who expressed it like this:

> Everyone should be able to look back in their memory and be sure he had a mother who loved him, all of him; even his piss and shit. He should be sure his mother loved him just for being himself; not for what he could do. Otherwise he feels he has no right to exist. He feels he should never have been born.
>
> No matter what happens to this person in life, no matter how much he gets hurt, he can always look back to this and feel that he is lovable. He can love himself and he cannot be broken. If he can't fall back on this, he can be broken.[9]

This experience of being loved, just being alive, can, and only too quickly will, change. We become loved rather more for secondary values—how we look, what we can do, or how we behave. Jesus' command, "Unless we become," seems to be inviting us in part to regain that deep sense of loving trust and dependency. From this we can take a sense that we are asked to believe that God loves us for just being alive and that amazingly our feelings are acceptable, no matter what they are, in his sight.

In infancy there is no formal speech, only the burblings or cries to convey what feels good or bad. Interestingly Thomas Merton thought that innocence, "consists in not having to answer, and therefore in not even thinking about an answer."[10] There is no conceptual thought. When we are happy we are happy, when we are sad we are sad, when we are afraid we are afraid. This vividness of mood, not tempered yet by self-awareness or injunctions about behavior or controlling our emotions, has been likened to the feelings of delight and desolation experienced by those who are mystics in their relationship with God. For the mystic the experiences are clear and unmodified in God's presence. There is no thought about it; we are at that point what we are. It has been suggested that for both adults and children the spiritual journey is about becoming "so lost in the mystery of God that we become permeable, available, vulnerable to what is real."[11] This, perhaps, is about becoming absorbed in God, especially during times of prayer, so that this self-consciousness begins to dissipate and become less important.

9. Laing, *Divided Self*, 172.

10. Merton, *Learning to Love*, 255.

11. Paulsell, "Lost in the Mystery," 83.

The experience of life as a mystery where things happen for no apparent reason and all is incomprehensible begins to change as the infant grows and when routines become recognized and a sense of order and consistency develops. It is not until babies are older that they understand they exist independently from the mothering person or indeed appreciate what "I" or "me" means. This realization of the separate self is discussed below. How this links with creativity and our sense of God is explored more fully in a later chapter. With language comes the sense of "being me" and so develops self-consciousness. We begin to understand our place in the world and adapt our behavior accordingly so that we can fit in and be valued for that. Our sense of being loved is then over time obscured by approval and achievement.

The Developing Sense of Self—"Me"

Two very different psychoanalysts offer intriguing insights into how the self develops in early infancy and also how precarious any sense of self is. Their psychological thinking can also contribute to a spiritual understanding of the self, and, indeed, what the implications might be of beginning to let go of a belief in the importance of the self presented to the world.

Donald Winnicott famously suggested that our earliest image of our self comes from looking at the face of the person who is caring for us; that "the precursor of the mirror is the mother's face."[12] In other words when the tiny baby looks at the mother's face he or she can see himself or herself, so how the baby feels is reflected back in the mother's facial response. This means that a huge amount depends on the response of the mothering person as this will affect the growing child's personal sense of self-worth and whether or not their needs were met in their early years. For example, if the mothering person is smiling and looking loving the baby can feel warmly held and loved, and so experiences themselves as loved and wanted. This of course has led to ideas about what might happen when the mothering person is preoccupied or angry or depressed and the baby only receives back how the mother feels and will not get anything back for themselves. So if the mother is unable or unwilling to respond to the infant's gesture of personal need "the central self suffers insult."[13] However if the infant is seen in a way that makes them feel that they exist, in a way in which they are confirmed, then they are free to go on looking.

12. Winnicott, *Playing and Reality*, 130.
13. Phillips, *Winnicott*, 129.

For Winnicott, the consequences of a failure of maternal provision are feelings of conflict and misrecognition. These become embedded in the inner landscape of the small child and affect not only feelings of self-worth but how the small child then develops and interacts with others and the world. He writes that "being seen is at the basis of creative looking." In other words unless we can somehow see ourselves we cannot begin to see others. Winnicott suggests a process in the development of the individual self that depends on being seen:

> When I look I am seen, so I exist.
> I can now afford to look and see.
> I now look creatively and what I apperceive I also perceive.
> In fact I take care not to see what is not there to be seen (unless I am tired).[14]

Being authentically seen by another allows the true self to flourish and it leads to creativity, imagination, the capacity for play, and to religious sensibilities. However if very small children are not recognized for who they are then they may turn to what Winnicott calls strategies of compliance. For Winnicott these are the basis of what he calls the false self organization. He saw this organization as primarily a way of surviving or at least conserving the true self that may be under threat from the maturational environment. If the infant is not seen in their own right then he or she has to be attentive to the needs of the mothering person and fit in with her. Therefore the creative originality that Winnicott considers an innate characteristic of infancy becomes muffled or indeed feels as if lost. In this way the false self does include, as Thomas Merton suggests in his analysis from the spiritual perspective, aspects of the unconscious. This compliance that results from infancy can be further exacerbated through the compliance that society and culture demands. It also leads to a false relationship with God. On the positive side the false self can also act as a caretaker self to something more real that remains. Both Winnicott and Merton call this the true self. In other words some children can only survive through a protective shield—a public self that presented to the world. It is this sort of experience that can then still be present in the adult mind.

In his thinking about the development of the self, the French psychoanalyst Jacques Lacan looks at what the small child experiences between the ages of six and eighteen months when the infant begins to observe her image in the mirror. This first observation refers to a particular moment of recognition and jubilation, when the infant is moving away from the

14. Winnicott, *Playing and Reality*, 134.

simple reflection of the mother's gaze. Such recognition of the self may be accompanied with pleasure. Lacan writes of observing "signs of triumphant jubilation and playful discovery that characterizes from the sixth month, the child's encounter with his image in the mirror."[15] However for Lacan the central point is that the small child initially confuses the image with reality and then confuses the existence of the image with its own properties. He thinks that this continues into adulthood. He explains the experience in this way: when the child looks in the mirror he or she sees a unified image of his or her own disarray. What does he mean by this? Though infants experience themselves as all over the place, in bits and pieces, when small children look in the mirror they observe that all the bits are collected into one image. This disparity between the image and the feelings has been called a formative misrecognition in that it offers the child the lure of a spurious image of completeness that will, in actuality, forever seduce and elude the child and later the adult. Lacan suggests that the mirror is deeply misleading as it gives the child a false promise.[16]

In both these theories there is a strong sense of the fragility of the developing sense of "me." In Lacan's idea there is an inbuilt misrecognition (the image is an illusion); in Winnicott's idea all is dependent on the consistency of the maternal provision. It is from such shaky beginnings that we build up the image of ourselves and so it is this false self or inauthentic image of an "I" that can be presented to the world. The sense of "I" is thus in part a cover up, but it also means that the self by definition "is what which is forever unfinished." More importantly whatever happens to us in childhood and all the emotions of love, hate, joy, sadness, anger, and so on, are still present within the adult identity. We just have better ways of managing them. The inner world is fueled by childhood experiences and emotions but these are usually shrouded or become largely shrouded by compliance and expectations. The primitive passion is tempered and managed most of the time; though what is repressed can always break through.

Learning from Children

One of the difficulties of growing older is our developing self-consciousness: What am I doing? How do I appear? What do others think of me? What does God think of me? It is all this and much more that Thomas Merton thought obscured our relationship with God. One way of approaching the lessening of self-consciousness is to look back at spirituality in childhood, and

15. Lacan, *Ecrits*, 18.
16. Ibid., 1–7.

recognize that the ongoing invitation from Jesus Christ to adults is about, in part, recovering some aspects of that state of mind. Our child remains within us no matter how sophisticated we become, and indeed all of us are reminded in all sorts of ways and at any time about our childhood. This includes those who write about religion and spirituality where the hidden child will have been affected by early religious teaching and experience.

While it is possible the small child spoken of by Jesus in the synoptic gospels was the pre-verbal child, expressing him or herself only through sounds and gestures, most contemporary studies on the spirituality of children tend to focus on experiences in children over the age of five or six who are fully verbal. They can be asked about what they are looking at or feeling and they can respond because their experiences can be put into words. The findings of such research on the spirituality of speaking children can offer some guidance and inspiration to adults. Predominantly this is to work towards becoming increasingly and appropriately receptive and open in our relationship with God: "Unless you become . . ." This is one way of beginning to get a deeper sense of what Jesus meant about this potential state of being.

From recent findings on studies with children there are three central aspects that prove especially relevant. The first is the idea of relational consciousness. In this term "relational" refers to the importance of God, other people, other creatures, things, and self as the focus of attention and interdependence. "Consciousness" emphasizes qualities of awareness, mystery, and value-sensing. In their ground-breaking work David Hay and Rebecca Nye understand consciousness as including awareness, being in the here-and-now with a quality of vividness in each experience.[17] It also includes tuning or feeling at one with nature. This can include a focusing on what is being looked at or on an activity the child is involved in, leading to a sense of flow where the child is so involved that there is the feeling of it happening without conscious agency. In other words there is a lack of self-consciousness and an absorption in the present moment. Mystery includes feelings of wonder and awe and imagination. This is often shown when children play. For Hay and Nye value-sensing involves an intensity including feelings that some things may be ultimately good, and meaning-making where children ask questions that are essentially spiritual such as "why" and "who am I?"

The second relevant aspect that has emerged from research on spirituality in childhood is about having the necessary space for experiencing and play. This suggests a freedom to both create and to explore without restriction of thought or circumstance. It is about allowing the imagination to have free rein.

17. Hay and Nye, *Spirit of the Child.*

The final significant characteristic of childhood spiritualty is the child's sense of being in a position of powerlessness. This may first become some-thing the child is gradually aware of in terms of family dynamics where the parent can be seen as all-powerful and therefore fairly or unfairly control-ling various activities. For older children there may be a dawning awareness of their exclusion from worldly power, participation, their place outside of money-making ventures, and indeed that they are denied much recognition in terms of worldly values. In religious terms this can be seen as a place of humility in terms of the world. Some commentators on the biblical read-ings about children have particularly emphasized this aspect, seeing how it complements Jesus' teaching on the poor and those seen on the edge of worldly success. The state of humility has been linked to the low status of children and thus God's identification with the least. Jesus asks us, his disci-ples, to journey in life towards a condition of complete simplicity and where all impediments to this are stripped away. It is a journey to become free in our relationship with God. It is an ongoing journey towards a potential state of mind and a way of being truly alive. It is not about going backwards to a state of pre-verbal impotency, but rather a way forward into being attentive in our present relationship with God.

Jesus' Command to Become as Small Children and Thomas Merton's Ideas on Rebirth

Thomas Merton thought that one way of reading the Bible and perhaps the most helpful for spiritual development was by responding not so much in-tellectually but rather at the level of our entire being. He thought the "whole climate of the New Testament is one of liberation by mercy"[18] and this com-mand from Jesus to become as small children is above all a command that will lead to liberation, a breaking away from some of the conventions and constraints of adulthood.

Thomas Merton understood that in some way Jesus' command was central to the spiritual life. As Merton understood it, this teaching is not about learning how to do something or how to follow instructions it is rather about experiencing. It is about changing and becoming more true to ourselves, the person that God wants us to be.

The accounts about Jesus' interactions with actual children in the gos-pels describe inclusion, acceptance, and tenderness:

18. Merton, *Love and Living,* 210.

> Then little children were being brought to him in order that he might lay his hands on them and pray. The disciples spoke sternly to those who brought them; but Jesus said: "Let the children come to me and do not stop them; for it is to such as these that the kingdom of heaven belongs." (Matt 19:13–14)

The children are brought, presumably by their parents, for a blessing. This extract can also be understood as a metaphor, for, as adults, we are invited to bring the hidden inner child part into the light and so into Jesus' presence, so that we can be held and blessed. The usual order of who is important and the accepted hierarchy of what happens in the grown-up world are overthrown. Here, in the invitation to intimacy with Jesus Christ it is the least powerful, the least defended and the most vulnerable and dependent, who are the most welcome. This is the part of each person that can be blessed, and here is the invitation not to deny and reject that part of ourselves. We are asked to be tender, accepting, and embrace that small child still present within us. Merton wrote in one letter: "we must be meek and loving even towards ourselves as, and because, God loves us. . . . Oh, the mercy of God. We are its ministers, even for ourselves."[19]

The children do not speak in the gospel accounts but are placed centrally: "Then he took a little child and put it among them; and taking it in his arms, he said to them, 'Whoever welcomes one such child in my name welcomes me'" (Mark 9:36–37). In this narrative Jesus' teaching is to place the silent child among the talking disciples. It is the open but non-verbal part of us that is the center of Jesus' concern. As it is the silent child who teaches by example, so, perhaps, this is a suggestion that it is through contemplation we can best approach Jesus. Perhaps all the words used in prayers get in the way of direct connection. We are invited to welcome the inarticulate, lost-for-words part of ourselves into Jesus' embrace.

In the gospels Jesus often calls his followers and disciples "children." There seems a deep identification by him with children. This term is then continued in the later books of the New Testament. Sometimes the term is used directly as in the relationship with Jesus Christ. For example, "Jesus stood on the beach . . . Jesus said to them, 'Children, you have no fish, have you?'" (John 21:4–5). In other contexts it is part of the guidance about increasing intimacy with God, "While you have the light, believe in the light, so that you may become children of light" (John 12:36).

Jesus' teaching tells us that the gift of being like a child is vital and necessary for entry to the kingdom—it is a command: "unless." This extraordinary teaching is consistent in the three synoptic gospels but the

---

19. Merton, *School of Charity*, 137.

meaning of the teaching is less clear. In fact the mystery of what it might all mean is revealed only to babies and toddlers, in other words those who are not yet able to speak: "At that time Jesus said, I thank you Father, Lord of heaven and earth, because you have hidden these things from the wise and intelligent and have revealed them to infants" (Matt 11:25). The message is that for us to see and to be close to God we have to relinquish the part of us that feels important and knowledgeable as a grown-up and turn in a state of not-knowing to God.

Merton believed that attempting to understand what is meant in Scripture can be helped by the Holy Spirit who "enlightens us, in our read-ing to see how *our own lives* are part of these great mysteries—how we are one with Jesus in them."[20] This complements another teaching by Jesus in John's Gospel, "Very truly, I tell you, no one can see the kingdom of God without being born from above" (John 3:3). Thomas Merton saw the idea of rebirth "as a central fact of Christian existence"[21] and "fundamental to Christian theology and practice."[22] He understood this as the whole mean-ing of baptism which is the process or journey of both monastic and indeed Christian commitment. In the command Jesus asks each disciple to adopt the vocation of self-renewal, liberation from separation from Christ and so "the transformation of one's entire mentality 'in Christ.'"

Rebirth is in part about a recovery of something and some quality of being that is still deep within us. Merton saw it as an inner transformation of consciousness and importantly as both a psychological and spiritual re-birth, and it is this that is the goal of authentic maturity. For Merton this was rebirth into the kingdom and so following Jesus' command a rebirth into becoming as a small child. Rebirth for Thomas Merton was a metaphor for contemplation involving an inner revolution: "It is the obscure but insistent demand of [a person's] own nature to transcend itself in the freedom of a fully integrated, autonomous, personal identity." He sees this as a deep spiri-tual instinct, an urge for inner truth that can be found through interior si-lence and contemplative prayer: "a continuous dynamic of inner renewal."[23] Merton also understood this as something found in other religious and spiritual traditions including Sufism and Zen Buddhism:

> Emphasis is placed on the call to fulfil certain obscure yet urgent
> potentialities in the ground of one's being, to "become someone"
> that one already (potentially) is, the person one is truly meant to

20. Merton, *Monastic Journey,* 29.

21. Merton, *Love and Living,* 202.

22. Merton, "Final integration," 454.

23. Merton, "New Birth," 62, 65.

be. Zen calls this awakening a recognition of "your original face before you were born."[24]

For Merton the person who is fully born has an almost entirely inner experience of life based on a deep inner spiritual freedom.

The suggestion in this book is that this is the freedom of the spirit of the child—something that in some way we have already known; it is a return to and recognition of our original face, before the world helped us lose sight of it. Another thought explored in the book is that Jesus commands us to unburden ourselves of the weight of adult responsibility in our relationship with him. Merton did not underestimate the difficulties of this and what regaining paradise through becoming like a small child might involve. He quotes St. Ambrose: "All who wish to return to paradise must be tested by the fire." Moving from knowledge to innocence regained is a way of temptation and struggle; "it is a matter of wrestling with supreme difficulties and overcoming obstacles that seem, and indeed are, beyond human strength."[25]

The state of innocence and the state of knowledge appear as opposites, but the spiritual journey to follow Jesus' command leads to a synthesis or what the analytical psychologist Carl Jung called the transcendent function. This is a third position that arises from intense and concentrated conflicts within the psyche. It is similar to the koan of the Zen masters where strange and upsetting paradoxes can breakthrough into new insight. The task is to hold the tension between the two apparent opposites for long enough so that the unexpected and creative new way can be born. It is an incarnation born from the two other ways of being and is fully explored in a later chapter.

If we consider Jesus' command to the would-be adult disciples to become as small children as equivalent to a koan, then the work is to hold the lost innocence and the knowledge until the breakthrough can emerge. The idea in this book is that the third new way to emerge is the spirit of the child or what Merton called the child mind. As Merton knew from his reading on the Desert Fathers and his own spiritual practice it is not possible as an adult to regain innocence without knowledge. He quotes from the Desert Fathers the experience of John the Dwarf who wants to reach a state in which there is no temptation and no further stirring of the slightest passion. But this is seen as merely the refinement of "knowledge" and only leads to a pure love of self and so is subject to deception.

Purity of heart is the recovery of divine likeness where the true self is lost in God. The spirit of the child, to use the language of this book, is one

24. Merton, "Final Integration," 454.
25. Merton "Recovery of Paradise," 58.

with the Christ child and this as Merton writes is "only a return to the true beginning." For this is where Christ is—in the beginning and in the becoming. This is the rebirth or a fresh start where Merton believed the preparation took place "for the real work of God which is revealed in the Bible: the work of the *new creation*, the resurrection from the dead, the resurrection of all things in Christ."[26]

The spiritual journeying required to follow Jesus' command is both struggle and breakthrough but we can be guided in part through our understanding of our relationship with God both as a parent to us and as a child within us. This paradox is shown to us in Scripture, and once again, paradoxically we have to use conceptual thought and psychological insight to glimpse again a state where we were conscious of neither. Despite the challenge we are reassured as Jesus tells us that we are not to be left orphaned as we seek and search for increased closeness and union with God.

26. Ibid., 63.

3

Thinking about God as Parent and God as Child

Can we love God as a parent? How confusing does this become if we also love God as the Christ child—indeed as the eternal child within us? Reading the Bible suggests that envisaging God as both parent and child, though a paradox, is yet conceivable and that the one does not cancel out the other. Both are about relationship; one way to understand the ever-changing relationship with God is to consider the psychodynamics.

Understanding the Psychodynamics

As Lancelot Andrewes (1555–1626) expressed it, "Christianity is a meeting."[1] Using the term "psychodynamics" implies that the relationship with God is never static. It involves emotion and change and this usually implies an active struggling with different feelings. It is the same in any relationship. As a child with parents there are conflicts especially over control and independence, and, as a parent with a child different feelings both loving and critical inevitably contribute to the relationship—a relationship which changes over time. This means that the relationship with God as parent and the relationship with the Christ child both involve mixed feelings and much interplay and change within and between them.

In analytic thought the term psychodynamics is traditionally used to characterize aspects of the unconscious and the relationship between what is conscious and what lies below the surface. This may be especially pertinent in Christianity where the social mores, perhaps particularly of the established church, tend to involve keeping certain more negative feelings from reaching consciousness and this may lead to inner conflict. Sigmund

1. Andrewes, *Ninety-Six Sermons*, 193–94.

Freud, the founder of psychoanalysis, wrote about resistance and defense mechanisms where unpalatable feelings are avoided, repressed, or managed in different ways, often through some sort of compromise formation. The term dynamic also implies an intensity and energy which is a crucial part of keeping the relationship alive within the psyche. For the relationship with God to remain dynamic there is a need for all the mixed feelings to be owned and brought into conscious awareness.

In our relationship with God the dynamics are framed by our earlier experiences, though they may be modified by church teaching and so on. If they are largely subjective this means that old attachments from significant figures from the past can become reawakened in the relationship. For example, past experiences with parents and care-givers will affect the quality of any future close attachment. The shadow cast by a troubled childhood is fully explored in chapter 8, but our ability to trust and love is central to how we relate. It is here that attachment theory could be helpful. This is because attachment theory suggests that intimate relationships have specific interactional psychodynamics. There are differing emphases for the self in relation to another and it has been suggested that these forms of attachment emerge from and can be identified in infancy. This means that children who have had enough good in their early infancy develop a secure attachment pattern, however for those who have had a more troubled experience the attachment experience may be damaged and so future relationships follow the early pattern experienced. This can take the form of feeling unable to trust in relationships so there are feelings of insecurity and this may mean the child has mixed feelings or is totally resistant to close contact with another. Another type of insecurity may take the form of avoiding all relationships, or following a pattern of disorganized relationships. John Bowlby who explored these dynamics believes that the attachment pattern continues throughout life, largely in an automatic unconscious way, and it certainly seems relevant in our relationship with God, and also between members of any church community. So for example in both avoidant and ambivalent attachment there is an underlying fear of intimacy, therefore it may be harder to trust in a loving God and easier to keep God at a distance. For those with insecure relationships there may be much anxiety in pleasing God through compliance and false "goodness." Unresolved difficulties from childhood will undoubtedly affect us as we consider God as parent.

God as Parent

> As a father has compassion for his children, so the Lord has
> compassion for those who fear him. (Ps 103:13)

St. Catherine of Siena (1347–1380) wrote about her understanding
of increasing closeness with God. She believed that the relationship has to
become parental; it cannot remain in a formal official way with a God out
there far from us. The first step is to move towards friendship and from
there to something more intimate. She wrote down a vision of God speaking
to her in this way:

> I want to show you how a person comes to be my friend, and
> once my friend, becomes my child by attaining filial love. . . .
> Filial love, I tell you, is perfect. For with filial love one receives
> the inheritance from me the eternal Father. But no one attains
> filial love without the love of friendship, and this is why I told
> you that one progresses from being my friend to becoming my
> child.[2]

Here she reflects the sentiment of biblical passages where God is as
parent. One such example is found in Hosea where God is filled with parental tenderness towards his people:

> When Israel was a child, I loved him, and out of Egypt I called
> my son. . . . I took them up in my arms . . .
>
> I led them with cords of human kindness, with bands of love.
> I was to them like those who lift infants to their cheeks. I bent
> down to them and fed them. (Hos 11:1, 3b and 4)

The psalmist in Ps 131:1–2 offers a quiet confidence in the way of spiritual childhood, and shows the way that he responded to such a tender God:

> O Lord, my heart is not lifted up, my eyes are not raised too
> high; I do not occupy myself with things too great and too mar-
> vellous for me.
>   But I have calmed and quieted my soul, like a weaned child
> with its mother; my soul is like the weaned child that is with me.

The medieval mystic Meister Eckhart (1260–1328) wrote about
God not just as parent, but more specifically as a birthing mother: "What
does God do all day long? God gives birth. From all eternity God lies on a

---

2. Catherine of Siena, *Selected Spiritual Writings*, 108.

maternity bed giving birth."[3] This extraordinary image offers another way of thinking about the idea of being reborn in our faith. With God as our parent the way of spiritual childhood is seen as an opportunity to begin again, a rebirth into spiritual infancy and from there to grow into spiritual maturity and to "the full stature of Christ" (Eph 4:13).

This is certainly a counter-cultural move, but one in tune with many religious teachings. For the gospel model of the full stature of Christ is not about worldly independence or worldly wisdom but, paradoxically, instead about an increased dependence on God that leads to spiritual wisdom. This is being-in-dependence with God. Jesus in the gospels turns to God as father, as *abba*. Jesus reveals his deep intimacy with God, and, as has been pointed out, by incorporating this into his adult ministry and teaching Jesus shows no embarrassment. He uses a word from his own childhood, *abba*, a word from the family, to describe the intimacy that is needed in relationship with God.

To take this brave move towards being-in-dependence with God there needs to be a good degree of trust, or instead one might need to be in a state of desperation where there is no alternative. Making this move involves some belief in a God who is aware of the smallest detail of what is happening, and a belief or at least a hope that suggests there is no need to be afraid. And in acknowledging our dependency, so there is comfort. As St. Hildegard (1098–1179) expresses it, "God hugs you. You are encircled by the arms of the mystery of God."[4]

The Catholic priest John Vianney, also known as the Curé d'Ars, who died in 1859 was was much loved by his parishioners, building a huge following of people who wanted his ministrations. In his own life he was seen as "the very model of the childhood which Jesus loved, the very impersonation of Christian infancy; and therefore it is that God is with him." The priest himself said that "our soul is swathed in our body like a child in its swaddling bands." Of our relationship with God he said in a poignant way:

> When He sees us coming, He leans His heart down very low to this little creature, like a father who bends down to listen to his child when it speaks to him. In the morning we should do like the infant in the cradle. As soon as it opens its eyes, it looks quickly through the room to see its mother. When it sees her, it begins to smile, when it cannot see her, it cries.

3. Meister Eckhart quoted in Fox, *Original Blessings*, 220.
4. Hildegard of Bingen, "Quotations."

Yet, alongside his joy, there is deep exhaustion, suffering and weariness.[5]

Here in this most maternal of images, Vianney also includes the experience of the adult who may be able to have the mind of the child but who is also beset by the reality of the adult demands of those around. In Vianney's situation this was the constant requests from the spiritually hungry and those who were suffering and longing for the same intimacy with God. As adults the joy of such intimacy is also tempered by another reality.

Such a degree of intimacy where God is as a parent, offers great comfort in times of loss and sadness. When the Quaker Rufus Jones was traveling to England from America in 1903 he wrote about this experience:

> The night before landing in Liverpool I awoke in my berth with a strange sense of trouble and sadness. As I lay wondering what it meant, I felt myself invaded by a Presence and held by Everlasting Arms. It was the most extraordinary experience I had ever had.

On landing he heard of the death of his fourteen-year-old son:

> When the news reached my friend John Wilhelm Rowntree, he experienced a profound sense of Divine Presence enfolding him and me, and his comfort and love were an immense help . . . nothing has carried me up into the life of God, or done more to open out the infinite meaning of love, than the fact that love can span this break of separation, can pass beyond the visible and hold right on across the chasm. The mystic union has not broken and knows no end.[6]

Thomas Merton writes of his experience of God as "the Father who fights to defend and rescue His child." The child in turn recognizes the need for obedience, but this recognition takes place "in solitude."[7]

The extraordinary breakthrough for some saints and mystics was that in becoming vulnerable in this way and allowing a deep dependency on God's love as a parent a further insight was born. This is the paradox where there is a relationship with God as parent but also the potential for a relationship with God as child, as an infant, for the Christ child to dwell in us.

St. Paul equates the birth of discipleship in this way, "My little children, for whom I am again in the pain of childbirth until Christ is formed in

5. Monnin, *Life of Jean-Baptist Vianney,* 213, 257, 298.

6. Jones, "Spiritual Experiences of Friends" in *Christian Faith and Practice,* 92.

7. Merton, *Dancing in the Water,* 334.

you" (Gal 4:19). In 1 Peter the emphasis is also on the very small child, "Like newborn infants, long for the pure, spiritual milk, so that by it you may grow into salvation" (1 Pet 2:2). When Paul (Gal 4:4–7) describes the process of such rebirth, he speaks of the process of adoption leading to an inheritance and embracing a deep intimacy:

> God sent his Son, born of a woman, born under the law, in or-der to redeem those who were under the law, so that we might receive adoption as children. And because you are children, God has sent the Spirit of his Son into our hearts, crying "Abba! Father!" So you are no longer a slave but a child, and if a child then also an heir, through God.

Here there is an acknowledgment that the spirit of the Son enters into the psyche. Perhaps in acknowledging ourselves as children in relationship with God, it becomes increasingly possible to identify with "the Beloved Son." Thomas Merton calls this realization "divine sonship" and sees it as "the likeness of the Word of God in us produced by his living presence in our souls, through the Holy Spirit."[8] He thought this central: "I realized that what is important is . . . my own self and my sonship as a child of God."[9] Quoting Karl Barth, Merton notes in a journal entry that through the cruci-fixion, Christ established the order for us "to live eternally as the redeemed, converted child of God."[10]

God as Mother

The use of maternal imagery in the relationship with God emerged strongly in the twelfth century particularly through the Cistercian monks Bernard of Clairvaux (d. 1153), Aelred of Rievaulx (d. 1167), and Guerric of Igny (d. 1157, among others, and also from the Benedictine, Anselm of Canterbury (d. 1109). The idea was that Jesus was mother to the individual soul who could then be reborn to life. The imagery used particularly by the Cister-cians was of nurturing and particularly of suckling. In St. Bernard's "Song of Songs" he writes how the breasts of Jesus as mother offer a "richness of the grace" that "contributes far more to my spiritual progress than the biting reprimands of superiors."[11]

---

8. Merton, *Life and Holiness*, 60.

9. Merton, *Dancing in the Water*, 287.

10. Merton, *Turning Towards the World*, 51.

11. Bernard of Clairvaux, *"Song of Songs,"* sermon 9, paras 5–6.

The idea of Jesus as mother was particularly strongly described by Julian (1342–1416) an anchoress from Norwich who is now valued as a theologian and great pastoral teacher. Thomas Merton ranked Julian as "the greatest of the English mystics . . . one of the greatest English theologians."[12] When Julian was thirty-years-old she received sixteen visions, she later expanded these over the next twenty years into eighty-six revelations. Julian's revelation of the Trinity is of the Trinity as Father, Mother, and our Lord— which she describes as might, wisdom, and love. In the vision granted to her she understood that in the one God there are three qualities: fatherhood, motherhood, and lordship. Christ is the second person of the Trinity and so becomes our mother holding both the spiritual essence and the physical self.

So Christ as our mother in whom our two natures are undivided, is a mother to us in different ways:

> In our Mother, Christ, we prosper and develop; in his mercy he corrects and restores us; and by the power of his Passion, death and resurrection unites us to our essential being. That is how our mother works in mercy for all his children who are yielding and obedient to him.[13]

Christ as mother heals and restores. "We have our being from him, the ground and source of all motherhood, and with it we have all love's sweet protection for ever more." God she writes is truly our mother as he is our father. The motherhood of God she believed came firstly from his creation of our human nature. Secondly, what Julian describes as "the motherhood of grace," stems from Christ assuming this human nature. Thirdly, the motherhood of God comes through the practical outworking of motherhood, what Julian called a "spreading out," where we are touched by mercy and grace. Julian sees that only Christ can perform this role, carrying creation within himself and through his death giving birth to a new state of being. Following our spiritual birth, we are, Julian says, sustained through "the blessedness sacrament." From her revelations Julian writes that as infants we are all led by Jesus "intimately into his blessing breast, through the sweet open wound in his side."[14]

In her accounts Julian extols Christ as the ideal mother fostering a secure attachment through tender and firm care which leads to a deep trust, "whose sole job is to attend to the welfare of her child." The result of this

---

12. Merton, *Mystics and Zen Masters,* 140.

13. Julian of Norwich, *Revelations of Divine Love,* 121.

14. Ibid., 125.

mothering is a loving relationship that extends to others. Julian's visions showed that when "our gracious Mother brings us up into our Father's bliss" there will be the revelation that "All will be well. You will see for yourself, that all manner of things will be well!"[15] Here is the similarity with the reassurance that a good mother offers to allay the small child's fear and insecurity.

Relationship with the Child Within—Incarnation

> Jesus was always the child. A child is totally dependent on its parents for simply everything.[16]

The incarnation is something eternal realized in time. Yet time allows for the unfolding of a gift which was already there in principle; it was given in the beginning and awaits the chance to be born—to emerge. In sharing our human birth, Jesus Christ comes close to us, allies himself with us. He offers us all a new birth and a potential becoming.

From the Jewish tradition Rabbi Abraham Heschel thought that each person carries the possibility for such insight, though it is usually vague and hidden. This for him is the presence of God within, and the awareness of such potential means that we too can become pregnant with God. For some this seed grows and in others it decays. "Some give birth to life. Others miscarry it. Some know how to bear, to nurse, to rear an insight that comes into being."[17]

This whole way of thinking turns the idea of being a child upside down so that we become parent to the part of us that is reborn. Meister Eckhart puts it in this straightforward way: "We are all meant to be mothers of God. For God is always needing to be born." Mary, the mother of Jesus, teaches us that God is not only parent, but God is also child. Mary, alone, is the mother of God, but we too can give birth to wisdom and compassion as we will explore later. Eckhart promises that through creating the image of God within us we will find great blessing. Here is the suggestion that God, born within each person, is eternally new. Eckhart uses the word *novissimus*, the newest thing there is. This is the infant at the heart of Christianity.[18] This is the true child of the self, the eternal child, the Christ child who lies deep within the psyche, waiting to be born anew.

---

15. Ibid., 128, 131.

16. Burrows, *Love Unknown*, 145.

17. Heschel, *Insecurity of Freedom*, 125.

18. Meister Eckhart quoted in Fox, *Original Blessings*, 222.

This is also, as Merton phrased it, the Christ of immediate experience. For each person's existence offers potential representations of Christ simply because of our humanity. "In becoming man, God became not only Jesus Christ but also potentially every man and woman that ever existed."[19] God envisaged his wisdom, as a human child, "playing in the world, playing before him at all times." Merton reflects on Wisdom's pleasure, "my delights are to be with the children of men 'rejoicing in his inhabited world and delighting in the human race' (Prov 8:31)."[20]

Mark Frank, a seventeenth-century preacher and follower of Lancelot Andrewes, writes in a sermon that one of the messages found in the nativity is about littleness:

> . . . to think and make little of ourselves; seeing the infinite great-
> ness in this day becomes so little, Eternity as a child, the rays
> of glory wrapped in rags, Heaven crowded into the corner of a
> stable, and He that is everywhere want room.

Frank's sermon is about paradox and the mystery of new life "as if to emphasise that it is when the opposites come together that something new can come to birth," for there is "wisdom in the infancy of a child."[21] The message of the nativity and the incarnation is that Christ can be born in us even in the poverty of our self. While the date of our actual birth is our birth in time, the date of the incarnation is our shared date of rebirth:

> Christmas night with the angels' songs
> Is the hour of our birth.[22]

So the fellowship of the crib offers a connection with all children, a connection with the child that once was, and, also, a connection with the potential spirit of the child still hidden in the adult. Irenaeus (130–202), known by some as St. Irenaeus, one of the early church fathers, wrote of the significance of the infancy of Jesus Christ: "In his own he sanctifies the infancy of all little ones and shows that every age is capable of the divine mystery."[23] Here in the birth of Jesus is the excitement and energy of potential, for the future, and for all new life and beginnings.

---

19. Merton, *New Seeds*, 190.

20. Merton, *Search for Solitude*, 182.

21. Frank, *Sermons*, 89–91.

22. Grundtvig quoted in Allchin, *Joy of all Creation*, 200.

23. Quoted in Saward, *Perfect Fools*, 10.

For Merton the nativity celebrates the renewal of all creation and the birth of the Christ child within each person. The nativity and incarnation offer "the indestructible kernel of hope that is in it."[24] We are reminded of

> the Child of God Who comes shyly and silently into the midst
> of our darkness and transforms the winter nights into paradise
> for those who, like the shepherds and the humble Kings, come
> to find Him where no one thinks of looking; in the obviousness
> and poverty of . . . ordinary everyday life.[25]

The paradox of experiencing God as parent and as child is ultimately a mystery but through growing self-awareness of this hidden but familiar child part within us we can develop the capacity both to dwell in God and to be a place where God dwells.

> See in heaven and earth
> In all fair things around
> Strong yearnings for a blest new birth
> With sinless glories crowned.[26]

Through rebirth and renewal the incarnation can take place within us—a process that can transcend dualities by making us one with Christ. Thomas Merton described it like this:

> For though evil and death can touch the evanescent, outer self in
> which we dwell estranged from him, in which we are alienated
> and exiled in unreality, it can never touch the real inner self in
> which we have been made one with him.[27]

Becoming one with Christ is about awakening the true self—the Christ child within—through accessing the deep realms of the spiritual unconscious. William Shannon's summary of Merton's writings on the self includes the following:

> The awakening of the true self marks the end of dualism, for
> the true self is my own subjectivity united to the subjectivity of
> God. My experience of God is an experience of total and radical
> dependence on God but at the same time an experience of the
> God upon whom I am so totally and radically dependent.[28]

24. Merton, *Road to Joy,* 108.

25. Merton, *Courage for Truth,* 93.

26. Pusey quoted in Allchin, *Joy of all Creation,* 149.

27. Merton, *New Seeds,* 190.

28. Shannon, "Self," 419.

Substitution of some of the terms in the first sentence helps explain this further so instead we can read: The awakening of the spirit of the child marks the end of dualism, for the spirit of the child is my own divine child united to the divine child of God—the Christ child. The Christ child needs and asks for our receptivity and hospitality in order to dwell within each person. Our vocation is to become "the fair one of the bright childbearing"[29] offering a home to the eternal child, the Christ child, in this way we "Live as children of light" (Eph 5:8).

The Example of Mary

Another way of envisaging this experience of opening ourselves to the Christ child is to use the example of Mary pregnant with Jesus. She creates a space for the Christ child to dwell and indeed to develop. In the sense that the word can be born in each person, Mary is the mother of us all and an example to us all. Mary whose childbearing stands at the heart of the life of the Church is the one in whom and through whom we come to know the mystery of the Word made flesh. Mary's maternal role speaks of the God-bearing capacity in the whole of creation; she presents human love and tenderness. In the person of Mary humanity—the flesh—cooperates actively in the incarnation. Jeremy Taylor, the seventeenth-century Anglican preacher, saw Mary as the exemplar for prayer and for silent contemplation, for receptivity and for fruitfulness. His writing exalts the "heights to which human nature is called, its true capacity, as revealed in the mystery of the incarnation."[30] In his work "Of Nursing Children," Taylor writes about the importance of breastfeeding so that higher spiritual acts and virtues are firmly rooted in our most basic bodily needs and instincts. Like all later psychotherapists, the preacher Taylor saw the importance of the relationship between the mother and child as a foundation for the child's capacity for relationship with other people, with the outside world, and with God.

Thomas Merton also saw in Mary this receptivity to the indwelling of the Word as a model of contemplation and, in his later writings, as a model for simplicity and hiddenness:

> Mary, who was empty of all egotism, free from all sin, was as pure as the glass of a very clean window, which has no other function than to admit the light of the sun. . . . The light has wished to remind us of the window, because he is grateful to

29. Allchin, *Joy of All Creation*, 181.

30. Ibid., 63.

her and because he has an infinitely tender and personal love for her.[31]

Without Mary there could be no incarnation of the Word:

> She it is, who, by her vocation to be the place of God and by her fulfilment of that vocation, reveals the true destiny of all places, indeed of all humankind and of all creation, which shares in that high calling to become the place of God's inhabitation. This again is why she is called the joy of all creation, because the whole creation finds its possibility of fulfilment in her.[32]

The Eternal Christ Child Is Already within Each of Us

> Christ, from my cradle, I had known You everywhere, And even though I sinned, I walked in You, and knew You were my world: You were my life and air, and yet I would not own You.[33]

The novelist Elizabeth Goudge writes about the eternal child that is present in us no matter what happens in life. As a novelist, in Christian terms, she is alluding to the presence of the Christ child within each person, even if religion has long been rejected. She proposes the mask that an adult shows to the world hides an often frightened child part, but it is the child who wins by living on after death. One of the adult characters in a novel she wrote reflects on this:

> He did not often come here now, but it seemed that the boy he had once been was still in the room, over there by the window . . . the eternal child in a man who had not yet needed to put on a mask, and who did not know that when the pleasure and pride he felt in himself and all that he did had parted company with his innocence he himself would become a mask . . .[34]

The analytical psychologist Carl Jung understood that this sense of an eternal child present within the psyche was an archetype, in other words an inherent and typical pattern common to everyone. He thought establishing an understanding and therefore a relationship with the child archetype enriched adult consciousness. It enriches spiritual understanding by offering

31. Merton, *New Seeds*, 118–19.
32. Allchin, *Joy of All Creation*, 204.
33. Merton, "The Biography," in *Collected Poems*, 104.
34. Goudge, *Heart of the Family*, 76

an extra dimension. In Jungian thought the child archetype is always more than the actual experience of having been a child, as there is an added dimension of depth and meaning common to everyone, something more than ourselves, something that is eternal and universal. This can contribute generally to the feelings of nostalgia about childhood. As in the quote from the novel above, sometimes the memory of what has been lost can return quite clearly—perhaps when revisiting a place from the past.

As we grow older we are expected to lay aside childhood, but the deep feeling within us of nostalgia are sometimes evoked when we are with small children, reminding us of what is still present but hidden. Carl Jung believes the conscious mind of we adult is one-sided, so inevitably memories or thoughts have to come up to remind us, sometimes quite suddenly and unexpectedly, of what we have lost. He also thought this understanding of something eternal that is found in the image of the child is deeply embedded in what he called the collective unconscious. By this he meant the inherited history we all carry within us from past societies and generations. It is usually deeply buried but can irrupt into conscious awareness at certain times.

When Jung researched religious experiences from the past he found that often mystics reported visions of a wonderful child. One such mystic was Meister Eckhart who had a vision of a beautiful, naked boy with whom he spoke. The medieval mystic recounts asking the boy where he came from. The reply? From God. And in response to where are you going? *To God*. The dialogue continues:

> Where do you find him? "*Where I part with all creatures.*"
> Who are you? "*A king.*"
> Where is your kingdom? "*In my heart*"
> Take care that no one divide it with you! "*I shall.*"
> Then he led him to his cell [and said] Take whichever coat you will. "*Then I should be no king!*" And he disappeared. For it was God himself—Who was having a bit of fun![35]

This is no vision of a doctrine or a parental command. It is a playful vision of the divine child—the Christ child who asks to play and to become central in the heart of the person. The vision is in the present, and presumably has some links with Eckhart's own childhood in the past, but is also about the future. Jung thought that such visions and images were deep symbols of healing. The child brings together things that have been separated. The child mediates and is capable of numerous transformations, a figure

---

35. Politella, "Meister Eckhart," 129

that is always changing as the child grows older, but a figure that makes things whole.[36]

In one account of the revelations given to Mother Julian of Norwich we read:

> During this time I saw a body lying on the earth. It looked heavy and horrible, shapeless and formless, like a swollen mound of stinking compost. And suddenly out of this body there sprang a beautiful creature, a little child, perfectly shaped and formed, agile and lively, and whiter than a lily, who at once glided up into heaven.

For Julian, using the language of her time, the smallness of the child stood for "the utter purity of the soul" uncontaminated by the wretchedness of "mortal flesh."[37] Her vision seems to be about the absolute newness of rebirth, and the restoring of the promise of childhood spirituality even out of the most unpromising situation.

Thomas Merton too dreamt of a child, a young Jewish girl named "Proverb," who embraces him "with determined and virginal passion. . . . She clings to me and will not let go, and I get to like the idea. I see that she is a nice kid in a plain sincere sort of way." Initially rationalizing and almost dismissing the dream, Merton later returns to reflect on it further some days later, including writing Proverb a letter. In it he sees the experience as healing and restorative and he thanks her, "for loving in me something which I thought I had entirely lost, and someone who, I thought, I had long ceased to be . . . your lovely spontaneity, your simplicity, the generosity of your love." Merton continues saying that what he holds most dear in her is "the revelation of your virginal solitude . . . your marvellous, innocent, love . . ."[38]

Visions of the Christ child have appeared throughout the ages; some are documented and others contribute to legends. One such is the well-known story of St. Christopher, a third-century martyr about whom very little is known. His name Christopher (Christ-bearer), rests on the legend that his Christian service was to help travelers cross a river. The story is told that once a child asked Christopher to carry him across, but Christopher found him so heavy that he was bowed down with the weight. The child then told him that he was Jesus Christ and that Christopher in carrying Christ had carried the weight of the whole world upon his shoulders.

---

36. Jung, *Archetypes*, 164.
37. Julian of Norwich, *Revelations of Divine Love*, 134.
38. Merton, *Search for Solitude*, 176.

Anthony of Padua (*c.* 1195–1231) was from the seventeenth century often depicted holding the Christ child who appeared to him. The story is told that when Anthony was visiting the Lord of Chatenaunef he was praying far into the night when the room became filled with a brilliant light—brighter than the sun. Jesus appeared in the form of a little child. Chatenaunef attracted by the startling light that filled his house was drawn to witness the vision but promised to tell no one of it until after the death of the saint. It has been pointed out that there is a similarity between this story and the story told in the account of the life of St. Francis where he re-enacted at Greccio the story of the birth of Jesus and the wooden carved figure of Christ child became a live baby in his arms. There are also other accounts of the appearances of the child Jesus to Francis and some companions. There is a link here with a sense of wonder and awe at the mystery of the incarnation and with the humility and vulnerability of the child.

In such visions the child is the beginning and the end, insignificant because small (and interestingly and unusually in Merton's dream female), powerless but divine. In many ways the divine child is a personification of all the vital forces included in a wholeness that covers the span before consciousness (the unconscious state of earliest childhood when there is no language or self-consciousness) and after consciousness as an anticipation of life after death. The symbol of the child anticipates a transformational process.

Carl Jung believed that such images of the Christ child will have to remain a religious and psychological necessity because the majority of people are unable to fulfil Jesus' command to become as small children themselves and so accept the infant as a part of what it means to become whole. Instead society encourages us either to deny the infant that we were or to encourage a false infantilism, or a superficial religious dependency. The divine child is the bringer of renewal and healing, the bringer of feelings of wonder, hope, life, energy, and spontaneity, "all that the wise men felt after their long, intuitive journey, when, guided by their eternal star, they found the Christ child. It brings with it the sense of individuality, eternity and immortality."[39]

The Christ child is then more than the baby in the manger; more than the child in the gospel; more than the child found in the adult disciples; and more than the child that each person once was. This eternal divine child welcomes each person into space, light, and freedom and anticipates a state of integration and oneness. As the mystics and saints have told us, the separation of the human and the divine is an illusion—it is all here, all now, in its entirety. We have only to see it.

39. Barker, "Healing the Child Within," 48.

4

The Influence of Monastics, Saints, and Theologians on Thomas Merton's Thinking on the Child Mind

Only one way to be a disciple—grow young again. That means learning how to die, to make oneself free, a traveler with almost no baggage. No acquired positions, no regrets, no decorations. Let the only dream of your life be—to wake up. Nothing is more revolutionary than childhood.[1]

Thomas Merton was living the scriptures through the monastic offices, reading extensively the works of the religious, the lives of the saints, and the work of theologians. In his writings and especially in the journals many are cited and some of these are selected here to be discussed in the context of the child mind.

Bernard of Clairvaux and Guerric of Igny on the Adoption of the Child Mind

Bernard of Clairvaux (1090–1153) was a French abbot and primary builder of the reforming Cistercian monastic order. Guerric of Igny (c. 1070/80–1157) was a Cistercian abbot. Thomas Merton was steeped in Cistercian monastic thinking. He wrote a book on Bernard called *The Last of the Fathers* and gave a series of talks to the novices about the teachings of Guerric of Igny so both men are significant in the development of Merton's understanding of mature spirituality in the context of the child mind.

1. Sulivan, *Morning Light*, 51, 124

Both of these twelfth-century monks used a synthesis of intellectual analysis and religious experience in their writings on the adoption of the spirit of the child. The intellectual approach tends to be speculative, defining and elaborating, so very much based on the conceptual. The experiential involves feelings of compunction, desire and love which allows for the unconscious, and may be harder to put into words. Such a synthesis of these two differing approaches has been called "wholespeak" as it includes both perspectives.[2] Religious experience fueled the monks' teachings with the focus on the mystery of the incarnation, and it is this that especially has implications for the idea of the child mind.

Guerric of Igny was influenced by the reforms of Bernard of Clairvaux and both men meditated and wrote extensively about the nativity and the meaning of the infancy of Christ in a way that conveys their lived experience. St. Bernard urges contemplation of the infancy of Christ, "The Word was made flesh, weak flesh, infantile flesh, young flesh, helpless flesh." He asks the question of why this would be so. The answer he gives is to be found in Christ's teaching and the example of his infancy that foreshadows the doctrine of his maturity, "the necessity of conversion to spiritual childhood, 'Why was it necessary that he should so empty himself, so humble himself, make himself so small but that you should do likewise.'"[3] Similarly Guerric, recalling similar teachings by St. Bernard, writes,

> But this birth in time is new in another way, in that the Child is born to renew us, he who as God is born eternally to make the angels blessed. The eternal birth certainly is more full of glory, but the temporal more lavish in mercy.

In a later Christmas sermon Guerric writes that Jesus Christ "has been born as a child for us . . . he has become our equal."[4] Both men write that through the incarnation comes renewal because innocence is restored. In the context of this book the incarnation is understood as a way that offers each person the experience of the child mind. It is a birth which can always bring about renewal in us. Early in his Cistercian monastic life Thomas Merton wrote about this as the "consciousness of innocence."

2. Allchin, *Joy of All Creation*, 21.

3. St. Bernard, Sermon 3 and Sermon 1, quoted in Saward, *Perfect Fools*, 63.

4. Guerric of Igny, first and third Sermon for Christmas, quoted in Morson, *Christ the Way*, 44, 46.

Another has taken over my identity, and this other is a tremendous infancy . . . as [if] I am one who is agelessly reborn . . . every day I am a day old, and at the altar I am the Child Who is God.[5]

For St. Bernard the story of the nativity and the birth of the divine child leads to the restoration of innocence and through this restoration he believed that each is led back to the fullness of life: "These things are mine, I am the one served, the food is set before me, the example held up for my imitation."[6] For Guerric there is a similar belief:

> O blessed childhood, whose weakness and foolishness is stronger and wiser than men; for it is, in truth, the strength and wisdom of God that works in us, does the work of God in man . . . O sweet and sacred Childhood, which brought back man's true innocence, by which every age may return to blessed childhood and be conformed to you, not in physical weakness but in humility of heart and holiness of life.[7]

For both Bernard and Guerric, and indeed for Merton, the state of childlikeness—the spirit of the child—is linked with simplicity, humility, and learned ignorance. Learned ignorance is the recognition that no one can know God rather one can know only what God is not. However one can learn something through this *via negativa* and so knowledge is attained of our ignorance: the unattainable is attained by its unattainment. (Some centuries later Nicholas of Cusa [1401–1468] wrote his book "On Learned Ignorance.") Guerric's use of the phrase "holy folly" and also "spiritual infancy" suggest the marks of a life thoroughly converted to Christ and unconformed to the world. The characteristics described in the contemporary research explored earlier of relational consciousness, playful imagination, and lack of status are implicated in both the phrases used by Guerric all those centuries before.

> Guerric's account of spiritual infancy is militant, with no trace of a sentimental or nostalgic cult of childhood. The Holy Child invades the fantasy world of Adam's adolescence and confronts him with the truth that seems like madness. There can be no substitute for the wild paradoxes of the gospel—littleness as the only way to greatness, death as the road to life, for this is the way taken by God himself, who emptied himself, to the point

---

5. Merton, *Entering the Silence*, 327.

6. St. Bernard, third sermon for Christmas, quoted in Morson, *Christ the Way*, 51.

7. Guerric of Igny, first sermon for Christmas, quoted in Saward, *Perfect Fools*, 64.

of almost seeming to be nothing, without whom nothing would have been.[8]

It needs to be emphasized that those monastics and religious who are able to live the way of spiritual childhood are not untouched by suffering or grief. It would be naïve and clichéd to see that restoration of the spirit of the child implies unalloyed joy and light-heartedness. Indeed in the same way a small child moves in an instant from a state of happiness to sadness, this can be seen as not dissimilar to the consolation and desolation sometimes described. The dread that only a child can feel, can be experienced in its same depth in an adult open to such bleakness. Those who have followed a way of spiritual childhood have implicitly experienced times of great suffering. This was undoubtedly the case for St. Francis of Assisi.

The Influence of Franciscan Spirituality

One of the important influences on Thomas Merton was undoubtedly the Franciscan intellectual and spiritual tradition. In a letter written in 1966 Merton wrote: "[I] will always feel that I am still in some secret way a son of St. Francis. There is no saint in the Church whom I admire more than St. Francis."[9]

Both Francis of Assisi (1181–1226) and Clare of Assisi (1194–1253), the founders of Franciscan spirituality, propose the words and deeds of Jesus in the gospel as the basic guide for their way of life. Of particular relevance in this context of the spirit of the child is the emphasis on the humility of God as revealed in the incarnation and in the goodness of all creation: Francis expressed his admiration for the humility of God revealed in the "Word made flesh." His desire to visualize the events of the birth of Jesus in order to enter more fully in to the experience of the incarnation led him to create an early form of the Christmas creation or nativity scene which he did in 1223—the story recounted in the last chapter of the baby Jesus coming alive in his arms belongs to this time. Like many religious his emphasis was on the littleness of the Christ child and the humility evident in the manner of his birth. In his *Admonitions* he writes, "Each day He humbles Himself as when He came from the royal throne into the Virgin's womb."[10]

In a similar way Clare—in the focus on the birth in the stable—emphasizes in her Order of Poor Sisters (later called Poor Clares) the bond

---

8. Ibid., 64–65.

9. Horan, *Franciscan Heart*, xix.

10. Short, "Franciscan Spirituality," 310.

between contemplation and poverty. She wrote in her letters about Christ as the mirror into which the sisters gazed and in doing so marveled at the "poverty of Him Who was placed in a manger . . . O astonishing poverty!"[11] It is not merely the poverty of the setting but the poverty within the person once stripped of all status, power, and prestige. This links to the humility found in the writings of other religious who upheld the status of childhood and Jesus' command—"Unless you become . . ."

Thomas Merton made an early decision to join the Franciscans, and while he was initially accepted, he subsequently was advised to reconsider following his own concern and disclosure of his past life. But it is to be noted that he did actually become a member of the Franciscan Third Order while working at St. Bonaventure College before joining the Trappists in 1941. During this time he read early Franciscan texts extensively and he commented and reflected in his journal written at the time on the impact these writings had on him. It has been noted that some of the early journal entries are "particularly evocative of his later spiritual teaching." This includes citations from St. Bonaventure, an early Franciscan theologian, with one "an outline of the entire journey, which moves from encountering God as reflected in the outside world to discovering the divine image and likeness within, to contemplative union with God as God is *in se.*" Merton was primarily interested in the Franciscan approach that the human person was created for contemplation—"the true paradise life."

In his analysis of the influence of St. Francis of Assisi on Thomas Merton, Daniel Horan explores in detail the Franciscan foundations of Merton's faith. He traces how Merton's thinking and development of the idea of the true self was shaped and inspired especially by both John Duns Scotus and St. Bonaventure. Duns Scotus like St. Bonaventure was a medieval Franciscan philosopher-theologian, and both men highlighted the necessity for the stripping away of the outer, transitory aspects of status and power to reveal the inner true core of the believer. There is a link between an early glimpse of Merton's central thinking and experience of the true self to a quotation from Francis which reads, "what a person is before God, that he [or she] is and no more"—"the conviction that our real identities . . . are found only in finding God, because God created us, knows us, and loves us for who and what we really are."[12] In Merton's search for the true self he understood this as our identity naked before God, in other words who we really are beyond the shadow and the disguise. In this book the suggestion is that this true self, this eternal potential, this state of "becoming" is the child mind.

11. Ibid., 311.

12. Horan, *Franciscan Heart,* 95–96.

In the context of the child mind the Franciscan tradition's theological reflection on creation is also important. The most significant idea is perhaps the concept of the kinship of all creation or as it has been called nature mysticism. In Francis's famous "Canticle of the Creatures" "all dimensions of the created world including planetary bodies, weather phenomena, elemental features of the Earth, vegetation, human beings, and death—are included." Francis, like the small child, created no distinction between different parts of nature, and nor did he judge the created order as reflecting human activity and reactions. He began with sameness and equality, seeing and believing that we are all created and so related. Again, like the small child "Francis's way of living in the world was one of intimate relationship. He lived *with* the world and not above and against it as others so commonly do."[13] Here there is deep connection with Merton's paradise consciousness which is explored in a later chapter. For in much of his writing on nature Merton came to see and understand that we are part of nature and members of the family of creation. For example he writes,

> The frogs have begun singing their pleasure in all the waters and in the warm green places where the sunshine is wonderful. Praise Christ, all you living creatures. For Him you and I were created. With every breath we love Him. My psalms fulfil your dim, unconscious song, O brothers in this wood.[14]

Whilst the popular contemporary images of Francis are sometimes presented as rather one-dimensional, for example being depicted as just a colorful lovable figure happily preaching to the birds and playing as a troubadour, Francis and Franciscan spirituality include great wisdom on the power of passion and love alongside Christ's suffering and death. The incarnation is concluded by the death and the resurrection of Jesus, which is all part of the "letting go" and the poverty. Francis writes in his Rule, "For our sakes, our Lord made Himself poor in this world." The stigmata, resembling the wounds of Christ's passion that, according to the account given by Francis' companion Brother Leo appeared on Francis two years before his death during an extended retreat on Mount La Verna, became an eloquent sign of his compassion with the suffering of Christ.

As Thomas Merton reflects in his extended meditation on the meaning of this experience, a tremendous and overwhelming change came upon Francis. He no longer said anything. In contrast the delightful figure that was so charismatic and joyous, preaching to the birds, singing and inviting

---

13. Ibid., 151.

14. Merton, *Sign of Jonas*, 285.

all to join him became a broken small figure. Instead he appeared, "strange" and "colourless" "a hunched up little man." No longer the troubadour he was quiet, almost unwell, "he carries upon him the stigmata . . . he bore the same insult as Christ—an insult beyond all comprehension, beyond all drama, beyond all speech, so extreme as to seem utterly neutral."[15]

The accounts of the life of Francis in all states of being—joy and playfulness, in his dependence, humiliation, and obedience, and also in his deep suffering and grief—show evidence that he became increasingly closer to Christ and in many ways his life is an exemplar of the child mind. Furthermore as has been noted, it is quite clear from the references to dancing and singing and playing, to being considered a madman, a fool, and a crook, Merton saw in Francis the pattern for his own life. He also understood from St. Francis the importance of humility. In trying to discern his vocation Merton wrote in his journal the following part prayer, part revelation:

> Holy Father, take away, by your prayers, this pride. . . . But for this pride, also, I wouldn't be so self-conscious about language to express what I feel . . . if I am humble, I will write better, just by being humble. By being humble, I will write what is true . . .
>
> Holy Father Pray for me, Holy Father Saint Francis, in all things to sing to God very humbly and childishly and sweetly . . . Only pray for me, my Father Saint Francis, to give up everything for my lord, to be the least of His children and the most insignificant of the poor for love only . . . Pray for me for enough humility to always pray for humility, poverty, and tears.[16]

St. Thérèse of Lisieux and the Little Way of Spiritual Childhood

Another saint who advocated humility, poverty, and littleness was St. Thérèse of Lisieux (1873–1897). She is also known as the Little Flower and is famous for her acknowledged way of spiritual childhood and the incorporation into this of deep suffering. Thomas Merton had a special relationship with this saint and writes mostly about the influence of St. Thérèse of Lisieux in his early journals, and in particular around the time of his entrance to Gethsemani Abbey, when he promises her, "I will be your monk."[17] In October 1941 Merton writes that he has just read the book about Thérèse called *The*

---

15. Merton, *Run to the Mountain*, 266.

16. Merton, *Run to the Mountain*, 407.

17. Merton, *Seven Storey Mountain*, 437.

Secret of the Little Flower, written by Henri Gheon, and "am knocked out by it completely."[18] Gheon had written of his horror at the mawkish nature and the "tinselled and sugary manifestations of devotion to the '*little* saint' (the abuse of this diminutive drove me frantic)," and his initial astonishment at the veneration of the young woman who apparently had done nothing for her short life.[19] Merton's own critique of the "scandal of cheap, molasses-art and gorgonzola angels that surround the cultus of this great saint"[20] does not prevent him, like Gheon, once initial resistance is overcome, from realizing her extraordinary nature. He describes her as "a great saint, one of the greatest: tremendous!"[21] From the reading of Gheon's biography, Merton gains "a faint glimpse of the real character and the real spirituality of St. Thérèse," and then is "immediately and strongly attracted to her."[22]

From his reading and reflections Thomas Merton sees Thérèse as "more extraordinary than even St. John of the Cross or Saint Theresa of Avila,"[23] partly because her simplicity includes the love and wisdom of both these earlier saints, but perhaps also because her simplicity and sanctity emerged, it appears, against such odds given her provincial and somewhat bourgeois background. This particularly struck Merton:

> The one thing seemed to me more or less impossible was for grace to penetrate the thick, resilient hide of *bourgeois* smugness and really take hold of the immortal soul beneath that surface, in order to make something out of it.[24]

It is worth noting that both Merton and Thérèse had suffered early maternal abandonment through death: Merton at the age of six and Thérèse at four and a half. Thérèse's autobiography *The Story of a Soul* describes both the pain of the loss, and, similar to Merton, the deepening of her relationship and dependency on her father (Merton's difficult childhood is discussed in a later chapter). Further identification that perhaps resonated with the newly converted Merton was Thérèse's devotion to entering the religious life, and the struggle, fully explained in her autobiography, to enter the convent despite the usual conventions.

---

18. Merton, *Run to the Mountain*, 431.

19. Gheon, *Secret of the Little Flower*, 11.

20. Merton, *Run to the Mountain*, 432.

21. Merton, *Seven Storey Mountain*, 423.

22. Ibid., 425.

23. Merton, *Run to the Mountain*, 432.

24. Merton, *Seven Storey Mountain*, 424.

In one of his early books, published in the same year as his autobiography, Merton, though writing about the French Trappistine Mother Berchmans, examines the influence of the simple and fundamental spirituality of Thérèse. He writes of Thérèse's path of spiritual childhood in this way:

> The soul that discovers the way of spiritual childhood is happy in a way that it had never before imagined possible, because, by discovering its own nothingness, it is at last liberated from the prison of futile introversion and fruitless self-consideration, and can devote itself altogether to . . . the knowledge and love of the great, immensely good God.[25]

Thérèse's "little way" was to surrender and to live as a child dependent on the mercy of God. She was reliant on her early life experiences alongside her religious tradition when she writes of her relationship with God as full of "the unconcern with which a child goes to sleep in its father's arms." She writes of remaining little so that she can be raised to heaven in the arms of Jesus. She asks herself:

> "Can't I find a lift which will take me up to Jesus, since I'm not big enough to climb the steep stairway of perfection?" So I looked in the Bible for some hint about the life I wanted, and I came across the passage where Eternal Wisdom says: "Is any one simple like a little child? Then let him come to me." To that Wisdom I went; it seemed as if I was on the right track; what did God undertake to do for the child-like soul that responded to his invitation? I read on and this is what I found: "I will console you like a mother caressing her son; you shall be like children carried at the breast, fondled on a mother's lap."[26]

Her initial ability to fall into this dependency with God may have been affected by the early loss of her mother. One biographer writes:

> She was affected by a nervous condition at this loss until . . . the age of 10 years. . . . She suffered from maternal abandonment even though she was surrounded by love. As a child and adolescent she suffered greatly from emotional distress . . . an affective weakness which would mark [her] whole life: *"Am I loved?"* asks Thérèse. She relates one year before her death that in one of her dreams she asks the question: *"Is the Good God content with me?"*[27]

25. Merton, *Exile Ends in Glory*, 159, 161.

26. Thérèse of Lisieux, *Autobiography*, 180, 195.

27. Ryan, *Edith Piaf and Thérèse of Lisieux*.

Her spirituality may have been energized by this early experience but it was reframed through prayer, experience, and life in a convent community into a personal and mature theology. Her life involved emotional suffering linked to loss and times of persecution and humiliation in the convent. She suffered acute physical pain with tuberculosis for a number of years before her death, and alongside this, doubt and perplexity about her faith. In all this, "She took comfort in the simplicity of 'The Little Way.'"[28]

The childhood spirituality of Thérèse has been questioned by some who suggest that the young woman could be seen as caught in a sort of perennial childhood, where she was not allowed by some of her interpreters and admirers to grow up. This critique perhaps fits with Merton's comments on Thérèse's spirituality where he writes:

> this mystery that being as a child was to be crucified, but crucified in a kind of innocence . . . a child whose childishness involves maybe a maturer mysticism than all Saint John of the Cross, something that rejoins the awful mystery of the Stigmatization of Saint Francis.[29]

Her way of spiritual childhood was based on self-knowledge and an awareness derived from thinking about what was happening in her and around her, even in times of pain. Living in community Thérèse developed an inner life instead of a defensive way of responding. Each personal experience when she was in the convent, no matter how apparently insignificant, led to insights that shaped her views and ultimately her theology. Her theology was still framed within tradition, from her rereading of the gospels and certain spiritual classics, but her personal experience distilled a simple set of insights within that tradition.

> The truly remarkable thing about Thérèse, however, is that she took her own very human failings—her longing for love and attention and acclaim, her overweening spiritual ambition—exactly as they were in all their silliness and childishness and began to work with them . . . she detached herself from the particular shame of such feelings by owning them . . . she took the scrap of life allowed to her and transformed it.[30]

In her work with the novices in the convent and her letters to missionaries outside, Thérèse did not use theory or deduction, but would offer practical solutions often based on her personal experiences: "she is properly

---

28. Furlong, *Thérèse of Lisieux*, 102.

29. Merton, *Run to the Mountain*, 433.

30. Furlong, *Thérèse of Lisieux*, 133–34.

experimental and intuitive . . . everything in her teaching is spirit and life . . . she considered that the hardest labour of all is that of self-conquest which we undertake within ourselves."[31]

Thérèse's way of spiritual childhood focuses on the personal as contributing to the theological so that the encounter with God becomes a dynamic and on-going encounter. Thérèse demonstrates a capacity to live in the present moment with awareness, her life is not static rather changing from instant to instant, but within a framework of the sacraments and prayer. She experienced great devotion to the Eucharist. Thérèse at her first communion writes, ". . . something had melted away, and there were no longer two of us—Thérèse had simply disappeared, like a drop lost in the ocean; Jesus only was left."[32] For her the way of childhood spirituality and living in the spirit of the child is about a deeply embedded relationship with the divine (like a baby with a loving mother), a form of inner merging with Christ. In turn this is fostered by the adult part of her through different forms of contemplative prayer that empowers actions.

Throughout there is self-examination and the consideration of everyday events, and so Thérèse demonstrates a process also found in Merton's writings, particularly in the journals, where he becomes a witness to his responses and experiences, then analyses and works with them. From this emerges in particular his personal understanding of the concept of the false and true self. For Merton the child mind is linked to the experiential, to a condition of complete simplicity and innocence without artifice, excluded from worldly power, status, participation, and recognition, in other words from ego-orientated identity. The crux for both Merton and Thérèse is a dependence on God framed within the concept of mercy exemplified by God's relationship with his creation and each one of us. Merton writing on God's mercy towards us reflects on mercy as the experience that binds us in relationship to God, and this grace does not depend on our perfection.[33] Similarly, for Thérèse the way of spiritual childhood "is nothing other than a mystical asceticism suited to God's action which revealed itself . . . as mercy."[34]

When Merton writes of "the tremendous experience" of his discovery of St. Thérèse of Lisieux he explains that this is then a relationship and a process of grace through which much may happen: "And so, now that I had this great new friend in heaven, it was inevitable that the friendship should

31. Petitot, "Spiritual Renaissance," 18, 20.

32. Thérèse of Lisieux, *Autobiography*, 82.

33. Shannon, "Mercy," 292.

34. Girard, "Spiritual Childhood," 75.

begin to have its influence on my life."[35] There is evidence from Merton's writings of this ongoing influence on his later spirituality. For both, their vocation was to live out what they discovered about themselves. As Merton writes, "Living is the constant adjustment of thought to life and life to thought in such a way that we are always growing, always experiencing."[36] Here then is once again the child mind—always in a state of potential and becoming—following the command: "unless you become . . ."

An Overview of Some Theological Interpretations of Jesus' Command

Thomas Merton would have been familiar with the various theological interpretations and commentaries associated with Jesus' command to become as small children. Most commentators agree that there are special qualities of childhood which are to be emulated by adults. Augustine of Hippo (354–430) takes the state of humility and links this to the low social status of children and thus God's identification with the least. In his *Confessions* Augustine saw the development of interior meditations on childhood as a spiritual practice and an acknowledgement of childhood experiences, the good and the bad, the desolation and the joy, as held in the mystery of God.[37] This practice then cultivates self-awareness, "critical self-presence," that develops the capacity both to dwell in God and to be a place-in-the-world where God dwells.[38]

Another example is Friedrich Schleiermacher (1768–1834), who wrote on the ability to live in the present moment, "The past disappears [for the child], and of the future he knows nothing—each moment exists only for itself and this accounts for the blessedness of a soul content in innocence." He also saw a child's experience of dependency as a key quality that he believed would give a "foundation for understanding their relationship to God." He praised their ability to experience "the full range of emotional life without repression."[39]

In Karl Rahner's work on "Ideas for a Theology of Childhood," he discussed that childhood, especially among Christians, has been seen as "a mere provisional conditioning for the shaping of adult life in all its fullness,"

---

35. Merton, *Seven Storey Mountain,* 426.
36. Merton, *Thoughts in Solitude,* 19.
37. St. Augustine, *Confessions.*
38. Frohlich, "Spiritual Discipline," 74.
39. Paulsell, "Lost in the Mystery," 88.

and so is left behind as quickly and completely as is possible. In contrast to this view he saw aspects of childhood, as "a field which bears fair flowers and ripe fruits . . . carried into the storehouses of eternity," but thought that what is already present in the child has still to be realized and so become actual in experience. Rahner believed that it is "the totality of this experience as summed up in the world 'child' that Holy Scripture draws on." In other words we are dependent on individual experience to understand what this might mean, and Rahner did acknowledge that this will include aspects that are "dark, complex and conflicting," but his emphasis was on the child as innocent and carefree in relationship with God. Jesus in his commands identified himself with children and for this reason Rahner saw childhood as ultimately a mystery, in the same way that life is mysterious and God is "utter mystery." The secret is then to remain open to mystery, including "trustful submission to control by another . . . a readiness to journey into the untried and untested."[40]

Contemporary commentators have questioned this emphasis on innocence and openness and whilst noting what an attractive picture they give of childhood have derided them as "general, ahistorical appeals" vulnerable to being filled, not with the lived experience of children but with adult fantasies about childhood and children. "If Rahner had lived through the exposure of the widespread sexual abuse of children in the church, it is hard to imagine he would have appealed to the 'readiness to be controlled by another,' as a characteristic of childhood to be cherished and imitated."[41] This is why the earlier definition of innocence discussed earlier as being "unwounded" can be more helpful than a superficial assumption of what it means.

In Thomas Merton's writing on "Barth's Dream" he is deeply moved by the account of the theologian Karl Barth's dream about Mozart in which Barth is appointed to examine Mozart in theology and Mozart does not answer a word. Merton in his reflections notes that Barth played Mozart every morning before going to work on his dogma. He suggests that perhaps Barth was trying to awaken "the hidden sophianic Mozart in himself" as Barth says:

> that "it is a child, even a 'divine' child, who speaks in Mozart's music to us." . . . Mozart, the child prodigy, "was never allowed to be a child in the literal meaning of that word." . . . Yet he was always a child in the higher meaning of that word."

---

40. Rahner, "Ideas for a Theology," 35–36, 40, 48.
41. Paulsell, "Lost in the Mystery," 89.

Merton comments: "Fear not, Karl Barth! Trust in the divine mercy. Though you have grown up to become a theologian, Christ remains a child in you."[42]

For both Barth and Merton "the 'divine child' belongs with this apprehension of divine *Sophia*, the wisdom at the heart of things."[43]

42. Merton, *Conjectures*, 11–12.
43. Williams, "Not Being Serious," 72.

5

Child's Mind is Buddha's Mind

Eastern thought has long understood the value of the child mind in the adult seeker for spiritual maturity. The child mind is seen as a place of surrender, alertness, and nakedness. It is seen as a space where there is little if any self-consciousness; there is no judgment of others. It is a time of humility. It involves an awareness of the person's nothingness—where the person is *no*-thing. The child mind recognizes the person's smallness and yet connection in the scheme of things, and in Eastern practices it is seen as a state that can be developed through silent meditation, and often in solitude. There can be glimpses or breakthroughs or longer periods of such awareness; it is experiential and not knowledge-based or a doctrine that can be learnt. For Merton part of the attraction of mystical teachings from the East was their convergence around the simplicity and freedom of not-knowing, a negative capability with similarities to the apophatic way in Christian mysticism. There are links here to the idea of not-knowing, learned ignorance, and negative capabilities which is like the small child's sense of life as ultimately mysterious and happening to them and around them. Merton saw the religious search as an authentic and deeply human journey leading to conversion to humility, spiritual poverty, and the nakedness of the child mind.

Mencius, the Chinese Confucian philosopher in the fourth century BCE, is reputed to have said that the wise person is one who doesn't lose the child's heart and mind.[1] Both Zen and Chinese philosophy describe an alert awareness, where the mind is unburdened by the past and especially by conceptual knowledge, where things are seen as they are without preconceptions or judgement. Merton found there are clear links here to the

1. Cohen, "Beginner's Mind," lines 27–28.

gospels. In Merton's introduction to the readings he made of Chuang Tzu, he wrote that "there is much in the teaching of the Gospels in simplicity, childlikeness, and humility, which responds to the deepest aspirations of the Chuang Tzu book and the Tao Te Ching."[2]

Buddhism teaches that there is a spark in each person that represents one's true nature; this is sometimes called Buddha Nature or the Original Mind. This spark is the child mind, fresh and always curious about experience. The Zen Buddhist concept "shoshin" is sometimes called "beginner's mind" and reflects the open and enthusiastic qualities of a child's mind in the present moment. One Zen master called the beginner's mind a child's mind, a mind that is empty and ready for new things so that the beginner's mind, like that of a child, is critical for the experience of the Buddha Dharma.[3] Here the beginner's mind is in a state of becoming: "unless you become . . ." Understanding the Eastern perspective confirms the child mind as a transcultural and transcendent experience—part of the communion underlying all spiritual traditions which includes Chinese philosophy, Taoism and Confucianism, Buddhism and Zen.

The Child Mind—A Communion of Authentic Experience across Spiritual Traditions

It is suggested that the authentic experience of the child mind in the adult contributes to a transcultural communion that spans the mystical aspects of all spiritual traditions. Merton's interest in the spirituality of religions other than Christianity did not emerge from his life as a Cistercian monk but has been traced back to the young Merton, who was influenced by Aldous Huxley's work *Ends and Means* with Huxley's argument that there is a:

> spiritual substratum to the material changing world, a substratum that took the form of a philosophia perennis. This notion that there was a transcultural structure of transcendent experience hidden under all religious systems made a profound impact on him. . . . Huxley, then, provided Merton with the notion that the religious search was an authentic and deeply human one.[4]

In his classic work *The Perennial Philosophy* Huxley writes of the universal and immemorial recognition of

2. Merton, *Way of Chuang Tzu*, 11.
3. Sa Nim, "Child's Mind."
4. Cunningham, *Monastic Vision*, 9.

a divine Reality substantial to the world of things and lives and minds; the psychology that finds in the soul something similar to, or even identical with, divine Reality; the ethic that places man's final end in the knowledge of the immanent and transcendent Ground of all being.[5]

Recognizing that rudiments of this belief are found in "the traditionary lore of primitive peoples in every region of the world" and in a more developed form "it has a place in every one of the higher religions," Huxley adds that the "being of a child is transformed by growth and education" but that one of the results of this is the change to more conceptual and systematic knowledge. He continues, "but these gains are offset by a certain deterioration in the quality of immediate apprehension, a blunting and a loss of intuitive power." The experiences of the numinous take place "immediately and apart from any vocabulary whatsoever. Strange openings and theophanies are granted to quite small children, who are often profoundly and permanently affected by these experiences."[6] Huxley appreciated the paradox that Reality, with a capital "R," is only available to those who have an inner poverty and humility, and that a theology based on the experience of such people reminded him of the saying in the gospel of Matthew that the revelation can only be experienced by infants rather than the wise and the intelligent (Matt 11:25).

Through reading Huxley, Merton understood that "all great philosophical thought" goes "immediately to the heart of things," and was attracted to "a certain mentality found everywhere in the world." However Merton writes that he

> came away from Huxley's *Ends and Means* with the prejudice that Christianity was a less pure religion, because it was more "immersed in matter"—that is, because it did not scorn to use a Sacramental liturgy that relied on the appeal of created things to the senses in order to raise the souls of men to higher things.[7]

Let loose in the library at Columbia University, where Merton was a student, he writes of being "turned on like a pinball machine"[8] to many writers including William Blake and, beyond the Christian tradition, to Ananda K. Coomaraswamy. However it was the Hindu monk, Merton's friend Bramachari, who told Merton that "I ought to turn to the Christian

---

5. Huxley, *Perennial Philosophy*, 9.

6. Ibid., 32, 9.

7. Merton, *Seven Storey Mountain,* 240.

8. Merton, *Love and Living,* 13.

tradition."[9] Merton met Bramachari, who was studying for a doctorate in the United States, through some mutual friends. In his autobiography Merton was struck by the fact that Bramachari never attempted to explain his own religion to him and guided him to Christian mystical books. Looking back he saw his contact with the Hindu monk as a special grace from God. Merton's open approach to other faiths also deepened as he held to the underlying truths found in all mystical writing.

One example of this is shown in a letter written in January 1961 to Dona Luisa Coomaraswamy, the widow of Ananda Coomaraswamy and a Sanskrit scholar in her own right. Merton wrote of Ananda Coomaraswamy as a "model of one who has thoroughly and completely united in himself the spiritual tradition and attitudes of the Orient and of the Christian West, not excluding also something of Islam." His thinking was that if some contemplatives could develop the capacity to hold within and personally experience "all that is best and most true in the various great spiritual traditions" they could become as "sacraments" and certainly "signs of peace" contributing to world peace and unity. Merton identified this as a task of "very remote preparation" that would lead to "new seeds of thought." Merton was not talking here about inter-faith dialogue that happened between two people, but something that could happen internally within the person.[10] In other words something that grew out of contemplative prayer and solitude.

This sort of individual pioneering Merton describes as "something more" a "communion in authentic experience which is shared not only on a 'preverbal' level but also on a 'postverbal' level."[11] Here are hints again of the child mind. The preverbal is the experience of the small child before language and the difficulties over conceptual meanings obscure and confuse, as in adult discourse but Merton takes this idea of "communion of authentic experience" beyond that and beyond the verbal into something that combines the experience of both and then transcends them: a place of authenticity. This is the child mind of the adult where there is the postverbal level beyond words and understanding, "the silence of an ultimate experience," which might also be described as *satori* or enlightenment.

Merton was not alone in such pioneering understanding that Zen in particular is about the deeply experiential rather than any rigid "reliance upon the authority of the scriptures." William Johnston, the Irish Jesuit, with whom Merton corresponded and wrote a preface for one of the books by Johnston, went to Japan in 1951. Johnston discusses his experience of

9. Merton, *Seven Storey Mountain*, 240.

10. Merton, *Hidden Ground of Love*, 126.

11. Merton, *Asian Journal*, 315.

practicing silent prayer and the time he asked the Jesuit Hugo Lassalle, known for his practice of Zen, "Where is Christ in Zen?" Lassalle replied almost sternly, "Father, practice Zen and you will find Christ." Someone else asked Lassalle, "But what about theology? Where does Christian theology fit in Zen?" and he answered, "I don't care about theology." "You don't care" said his questioner, "but other people do." It is documented how Lassalle's outlook led to trouble with Rome.[12]

It would seem that the trouble and difficulties that ensue over the search for such a communion of experience among those who undertake this depend in part on the adult mind's external and internal attachments to constructs, representations, symbols, status, and aspects of self-identity. The spiritual journeying that Merton describes is an increasing process of interiority, a stripping away of external representations and false selves, and, for him as a monk, struggles with, yet firm loyalty towards and changing interpretations of, obedience towards the institutional church.

Henri Le Saux, Benedictine monk turned Indian hermit known as Swami Abhishiktananda, wrote poignantly of the same dilemma. After many years of such pioneering he found that what mattered was the experience within, the being there simply, and the awakening to what he calls "real prayer," which is the interior silence of Jesus, "awakened in the depths of the heart." He wrote that the life of silent prayer, the life of contemplation, is "the awareness of the Presence, and when that is experienced, one is free . . ."[13]

Merton saw such authentic experiences as part of his faith and the overcoming of doubt, what is referred to in Zen Buddhism as "the Great Doubt," by going through it beyond the irrelevance of our personal life and situation, beyond the dichotomy of life and death into the ultimate reality of God. As Merton puts it: "free-floating existence under a state of risk."[14]

This is recognized as the last great struggle between feeling and thinking within the person—involving the mind full of logical thought and the heart holding onto trust. It inevitably involves confusion and the letting go of long held certainties into a deep unknowing.

This then is also the marginal place of the small child where power and conceptual thinking and constructs have no meaning. This could be called also the place of the poet, where the constraints of external position and status are increasingly dissipated. In this liminal place experience is all, but for the adult such a stripping away of external supports can be unsafe and troublesome. It sounds more like spirituality than religion. It is clearly

12. Johnston, *Mystical Journey*, 76.

13. du Boulay, *Cave of the Heart*, 222, 208, 212.

14. Merton, *Asian Journal*, 308.

a move away from the masculine dualistic model of Western Christianity towards the monistic or feminine spirituality found in the Christian and Eastern mystical traditions. Yet at the deepest level such pioneering in the realm of transcendence of differences and opposites within the person can bring a consciousness that includes a deep belonging and identity outside of the known. This is the communion of those with the child mind. As has been said of this openness in Merton:

> A tree has many branches. All lead down to the root, all are nourished by the same sap rising from the root.
> Thomas Merton went down the Christian branch of religion to the root. Nourished by that he saw the other branches.[15]

Spiritual Childhood, Tao and John Wu

> He who has in himself abundantly the attributes (of the Tao) is like an infant.[16]

It was in a letter written 1 April 1961 that Merton wrote to John Wu asking "the Lord to give you every blessing and joy and to keep ever fresh and young your 'child's mind' which is the only one worth having." Merton continued, "May he grant us (as you so well say) to be both inebriated and sober in Christ, Confucians and Taoists. It is all-important for us to be in Christ what the great sages cried out to God for."[17]

John Wu, both a scholar and diplomat, was, together with Paul K. T. Sih, "deeply influential in guiding Merton towards some of the classic Taoist texts and in enabling him to delight especially in the writings of Chuang Tzu, the Chinese Taoist master of the 4th century BC."[18] Wu described in a beautiful analogy the Chinese culture as the gifts of the Magi to Christ: "I often think of myself as a Magus from China who lays before the Divine Infant in the arms of the Blessed Virgin the gold of Confucianism, the musk of Taoism, and the frankincense of Buddhism." He claimed that Christ purified them and lifted them up into supernatural values with His divine hands.[19] John Wu understood the communion of those who experience the child mind.

15. Schloegl, *Thomas Merton on Zen*, vii.
16. Lao-Tzu, *Tao Te Ching*, 55 lines 1–2.
17. Merton, *Hidden Ground of Love*, 614.
18. Moses, *Divine Discontent*, 146.
19. Tang, "Meeting Wu and Thérèse," 10.

Again as with Zen, Merton wrote of finding in Taoism "a full awareness of the transcendent dimensions of everyday life in its very ordinariness."[20] In the correspondence with John Wu, Merton emphasizes his own need for humility and his appreciation of the simplicity found in Chuang Tzu. Merton, helped by Wu, offered a compilation of stories by and about Chuang Tzu from the fourth and third centuries BC. Merton found in this teaching "simplicity," "humility," "self-effacement," "silence," and in general, "a refusal to take seriously the aggressivity, the ambition, the push, and the self-importance which one must display in order to get along in society. This other is a 'way' that prefers not to get anywhere in the world."[21] Merton sees that the Taoism of Chuang Tzu is manifested by what he calls "a Franciscan spirituality and connaturality with all living creatures," frogs, birds, and fishes are among the "characters" that speak the mind of Chuang Tzu, who "is nostalgic for the primordial climate of paradise in which there was no differentiation,"[22] where humans could be simple and living unselfconsciously in peace. While still ours, in some part of our being, this paradise has been lost, and can only be regained through redemption.

> You want the first elements?
> The infant has them.
> Free from care, unaware of self,
> He acts without reflection,
> Stays where he is put, does not know why,
> Does not figure things out,
> Just goes along with them,
> Is part of the current.
> These are the first elements!

The disciple asks whether this is perfection and Lao replies that such awareness can only be the beginning.

> This melts the ice.
> This enables you
> To unlearn,
> So that you can be led by Tao,
> Be a child of Tao.[23]

For Merton, Chuang Tzu "demands the Resurrection, for the Resurrection goes beyond all moralities and moral theories, it is a totally new life

20. Moses, *Divine Discontent*, 147.

21. Merton, *Way of Chuang Tzu*, 11.

22. Ibid., 27.

23. Ibid., 132–33.

in the Spirit."[24] As Merton became increasingly immersed in the words of the Chinese writer, he explored with Wu the carefree nature of the work, which for Merton reminded him of the liberty of spirit found in St. Paul's Epistles and in St. John.

> We underestimate St. Paul. We do not realize what a liberation he went through and how carefree and undetermined a Christian really should be, with no care save to listen to the Holy Spirit and follow wherever He beckons! Let us seek more and more to do this in the gaiety and childlike joy of Chuang Tzu. I think spiritual childhood must be characteristically Chinese grace. I mean one which the Chinese temperament was prepared for . . .[25]

Given Wu's understanding of this spiritual childhood it is no surprise that writing to him about his interest in Wu's work on St. Thérèse, Merton adds, "I am sure you will have a very special insight into the Little Way."[26] Both men recognized that St. Thérèse was indeed a kindred spirit and connected through this communion of the child mind. Indeed in one of Wu's published works, discussed in the correspondence with Merton above, Wu writes of his appreciation of St. Thérèse's spiritual childhood:

> If she is a child, she is a subtle one. If she is as simple as a dove, she is also as wise as a serpent. Her little way of spiritual childhood is really the most mature way, and she seems to be aware of it. During her serious illness, she once said, "Let God play the part of Papa; he knows what is best for baby." Her eldest sister Marie asked her, "Are you a baby?" Thérèse looked serious and said, "Yes,—but a very wise baby! A baby who is an old man."[27]

Wu understood that to get to the spiritual childhood the saint lived and wrote about is not a sentimental regression but rather to "go a step forward until we find God in the most secret chamber of our heart." He uses the analogy of a cure for urbanity where a dream of returning to the country is useless, for even back in the country from the city "we would still carry the city with us. We have already gone too far to retrace our steps." The only route to take is to "be so urbane that we become citizens of the City of God, which exists before both the city and the country ever did." The way is then to move beyond, transcend, while encapsulating and integrating earlier

24. Merton, *Hidden Ground of Love*, 614.

25. Ibid., 615.

26. Ibid., 616.

27. Wu, *Science of Love*, 12

experiences. Beyond is to something greater than ourselves. Wu returns to the wise baby when referring to St. Thérèse: "nor is it for nothing that this time He has raised 'a baby who is an old man.' For our century is an old man who wants very much to be a baby." For Wu it was Thérèse's humility and awareness of her own nothingness that reminded him so much of the Tao and Confucianism: "her vison was so clear she had to resort to parables." He references Lao Tzu who said:

> To be the Brook of the world is
> To move constantly in the path of Virtue
> Without swerving from it
> And to return again to Infancy.[28]

A different translation phrases the same verse in this way:

> Thus he the constant excellence retains;
> The simple child again, free from all stains.[29]

In Merton's writing on the sage or the person who has discovered the secret of the *Tao*, he emphasizes that the person is not especially wise or has acquired any special knowledge. Rather the opposite:

> Whilst everyone else exults over success as over a sacrificial ox, he alone is silent "like a babe who has not yet smiled." Though he has in fact "returned to the root," the *Tao*, he . . . is bland like the ocean, aimless as the wafting gale. Again we remember the Gospels: "The wind blows where it pleases . . . even so is every man who is born of the Spirit." (John 3:8)[30]

The correspondence between Merton and John Wu begun in 1961 only ended with Merton's death in 1968. The central motif remained almost throughout the child mind: "Thus we go along gaily with littleness for our Mother and our Nurse, and we return to the root by having no answers to questions." One especially lovely Christmas letter from Merton confirmed his view that Chuang Tzu acts as a reminder of the need for continual "debunking" to return to the "essential element in the Gospel . . . the crib full of straw, in which the Lord of the world laughs and says, 'You should worry!'" The letter ends:

28. Lao-tzu, quoted in Wu, *Science of Love* (different translation of the same verse but referenced as Tao Te Ching chapter 29 lines 1–4).

29 Lao-Tzu, *Tao Te Ching*, chapter 28 lines 5–6.

30. Merton, *Thomas Merton on Zen*, 42

Every blessing in this holy season when the animals and the shepherds show us the way back to our child mind and to Him in Whom is hidden our original face before we are born. Be of good cheer. They cannot silence either Chuang Tzu or this Child, in China or anywhere. They will be heard in the middle of the night saying nothing and everybody will come to their senses.

In a later letter, after both men met the Zen scholar D. T. Suzuki in 1964, they agreed that Suzuki, as Merton puts it, has "a child's mind and heart. It is perfectly true and that is his greatness." In writing about a haiku and calligraphies, Merton writes "I have the privilege of being reduced to a state of complete infancy."[31] This state of concentration seems to link to the image found in early Chinese depictions of the sage in deep meditation and in whose heart a small child is forming. "The little child is nourished and cared for there until at last it is ready to float through the cranial cavity out into the heights as the new divine birth."[32]

"To be absolutely naked"—Zen and the Child Mind

Merton wrote that the true inheritors of the thought and spirit of Chuang Tzu are the Chinese Zen Buddhists of the T'ang period from the seventh to tenth centuries CE. He writes that it is clear that the kind of thought and culture represented by Chuang Tzu was what transformed "highly speculative Indian Buddhism into the humorous, iconoclastic, and totally practical kind of Buddhism that was to flourish in China and in Japan in the various schools of Zen. Zen throws light on Chuang Tzu, and Chuang Tzu throws light on Zen."[33] Furthermore the unconditional experience that is the essential core of Zen has been seen also as the core of all mystical traditions. Less a religion it is more a way of looking at life and being alive. Thomas Merton, whilst recognizing that Zen developed from and within Buddhism, saw it as ultimately encompassing and extending across cultures and other religions as "trans-formed consciousness."[34] He agreed with the teaching of the great Zen scholar Dr D. T. Suzuki, "that the 'perfect poverty' of Meister Eckhart, in which there is no 'place' for God to work, and therefore no separation between the self and its divine Ground, is an expression of Zenlike awareness." In this way Zen is about an emptying out, in the way that Christ

31. Merton, *Hidden Ground of Love,* 618, 624–25, 633.

32. Hannah, "Beyond," 122.

33. Merton, *Way of Chuang Tzu,* 16.

34. Merton, *Zen and the Birds,* 4.

"emptied himself, poured himself out, and clung to nothing."[35] However it is worth noting that Merton writing of the difficulty of comparing Zen to Christianity in his introduction to John Wu's *The Golden Age of Zen* tells us that to compare them is like comparing tennis to mathematics.[36] Where the convergence exists is through contemplative prayer and the letting go of reasoning about concepts.

Merton corresponded with the Zen scholar D. T. Suzuki and the two men established a real friendship and indeed later met. In one letter Merton wrote quoting a Syrian Christian thinker of the fifth century:

> Simplicity is completely absorbed in listening to what it hears. All its thought is mingled with the word of him who speaks. It is like the little child, completely absorbed in the person speaking to it.[37]

For Merton "Zen is your everyday mind." It is about detachment, and without this cutting "one's umbilical cord to mother, father, family, race, state, status, money, and gods. One can never emerge fully as oneself. One can never be fully born."[38] Paradoxically to move towards the child mind there has to be a letting go of attachment to the actual past childhood and to the achievements of adult identity.

Similarly, Irmgard Schloegl, later known as Ven Myokyo-ni, a Zen Buddhist nun who also undertook a Jungian analysis, wrote in her introduction to the collection of Merton's writing on Zen, that Zen understands that life is a process and puts this in stages. She quotes the Zen saying, "to begin with, we see trees as trees and water as water; then trees are no longer trees, and water is not just water; but in the end, trees are trees again, and water is water." Schloegl links this to the innocence of the child that takes things as they are. With the loss of innocence there comes a questioning and a need to check things out and understand. If, she believes, this goes well, there is what she describes as "a settling down in ripeness" and adds, "Christ said: 'Unless you become as little children . . .' which is surely different from being merely childish." A commentary on this analogy with the small child points out that although the first and the last stage seem so alike on the surface, there is a difference between them:

> A small child will play happily when all goes well; but the slightest difficulty is a threat from the great unknown, and it will yell

---

35. Kennedy, *Zen Spirit*, 14.

36. Merton, "Introduction" to Wu, *Golden Age of Zen*, 1.

37. Merton, *Hidden Ground*, 571.

38. Kennedy, *Zen Spirit*, 33.

out: "Mummy!" In the third state there is no need for such a yell anymore.[39]

Here she is writing about the state of the being-in-dependence with Being, the being-in-love with God characteristic of the child mind. There is no conscious duality of a state of dependence or of independence on God— it is about being and becoming—the dependence is implicit, fully integrated into the adult psyche. Zen reminds those open to it, as does Eckhart, Merton and many other contemplatives "that the highest point of our Christian mysticism is reached not in the experience that I know God or that I love God—not in any I-Thou experience—but in the experience that God lives in us."[40] In this sense Zen is a reminder of contemplation as transformation into Christ, into the Christ child.

William Johnston summarizes this understanding and compares the mind of a child to the "mirror mind" about which Zen constantly speaks. He writes:

> One of the aims of zen is to come to possess the mirror mind. Just as the pure and polished mirror is completely transparent, receiving everything into itself without distortion and reflecting all objects as if they were appearing in it for the first time, so the enlightened mind is completely receptive and filled with wonder, seeing everything as if for the first time.[41]

The mirror mind is also called no-mind, partly because of the quality of openness but also because it is never fixed on one thing. As Johnston explains this is achieved by mindfulness, or as discussed earlier present moment awareness. It is about living the gospel and about becoming the mirror and becoming the child. He also reminds the reader that in Christianity it is also about the relationship between the child and the maternal father. The child is open to receive love:

> When I become the child I realize existentially in the depths of my being that God my Father is love and that we did not first love him but that he first loved us. And having realized this I cry out "Abba, Father!"
> It is truly an extraordinary thing to become a child of God . . . For in this way I become an image of the Father . . . and I realize my true self.[42]

39. Schloegl, "Introduction" in *Thomas Merton on Zen*, vii.

40. Kennedy, *Zen Spirit*, 36.

41. Johnston, *Mirror Mind*, 36.

42. Ibid., 37.

The word Buddha means "I am awake" and the last words of Jesus before his arrest in the garden were also "Stay awake" (Matt 26:38). This is about being fully conscious—open to whatever may be experienced. This, then, like the small child, is a state of consciousness where we are not conscious of anything in particular but rather of everything in general. It is a panoramic receptive awareness, so that you take in all that the moment offers without eliminating anything or attaching to anything. You are there. Schloegl in her translation of *The Zen Teachings of Rinzai* puts attention to the present moment like this:

> Far better to have nothing further to seek, and to put oneself at ease. When hungry, I eat my food. When sleepy, I shut my eyes. Fools laugh at me; the wise understand. Followers of the Way, do not seek for anything in written words.[43]

Thomas Merton understood this as is found in his essay "Day of a Stranger" when he writes:

> What I wear is pants. What I do is live. How I pray is breathe. Who said Zen? Wash out your mouth if you said Zen. If you see a meditation going by, shoot it. Who said "love?" Love is in the movies. The spiritual life is something that people worry about when they are so busy with something else they think they ought to be spiritual. Spiritual life is guilt. Up here in the woods is seen the New Testament: that is to say the wind comes through the trees and you breathe it. Is it supposed to be clear?[44]

A classic Zen teaching tells of the small child who could only talk a little but who watches the monks meditating in the Zen center all facing the wall. The child tells his mother:

> "Oh! Snake! That time a snake! Oh, Dog!" The mother thought this was very strange and asked, "What are you doing?" "I'm watching the dog." "Where is the dog?" "Over there, over there!" But the mother could not see a dog, only a great monk.... Then the mother asked the Zen Master, "My child said he saw dogs and snakes appearing inside the Zen Center."
>
> The Zen Master said, "Yah, correct. All people have these consciousnesses—god, ashura, human, animal, hungry ghost, demon. They all have these minds. If you are attached to something, then you become a dog or a snake; you get heaven or hell. Your child is very clear, so he can see other people's

43. Schloegl, *Zen Teachings*, 23.
44. Merton, "Day of a Stranger," 235.

consciousnesses. Normal people cannot see them. Why? Their minds are dusty, not clear, so they cannot see the consciousness body. Your child can see these monks' consciousness bodies, their attachments. These monks are attached to something. They have their minds. So they must clean their minds. So they sit Zen . . ."

Child's mind is Buddha's mind. Just seeing, just doing is truth. Then, using this mind means when you are hungry, eat. When someone is hungry, give them food.[45]

In Buddhism the beginner's mind, or the child's mind, is really just about seeing things as they are. "To have some deep feeling about Buddhism is not the point; we just do what we should do, like eating supper and going to bed. This is Buddhism."[46] Once again this does not mean a regression or a retreat to the naiveté of a child. It is not about being simplistic, stupid or ignorant; rather it is about approaching awake and alive with curiosity and enthusiasm. So this is the mind emptied of preconceptions and expectations, judgments and prejudices. In other words there is the sense that anything is possible; a sense that is there for most children but eventually all but lost as enthusiasm and optimism tends to be mocked and experience creeps in. A child says "why not?" "In the beginner's mind there are many possibilities, in the expert's mind there are few."[47]

Zen is a process of letting go of both subjective and psychological consciousness. This is a state entirely natural in the small child but it cannot be returned to by the adult it can only be transcended. Merton's deepening interest in Zen and his relationship with John Wu clearly contributed to his appreciation of the idea of the adult becoming as a small child and having the child mind, the only mind worth having. Eastern mysticism is needed to help us penetrate more deeply into the gospel of Jesus Christ. "Now more than ever the world cries out for wise men and women from the East, people who will follow the star bringing gifts of gold, incense and myrrh to the child who has been born."[48]

---

45. Sa Nim, "Child's Mind," lines 24–48.
46. Suzuki, *Zen Mind*, lines 32–33.
47. Ibid., lines 2–3.
48. Johnston *"Arise My Love,"* 40.

6

The Shadow and the Disguise

The Adult Life of Care

Shades of the prison house begin to close
Upon the growing Boy.[1]

From both the Western and Eastern traditions it is acknowledged that characteristics of childhood are seen as essential for the spiritual life. So what goes wrong as we get older and why is it so hard to hold on to the promise of childhood spirituality? One helpful way to begin to think about it is to understand that as we grow as children we become increasingly compliant and then turn away from the vivid feelings we knew as children. As we learn to fit in and pick and choose certain words and phrases to describe what is happening and what we are doing, gradually the openness and immediacy of pre-verbal experiences without the constraints of conceptual thought become a closed way. Ironically, as children, most of us longed to be older and be seen and treated as grown up, and imagined that this might lead to freedom, but as we grow older so the experience of the radiance of the world around us, our absorption into the present moment, and our closeness to God becomes a distant memory.

A story in contemporary use recounts the infant sister who has been "difficult" since the birth of a new brother, continually asking to be alone with him. Fearing that she might hurt him the parents resisted, but eventually placed a baby monitor in the baby's room and let the small child have time alone with him. There was no sound of violence or anger, and if envy was present it was, "tinged with melancholy as the little girl said to her baby

1. Wordsworth, "Ode," stanza v, lines 10–11.

71

brother, 'Tell me about God; I'm forgetting . . . '" Here is the imperceptible memory of our original blessing, a frayed but still undying umbilical cord linking us to a lost paradise, the garden where we walked with God free from fear or artifice.[2]

As we walk out of the garden of innocence towards the world, we move away not only from intimacy with God, but we change from an authentic to an inauthentic relationship with our self. A number of religious writers and psychotherapists have used the phrase false self to describe this development. There are many reasons, most of them inevitable, why this takes place. As the child becomes more involved with the world they seek to conform and to fit in with what seems normal and conventional. Therefore the false self can partly be seen as the social self or the persona or disguise that we present to the world. It can also include parts of our self that we would rather not think about or difficult experiences that we seek to push out of consciousness and this may partly be for self-protection and as a way of coping. The danger is that in our at times necessary adoption of this false self the true part of our self becomes obliterated almost like a stranger that still lives inside us but that we rarely meet. Jesus' command: "unless you become" takes us back to our true self—the potential child who remains still within us.

The Shadow and the Disguise

The words shadow and disguise are used by Thomas Merton in the description of an epiphanic moment explored in a later chapter. The two words give a helpful frame to use for understanding what happens to the spirit of the child. Alongside considering the way that Thomas Merton used the words I am including the thinking of the analytical psychologist Carl Jung as the contribution of both spirituality and psychology is needed.

Thomas Merton's phrase "the false self," used above, describes both the shadow (the parts that we keep hidden or would rather not know about) and the disguise (the mask or persona that we present to the world about who we are). It is the effort of keeping the shadow repressed and the disguise maintained that contributes to our separation from the spirit of the child and from God. For Merton the false self was more than the social self or the mask, it also included the repressed and unconscious self—any part of us bound by space and time. He thought it was all part of the illusion of who, as adults, we think we are. In a letter to a friend Merton wrote,

2   Hall, "Child in the Rain," 33.

It is true we do not know where we are . . . children can, if they still will, give us the lie and show us our folly. But we are now more and more persistent in refusing to see any such thing. All we will see is the image, the image, the absurd image, the mask over our own emptiness.[3]

The false self is partly an ego-self affected by life's ups and downs but under this disguise there is another presence within us. Merton referred to this as "a disturbing stranger the self that is both 'I' and someone else."[4] It is suggested in this book that one of the ways that the disguise can be recognized and unravelled is through the active return as an adult to aspects of childhood spirituality, to the way that the child can see through the image to how things actually are.

Carl Jung offered definitions of both the disguise, which he called persona, and of the shadow. The persona, used in his exploration of individuation, which Jung saw as the life-long process of personal development, was originally the name for the mask worn by actors in antiquity. In terms of psychology Jung saw it rather as a packaging of the ego. It begins to develop as the small child learns to adapt to the expectations of others. For some children seeking approval, and perhaps for those with critical or withholding parents, this leads to the formation of a compliant personality where spontaneous gestures and feelings become repressed. For all children, in varying degrees, while desirable traits are built into the persona, qualities seen as undesirable or reprehensible are repressed and hidden from view and come to form the shadow. The psyche learns to become civilized so the primitive parts become assimilated and managed, or split off and denied. Somewhere in the heart of every person is what Jung called the self (sometimes given a capital "S" and sometimes not), which is the personal part of what he saw as the universal God image and what Merton called the true self, a part of the inner life that is potentially spontaneous, alive, and able to wonder at life.

The persona is also a disguise because it fails to acknowledge the repressed and denied parts that may not fit with the image we want to, or are asked to, present to one another and in the world. All these aspects of our selves contribute to the personal shadow. However for Jung the shadow not only included the individual person's repressed and dissociated memories and emotions that come to form the personal unconscious, but could also include societal and collective aspects passed down over generations that remained discarded, unrecognized, and unwanted. Jung called these

3. Merton, *Road to Joy*, 45
4. Merton, *Love and Living*, 40.

archetypal contents and was at pains to emphasize that they could be good or bad.[5]

For Jung, the analytical psychologist, it was essential that as much as could be is assimilated and brought into consciousness—into the light. It is a resource of the personality without which we are diminished. The shadow may be strange, frightening, or unacceptable, to us or to others; but often it is our denial or rejection of that shadow which is a source of what is wrong with us, not the shadow itself.

The illusory false self then includes both the disguise we adopt as our persona and the shadow, and both Merton, through contemplation, and Jung, from depth analysis, realized that there is a deeper true self within us. This is a realization that has been known throughout the ages and described in different ways, for example the Quakers call this "that of God" which is present within each person. Many novelists, poets, and artists know this through the creative process. One was Tolstoy, who describes the double life of man, "the outwardly conditional, unreal life, replete with falsehood, which he brings into relation with society, the state, and civilisation, and his inner real life in which man confronts primary reality and the depths of life."[6]

So we are in many ways divided creatures. A part of us, rarely evident, is contiguous with God, while the balance remains categorically different from him. The question is then "with which part do we identify?" The spirit of the child places us back in allegiance with God who asks us to lay aside our worldly concerns, our worldly disguise, and the burdens from the past, and stand spiritually mature as small children, open, aware, trusting, and alive in relationship with him. It could be said that the mind of the small child, the pre-verbal child—is a state of mind *before* the shadow and the disguise. Clearly adults cannot return to a time before the development of their personalities, but through the spiritual practice of becoming as a small child they aim to go *beyond* the shadow and the disguise.

A Life of Care

As we grow out of childhood and become grown up, we take on increasing responsibility. One of the usual characteristics accepted about small children is that they are carefree. This might be in itself an illusion, and indeed psychotherapists would suggest that small children undoubtedly have their own troubling concerns, but it is acknowledged that early childhood ought

5. Jung, *Archetypes.*
6. Berdyaev, *Slavery and Freedom,* 25.

to be a time without responsibilities. It is the grown-ups who are and should be in charge with all that that implies.

In the serious grown-up world filled with responsibility and routine it is hard to see where there might be a time or place to going back to being carefree—indeed free of care and to just "be." Being grown-up can become a weighty and onerous state of mind. The commandment of Jesus—to become as small children—is partly then about letting go of care: physically, emotionally, and spiritually.

However the idea of being like small children immediately carries aspects of negativity which are worth exploring, for they can affect our response to the gospel command. For despite our apparent love of children there is also a different attitude that could be called "childism," which is a form of prejudice against children. This is not so much to do with individual acts of cruelty or neglect or abuse but rather a societal or collective attitude where the status of children has been undermined and the state of childhood has been exploited. This is a prejudice that is also built into the very way that children are imagined or fantasized about. It is a child's inherent immaturity and dependency that sets them up as a target group, and yet at the same time they are envied for their youthfulness and energy with life all before them.

Children are seen by some adults as a burden and an interference with getting on with real life. It was the critic and author Cyril Connolly who famously wrote, "There is no more sombre enemy of good art than the pram in the hall."[7] While the poet Rainer Maria Rilke, who longed and tried very hard at certain times to regain the mind of the child while working, when staying for a brief time with his actual wife and actual child, found himself inhibited alongside what he saw as the child's self-absorbed existence seeming like "the next life, almost denying ours in continually consuming it."[8] Here is something that anyone around small children for any length of time can recognize.

Alternatively there is an almost endless capacity for sentimentalizing, identifying with, projecting onto, and indeed reifying children. This is often what happens in faith groups especially where children are deemed innocent in a sentimental way or stereotyped according to gender with no recognition of individuality. Perhaps sometimes what the adults in the church want the children to do as part of the faith group is more about what the adults want *from* the children. This may be a reassurance about our own experiences as children or some sort of reassurance that our faith has a future.

---

7. Connolly, *Enemies of Promise*, 109.

8. Prater, *Ringing Glass*, 136.

Given this, it is not surprising that Jesus' command has been some-times sidelined or misheard and superficially understood. For the biblical command asks something beyond our prejudice, misgivings, and stereo-types. Despite the history and influence of our own earlier experiences as children the command is "to become"—and that's here and now as adults! It is an ongoing journey towards a potential state of mind and a way of being truly alive. It is not about going backwards to a state of pre-verbal impotency, but rather a way forward into being attentive in our present re-lationship with God and to spiritual maturity.

In August 1965, in the last talk Thomas Merton gave as novice master to the novices at the monastery in Gethsemani, he reflected on a life free from care. In the talk he described the need for absolute surrender. This can be understood as total dependence on God, where the person is able to let go of self-importance and to some extent self-consciousness. This is a state of being-in-dependence with God, where we have let go of our fierce independence *from* God and are conscious of being in a state of dependency *with* God.

Merton urged the novice monks to unclutter themselves from fears, regrets, desires, and endless reflections—both trivial and seemingly impor-tant. He thought that all these distracted the novices from being awake and open to God. Even in the solitary life, "you can be devoured by care too . . . we have filled it with care."[9] Living full of care means that everything, and that includes our relationship to God, becomes opaque and crowded with concerns, conceptual thought, and anxiety. It is clouded by worry. Yet as Merton reminded us, God offers to take on the care of our affairs. This is like a parent taking responsibility for the life of the infant, and so this would then be a relationship that frees us to live life to the full. If such a life is pos-sible then we are able, Merton believed, to see that God is shining through an almost transparent world.

As suggested in this book this is the quality found in childhood spiri-tuality and this is the spirit of the child to which Jesus asks us to return. We are told, by those who see clearly, that truth is of a dazzling simplicity, but the ways in which it may be perceived are vastly complex. The idea of the child mind in the adult offers one way to approach this paradox. The gospel command to become as a small child is given as the way to the kingdom, to Christ. It is important to reemphasize as mentioned earlier that rather than regression or sentimentality the recovery of this promise of childhood spiri-tuality is seen as the essence of mature spirituality. Clearly then the child

9. Merton, "Life Free from Care," 69.

mind of the adult is not the same as the mind of say a baby or a two or three year old child but it is, strangely, the way to mature spirituality.

In his writing on wisdom Merton returned repeatedly to the figure of Wisdom at play in creation taken from Proverbs 8. "Sophia, the feminine child, is playing in the world, obvious and unseen, playing at all times before the Creator. Her delights are to be with the children of men" and where there is "One consciousness in all and through all: one Wisdom, one Child, one Meaning, one Sister."[10] For Merton the inner self remains an eternal child—a dweller who can play in paradise—but we lose our path to this inner self. This child mind for Merton was the essence and in many ways the only way to closer union with God.

The theologian Robert Orsi raised the problem that if children are more suited for the kingdom of heaven than adults, then "maturation can only be seen as a fall from grace."[11] However it is the suggestion in this book that adults through adoption of the spirit of the child can combine aspects of the promise of childhood spirituality with the experience of mature spiritual and psychological insight.

"Shades of the Prison House"—The Need to Be in the Know

In a life of care we are caught in the shadow of what we would rather not acknowledge and assimilate, and therefore captivated by the disguise which is what we present to the world. Part of the captivity of the disguise is the pressure to remain sharp, "in the know," on top of everything, in charge, so that one can give the impression of understanding what is happening around us and who and where one is, so that we are not caught out by the unexpected or surprised by something outside our known selves. This contributes to insecurities. It means that we are then careful/care full and are left in some ways missing the point, the real thing about life. All has to be carefully contained within the accepted, and the rationalized, and the explained—it is the opposite of the life of the spirit and especially it is the opposite of the spirit of the child and the injunction to "become as small children."

In his lecture as novice master in the Abbey of Gethsemani Merton calls the "life of the world, in the bad sense of the word" a life of useless care, which is self-defeating because it is a life that "cannot confront the inevitable fact of death." He writes about it in this way:

10. Merton, "Hagia Sophia" in *Collected Poems*, 368, 366.
11. Orsi, "Crisis," 29.

A life that has nothing but a straight line towards the grave and a
lot of little circular lines to forget the grave as you travel towards
the grave is a life of care, and it is a life of ever-increasing care
and it is a life of frustration and it is a life of futility. And this is
what is meant by the "world" in the bad sense of the word.

Our thinking, our obsessional worries and rituals make the world
opaque. Again, as Merton writes, "Everything becomes opaque in propor-
tion as we regard it as an individual object and become concerned with it."
He gives the example of building up to an event where we are consumed
by worry about how we might do or what might happen. As Merton calls
it "this day we have to live through," but at the end of the day when we go
through what did or did not happen there was nothing in it and so we move
in our worry onto the next big concern.

I get the job of teaching something to the rabbits. It becomes a
great thing, and I take the paper off this, piece by piece by piece,
and then there's nothing in that either. So you have to leave the
rabbits what they are, rabbits; and if you can see that they are
rabbits you suddenly see that they are transparent, and that the
rabbitness of God is shining through, in all these darn rabbits.

Merton thought even a monastic or solitary life of contemplative
prayer can still be filled with care and thus the false self:

We are devoured by care—care about our job, care about our
life of prayer, care about how we are getting on, care about what
other people are doing, care about this, care about that . . . And
then the thoughts "fears, reflections, regrets, and anxieties," this
constant business.

Merton believes that to get rid of this obsession with care it has to
be gone through. He quotes the French Jesuit de Caussade (1675–1751) as
having the solution: "Since God offers to take upon Himself the care of our
affairs, let us once for all abandon them to His infinite wisdom, that we may
never more be occupied by aught but Him and His interests." In other words
the entrusting of life and the associated cares onto God—"you cast your
care upon the Lord."[12] Merton writes that in his experience it is possible to
sometimes try to live like this, and that when this happens the opacity falls
away, and what he describes as the transparency of God shines through.
These are the glimpses of true life that are sometimes granted when for a
moment thinking stops, and real looking or listening or presence is possible.

12. Merton, "Life Free from Care," 68–71.

This real looking and listening is modelled for us in small children who can find fascination in the smallest stone or leaf on the ground. As will be explored later in the book, for adults to encounter the mystery of existence with feelings of wonder and awe, especially in the middle of rational activity, can be a surprise, and it can still happen. Education, the need to know, with its emphasis on answers to everything gradually erodes that sense of mystery, for part of the problem is societal or collective; one might say pressure from the external world from outside as well as inside each person. The adult is expected above all else to know—always remaining sharp in order to understand.

The Sharp Destructiveness of our Techno-Materialistic Age

In the contemporary world of science and technology there is the powerful illusion that the reality of the world is what can be defined and dissected, and from this belief comes the seduction of materialism. So in actuality what you see *is* what you get. This then becomes part of what could be called the collective disguise of contemporary society that befuddles everyone. It is also the denial of the irrational, the different, the unseen, and the unconscious and so there is no sense of different dimensions and realities. Instead there is a preoccupation with the material order which has been called the celebration of the commonplace, unapparelled in celestial light and without the fullness of imaginative vision. As William Blake fervently and with prescience begged in a letter written centuries earlier, that God keep us from a blinkered and one-dimensional view and from the sleep inducing effect of science.

The disguise as part of collective consciousness fuelled by science and technology is the belief that the material world is the only reality. Then the acceptance is that for a person: ". . . the human mind can examine this world objectively and so arrive at a knowledge of "reality" which will give him control over the world."[13] This very view has been proved false by science itself, but the belief in such a disguise remains dominant. The shadow of such a belief in control is the undermining of western civilisation, and the devastating effects of the full force of science and technology on the earth, on our continuing survival and on our psyches.

Over the last four hundred or so years, science in the form we recognize it promised to augment our power and control through knowing, and it proceeded to deliver on that promise dramatically. Yet the scientific

13. Griffiths, *Golden String,* 7.

method is restricted in principle to "telling us about a part of reality only; that part . . . that is beneath us in freedom and awareness."[14] Things more than ourselves or outside our knowledge range cannot be entertained as mattering/matter. For scientific knowledge, pure or applied, emerges only in regions where scientists can control or rather have power over the materials they work with.

This has been helpfully exposed in an analysis of primatology where the significance of animals has been interpreted as a way of understanding human life only in terms of sex and economics. The science and technology scholar Donna Haraway's interest was in exposing how knowledge is defined through the perspective of the often male, white, scientist or researcher giving just one view on the results. In other words so called "objective knowledge" is always and inevitably filtered through the human who has control over it. Instead Haraway notes the revolutionary insight that "we are not in charge of the world." She writes that the history of science has been "tied to militarism, capitalism, colonialism, and male supremacy—to distance the knowing subject from everybody and everything in the interests of unfettered power. The instruments of visualization in multinationalist, postmodernist culture have compounded these meanings of dis-embodiment."[15] She advocates "situated knowledges" where the context and influences are understood and where limitations are acknowledged, and where the word vision becomes metaphorically emphasized rather than a false vision promising human transcendence of all limits and responsibility.

However the current collective societal approach to machinery and technology almost in itself conveys a sense of transcendence. Thomas Merton noted how human beings in the modern age always expected a technological fix that could solve all problems. In this way he foresaw how in contemporary culture technology has become a form of idolatry where all the problems are apparently able to be solved through miraculous solutions offered by inventions. This means that the making or using of such artifacts through technology is a largely unthinking activity.[16]

In the talk "The Christian in a Technological World," Merton explains some useful technological changes. For example, the lawnmower was

> a good thing, it's fine, there is nothing wrong with this, monastic life allows us to do the lawns. . . .Technological society around a place like this requires cutting a lot of grass. . . . We used to have many creeks around here, and now we have one creek. When it

14. Smith, "Preface" in Meister Eckhart, *Essential Sermons*, xii.
15. Haraway, *Simians, Cyborgs, and Women*, 187–88, 199.
16. Shaw, *Illusions of Freedom*, 5.

rains, then you have plenty of creeks where the old ones used to be. But this is a problem that technology doesn't solve. Instead of five fields, you have one; you can go down the creek and clean it up in one operation. But that's exactly how technology operates. You can simplify everything and get at it faster.[17]

Technological attempts to control nature worried Merton, along with the concern for the effects of technology that he understood were linked to a "whole instinct of man to gain mastery over the environment." Instead he called humans to accept limitations and understand that we are part of nature: "It is not Christianity, indeed, but post-Cartesian technologism that separates man from the world and makes him a kind of little god in his own right, with his clear ideas, all by himself."[18]

Merton realized that there was no escaping technology and he anticipated both the advantages and inherent problems involved. He raised the issue of whether technology demeans or affirms life. He thought that along with inventions there could develop a mentality destructive of "authentic human ends."[19] The danger is that this mentality is not balanced by other aspects thus leading to a restriction of human life into a material force and ultimately to "cultural disintegration." The progress of technology and the associated increase in production and consumption bolsters the illusion that "mechanical progress means human improvement, and this alienates us from our own being and our own reality."[20]

In "Exploits of a Machine Age" Merton captured the emptiness of modern, technological society where a couple awaken one morning, and are dismayed by their own thin faces and the empty lives they lead. "The couple flee to their 'protected work' but 'unsafe machinery' by which their employers lived well, while they lived empty lives. At the end of the day 'the machines were safe' and they carried on. . . . The couple return to their grim dwellings, muttering, 'better luck tomorrow!'"[21]

Merton believed that nowhere was this alienation more so than in the production of nuclear weapons and ways to wage what Merton calls "modern technological mass murder" which is "abstract, corporate, businesslike, cool, free of guilt-feelings, and therefore a thousand times more deadly and effective than the eruption of violence out of individual hate."[22] Merton's

17. Dekar, "Technology," 67.

18. Ibid., 68.

19. Thompson, *Returning to Reality*, xix.

20. Merton, *Conjectures*, 73, 222.

21. Dekar, "Technology," 70.

22. Merton, *Faith and Violence*, 7.

thinking on peace in the nuclear era was grounded in the Christian tradition of peace making and an understanding based on deep contemplative
prayer. He expressed this in different ways. For example, in his book *Peace
in the Post-Christian Era* Merton describes the "tribal-totalitarian war dance
and . . . the idolatrous worship of the machine." He thought there were powerful forces that benefited "from the plunge into darkness. The machinery
of war undergirded national influence. . . . These weapons were . . . the result
of a moral callousness in the fabric of a technological society that placed a
priority on efficiency and progress."[23]

He also expressed his thinking on nuclear war in poetry. In Merton's
poem "Original Child Bomb" he observes that the nuclear weapon had become an end in itself, and an idol. As has been noted:

> Moreover language was distorted on behalf of the atomic
> project. Merton recalled the allied code names on the mission
> that employed terms from birth, motherhood, and religion.
> Churchill was cabled after the first successful Los Alamos test
> that "babies satisfactorily born." The scientists called it "little
> boy" and placed it in the "womb" of a B-29 named after the pi-
> lot's mother. The original atomic bomb was code named "Trin-
> ity" as it would bring a new beatitude, and vision of ultimate
> destruction instead of eternal life.[24]

So here, revealed through the language used in the technology of destruction is the complete perversion and denial of creation, of new life, of
infancy, of our vocation as children of God. Merton urged and argued that
we must align ourselves instead with truth and humility.

Finally, it has been said that we are living in an age of science and
should understand that the bitter message of science is that the universe
offers no consolations. It does not exist for a reason, but exists thick-witted,
mute, gormless, and callous. This is the paradoxical outcome of remaining
in the know. Perhaps then as Turkington writes, "science's worst crime is
that it ventures no answer to why there is a universe at all."[25] The mystery,
the wonder, and awe that each small child experiences is forgotten and all
sense of there being anything more to life than surface is expunged.

23. Thompson, *Returning to Reality,* 24.
24. Ibid., 26.
25. Turkington, *There's More to Life,* 5.

PART TWO

RE-FINDING

7

The Enchanted World, the Tendency towards Dis-enchantment, and the Possibility of Re-enchantment

Our birth is but a sleep and a forgetting:
The soul that rises with us, our life's star,
Hath had elsewhere its setting,
And cometh from afar:
Not in entire forgetfulness
And not in utter nakedness,
But trailing clouds of glory do we come
From God, who is our home:
Heaven lies about us in our infancy![1]

For all small children life is mysterious and mostly incomprehensible until the adults caring for them begin to help them form a pattern, a routine, and then a sense of coherent order, and, so, purpose gradually emerges. The small baby is subject to strong and sometimes overwhelming feelings, both good and bad, and hopefully is helped to manage this by the containing presence of a caring and loving adult. In the next chapter we will discuss what happens when this is not the case. As small children begin to play and if their imaginations and creativity are allowed to flourish, then the world is seen as a place of wonder and surprise—enchanted and mysterious—where animals speak and there exists different beings and other worldly creatures, both bad monsters and good fairies.

Somewhere in the deepest parts of the adult psyche (no matter what the chronological age and no matter what has happened in life), there remains

---

1. Wordsworth, "Ode," stanza v, lines 1–9.

85

some memory of enchantment and mystery and the mystical. Children as they grow older are pressured to take on the rational and to explain away the spiritual and the irrational aspects of life. Part of our developing persona and disguise is gaining this overly rational, materialistic, and logical sense of what is seen as real, and so the glimpses of enchantment become relegated to the shadow. However, many myths and stories remain to speak of this vestigial sense. This is one of them:

> There was not one amongst us who looked forward to being born. We disliked the rigours of existence, the unfulfilled longings, the enshrined injustices of the world, the labyrinths of love, the ignorance of parents, the fact of dying, and the amazing indifference of the Living in the midst of the simple beauties of the universe. We feared the heartlessness of human beings, all of whom are born blind, few of whom ever learn to see. . . . There are many reasons why babies cry when they are born, and one of them is the sudden separation from the world of pure dreams, where all things are made of enchantment, and where there is no suffering.[2]

That passage is about spirit children, children whose true home belongs elsewhere, but as human children grow out of infancy we, too, as "people of the flesh, as infants in Christ" to quote St. Paul (1 Cor 3:1) become disenchanted and separated from the world of pure dreams.

Another description of this process comes from an old Jewish legend that speaks of this knowing and then the forgetting that we ever knew. According to this myth when the soul of Adam was created so were all the future souls for the myriad of generations to come and these all were stored in the seventh heaven. As a baby is conceived, God decides its gender, size, and looks, but goodness and badness are left to be determined by the person. The angel who is appointed to souls is asked by God to fetch a soul from the seventh heaven and carry it to the mother's womb. Reluctantly the soul is dragged away and placed in the womb with two other angels set to watch that the soul does not escape. The next day the first angel takes the soul on a tour of paradise and explains how the righteous were also formed in the womb of their mothers, and, once born, obeyed God's commandments. The next day the same angel returns and takes the soul on a tour of hell, explaining again that these sinners were also created like her but then in the world did not follow God's commandments and so ended in this sad state. On the third day the angel in charge of souls returns and shows the soul what will happen in her life, where she will live, and where she will die, and many

2. Okri, *Famished Road*, 3–4.

other things. Then the soul is replaced in the womb for the nine months. At the time of birth the first angel returns one last time and says, "and now you go out into the world." Again the soul objects, but the angel responds, "As you were formed against your will, so you shall be born against your will and you shall die against your will." The soul carries on protesting until the angel strikes the baby on the nose and so extinguishes the light at its head and the baby arrives in protest, kicking and screaming forgetting all that she has learned.[3]

However what always remains, in some form or another, is a sense of something else, a glimpse or feeling of something forgotten that is encapsulated in the question that all children ask at some point: where did I come from? The factual biological answer to that universal question can never be the whole story, for underneath lies the deep archetypal memory of what might be called enchantment. And this vestigial sense of enchantment can sometimes spontaneously and unexpectedly return as one writer witnesses:

> For a brief and extraordinary moment there came again that freshness, this time within himself, welling up from that fountain down at the roots of things. . . . He supposed he had once known it, because there was a feeling of familiarity about it, but he had utterly forgotten it.[4]

Enchantment and Dis-enchantment

Enchantment also is a term used by some sociologists and theologians, amongst others, to characterize the time before the Renaissance and the Enlightenment. Charles Taylor, writes that the people who lived in this world, including the "European peasants in 1500 believed that the Christian God was the ultimate guarantee that good would triumph or at least hold the plentiful forces of darkness at bay."[5] In a world with God acting in the cosmos, founding and sustaining societies, acting as a bulwark against evil, atheism comes close to being inconceivable.

The expression dis-enchantment is used as a description of the modern condition. The dis-enchantment of the world that began in the Renaissance ran through the Enlightenment, and up until roughly the 1960s puts spirit all on one side and matter on the other. It has been described in this way:

3. Singer, *Seeing Through the Visible World,* 7–8.
4. Goudge, *Heart of the Family,* 15.
5. Taylor, *Secular Age,* 26.

Left to itself, the world had no meaning. It was solely the human design that injected it with sense and purpose. So the earth
became a repository of ores and other "natural resources," wood
turned into timber and water—depending on circumstances—
into an energy source, waterway or the solvent of waste.[6]

In this way nature was de-animated, and our human subjectivity denied as we were prepared for instrumental meaning. So that, in other words,
we too came to be dis-enchanted, and like timber and waterways rather
than like forests and lakes. Our subjectivity is limited as we are seen as con-
sumers and customers.

Disenchantment means that the world became one where the locus of
thoughts, feelings, and spiritual élan was seen to be in what are called minds
and the only minds in the cosmos were seen to be those of humans. Minds
were then bounded, with thoughts, feelings, etc. all firmly situated within
them. This is Wordsworth's prison house mentality quoted in the previous
chapter. This way of thinking, which is heavy and opaque with definition
and concepts, is designed to place us, humans, at the center of everything
that is, and pre-eminent among all creatures.

It is the opposite of the spirit of the child as we are weighed down by
conceptual thought and heavy with self-importance. One outcome of this is
then that we are alienated from nature and, as nature is basic to our recognition of ourselves as human there is a double loss. Despite the realization
of the inherent limitations of this view of reality, science, and technology
still remain the reigning orthodoxy. In mistaking this reductive and restrictive means of knowing for one that is assumed to be not only unrestricted
but also reliable, we skew our real world view only registering what is then
known and so controlled. This is dis-enchantment, with no place for the
mysterious, the unknown or the child mind. Indeed any such ideas are to be
ridiculed, denied, and dismissed.

A direct consequence of this mistake is spiritual decline which has
been defined as "the eclipse of God sloping into the death of God with the
correlative decline in our sense of transcendence and the sacred." It seems
that in particular "the West has lowered the ceiling on its worldview, forcing
us to live in a cramped, inferior world."[7] This too is the dis-enchantment of
the world and disenchantment for those living in it. This is where the so-
called real world is dis-spirited with a dis-qualified existence. In other words
it can contain little possibility of things that are unknown, that are bigger
than ourselves, or that exceed or are different from us in terms of freedom,

6. Bauman, *Intimations of Postmodernity*, xi.

7. Smith, "Preface" in Meister Eckhart, *Essential Sermons*, xii.

intelligence, and purpose. And so because of this our very self-image is diminished and the life of care for who we are and how we fit into this heavily defined world becomes paramount. Even in stating this insight there can be little change. After all it is very difficult to argue against a system from within that system, and usually most attempts to look at things from a different point of view, or from outside the main frame can get translated in a way that explains by explaining it away.

Enchantment in Early Childhood

As described above it was not always like this. Each person knows implicitly, whether acknowledged or denied, that there is more and has had experience of something more. For all small children there is initially a sense of awe and wonder as they begin to explore the world, there is an enchanted feel to all discoveries. This is the heightened amazement of encountering something new and fascinating—watch a small child really looking and touching and exploring—and sometimes as adults too one can briefly recapture that intensity and immediacy, even if only for a second. For those children with kind and sensitive parents the early months and years can include much enchantment.

> We glimpse reality in childhood, in those sudden flashing moments when the veil of appearance suddenly slips and we are aware of something behind, something indescribable and incomprehensible, but incomparably lovely. If you remember your childhood at all you will remember those moments. All our life afterwards is a search for the reality we saw then—saw without understanding and then lost. We think of it as a place, a person, a state, according to our temperaments.[8]

Kathleen Raine, poet and writer, describes remembering this state of consciousness beautifully, albeit using adult sensibilities:

> The pink aromatic clusters of the flowering currant bush hung over my pram. I looked up at those flowers with their minute perfect forms, their secret centres, with the delight of rapt knowledge. Not discovery but recognition; recollection. . . . To see was to know, to enter into total relationship with, to participate in the essential being of each *I am*. . . . The language of Eden—do we share it in some measure with the animals and birds and all the conscious creatures of the earth?—may be forgotten, but it is

---

8. Goudge, *Green Dolphin Country*, 280.

not to be learned; it is innate knowledge, and each recognition is like a remembrance of something for ever known.[9]

Similarly the analytical psychologist Carl Jung writes about the earliest memory of his life as rather a hazy impression:

> I am lying in a pram, in the shadow of a tree. It is a fine warm summer day, the sky blue, and golden sunlight darting through green leaves. The hood of the pram has been left up. I have just awakened to the glorious beauty of the day, and have a sense of indescribable well-being. I see the sun glittering through the leaves and blossoms of the bushes. Everything is wholly wonderful, colourful and splendid.[10]

Thomas Merton too remembers moments of wonder. This is from a memory around the age of five years:

> From across the fields, and beyond the red farmhouse of our neighbour, I could see the spire of St. George's church, above the trees. The sound of the churchbells came to us across the bright fields. I was playing in front of the house and stopped to listen. Suddenly all the birds began to sing in the trees above my head, and the sound of the birds singing and churchbells ringing lifted up my heart with joy.[11]

Merton's mother recording his infancy in "Tom's Book" for his grandparents wrote, "When we go out, he seems conscious of everything. Sometimes he puts up his arms and cries out 'Oh Sui! Oh joli!'"[12]

When Wordsworth famously described the baby as "trailing clouds of glory," he thought that the newly born brought the sense of and openness to, heaven with them. He also understood that as we grow older we are gradually reclaimed by the realities of life and we lose contact with what we have once known. Gradually the child loses that sense of oneness and connection with creation, and so becomes disenchanted and increasingly part of the adult world and in time prepared for "instrumental meaning" and materialism.

Kathleen Raine remembers a recurring dream from early childhood of "a place of perfect happiness, filled with the bright sun of Easter, pure living light and warmth. My place was my state and therefore in it I knew

9. Raine, *Autobiographies*, 1–2.

10. Jung, *Memories, Dreams, Reflections*, 21.

11. Merton, *Seven Storey Mountain*, 19.

12. Shannon, "Tom's Book," 489.

myself where it was mine to be. . . . So it always began." Raine describes how the dream then becomes increasingly frightening as she moves from floating in a peaceful river towards rocky cliffs and then towering buildings, "swept along against my will, my fear increasing as I was carried towards the machines, throbbing and grinding."[13]

So is it possible to once again recapture such moments of childhood enchantment? The child psychoanalyst Donald Winnicott thought that it was certainly possible to revive the wonder of what life is all about, and so enter again the enchanted world by re-experiencing and recognizing what he described as the tremendous penetration of childhood mysteries into mystery itself. This marveling of what life is all about, which we all knew as children, has just remained dormant and can be easily revived again because the experience of what happens inside us as we play as children extends into our adulthood and even unto death and across its unknown borders.[14]

Later we will explore this space, sometimes called a transitional space, where creativity and play and a sense of the divine can be genuinely experienced. This is about both action and being. It is about a process that involves emotional dependence and abandonment of an adult sense of self, and an awareness of the equivalence to a pre-verbal but absorbed state of mind in prayer and contemplation.

The Possibility of Re-enchantment through Seeing Things Differently

The breakthrough into re-enchantment comes not through wordy arguments or doctrine but through vision—a new way of seeing the world. Merton spoke to the novices about casting all cares onto God and abandoning the control that appears so important to maintain:

> We are living in a world that is absolutely transparent and God is shining through it all the time. . . . God manifests Himself everywhere, in everything—in people and in things and in nature and in events and so forth. . . . The only thing is that we don't see it.

For Merton our vocation is the same vocation as that of the original disciples and of all disciples since then, which is to see through the opacity of the apparently visible world, to lay aside the weight and deadness of care and much conceptual thought. This is what happened to those disciples on the road to Emmaus who were blessed with a new vision that was against

13. Raine, *Autobiographies*, 1.
14. Winnicott, *Playing and Reality*.

all common sense and rational reasoning.[15] Mary Magdalene was also able to see through the opacity and so shouted with joy and happiness, "I have seen the Lord." As at that moment of supreme spiritual maturity Mary Magdalene saw with her child mind directly to the heart of it all. She saw the new vision of what was previously unimaginable as an adult but with the spiritual maturity and the power to imagine it.

Clearly thinking is not all bad; we need it to survive as older children and as adults, and indeed it can guide us towards such a re-visioning. Some accounts from childhood show that older children using conceptual thought can tap into a realization of this difference between the opacity of the visible and the invisible worlds. The Jungian analyst June Singer recounts her first spiritual experience at the age of seven. She intently watches a large black ant walk slowly across the wooden floorboards then crawl along the edge of the door before beginning the long vertical journey up the door post. The ant strays slightly to the right and the left but seems to the small girl to be aiming for the door knob, and although the ascent would be long and arduous, when the ant arrived at that destination, it would have no possible way to open the door and enter the house. The seven-year-old girl, knowing that she could turn the knob and walk into the house realized:

> I am so much more than this ant. What I can do, the ant cannot even imagine. If the ant observed me as I got up and walked over to the door, put my hand on the doorknob, opened the door and stepped inside, it would surely wonder at my marvellous powers. From the ant's point of view I would be accomplishing a miracle! Then a great realization struck the child. The way the ant is in relation to me, must be the way I am in relation to God. Just as my acts are great mysteries to the ant, even so are God's acts great mysteries to me. As the ant doesn't have the ability to understand what I do, much less why, so I don't have the ability to understand what God does, much less why.[16]

The child that June Singer was at seven realized that there might be more beyond the familiar world than she had thought; only she could not see it. As an adult she held on to that experience with the recognition that there is much in life which is unknowable through the mechanisms of ordinary human awareness. For her there is a visible world and equally real though infinite and unbounded is the invisible world. Singer's later vision of re-enchantment in the adult initially came through her remembered imagination as a child.

15. Merton, "Life Free from Care," 70.
16. Singer, *Seeing Through the Visible World*, xi.

This new way of seeing the world can also come through something external, and an external change of vision can be something quite simple and quite common. For example on one occasion while Elijah Mohammed was schooling Malcolm X in the teachings of the Black Muslims there was a glass of dirty water on the kitchen counter. Mr. Mohammad placed a glass of clean water beside it. "Don't condemn if you see a person has a dirty glass of water," he said. "Just show them the clean glass."[17] In other words seeing an alternative way of being can lead to an awakening.

Thomas Merton in his famous autobiography describes himself in his late teens and early twenties as feeling free and apparently enjoying all that contemporary life had to offer:

> And so I became the complete twentieth century man. I now belonged to the world in which I lived. I became a true citizen of my own disgusting century: the century of poison gas and atomic bombs . . . a man with veins full of poison, living in death.

He saw that any last traces of religion were squeezed out in order to devote it to the worship of what he describes as "my own stupid will." Interestingly it needed a vision from medieval philosophy to open up the possibility of a different perspective and ultimately to re-enchantment. Merton bought the book *The Spirit of Medieval Philosophy* by Etienne Gilson not realizing initially that it was a Catholic book but needing it for his studies. However reading the small print he saw "Nihil Obstat . . . Imprimatur" on the first page—the mark of a book that has passed the Catholic censors. He writes:

> Then I would never have bought it. As it was, I was tempted to throw the thing out of the window . . . to get rid of it as something dangerous and unclean. Such is the terror that is aroused in the enlightened modern mind by a little innocent Latin and the signature of a priest.

In the light of his terror at the implications of reading a Catholic book Merton considered it a work of grace that he actually read the book at all. The epiphany that came to him was the realization of a big idea where thinking about what he had read opened the door into a new way of seeing. This came from reading in Gilson's book about "aseitas" (or "aseity" the English equivalent)—the power of a being to exist absolutely in virtue of itself, "not as caused by itself, but as requiring no cause, no other justification for its existence except that its very nature is to exist. There can only be one such Being: that is God." Merton goes on to express the relief he got from this idea, "to discover not only that no idea of ours, let alone any image, could

17. Smith, "Preface" to Meister Eckhart, *Essential Sermons*, xiii.

adequately represent God, but also that we should not allow ourselves to be satisfied with any such knowledge of Him."[18] While this conceptual thinking gave Merton a portal into religion it needed times of prayer, silence, and contemplation once he had joined the Trappists at Gethsemani Abbey before he began to see differently and reveal glimpses of the re-enchantment that was taking place within him.

> So much do I love this solitude that when I walk out along the road to the old barns that stand alone, far from the new buildings, delight begins to overpower me from head to foot and peace smiles even in the marrow of my bones.[19]

His journals are full of descriptions confirming his experiences of re-enchantment. He later wrote:

> The world has been given by God not to a theoretical man but to the actual beings that we are. If we instinctively seek a paradisiacal and special place on earth, it is because we know in our inmost hearts that the earth was given us in order that we might find meaning, order, truth, and salvation in it. The world is not only a vale of tears. There is joy in it somewhere. Joy is to be sought, for the glory of God.[20]

A new way of seeing the external world, re-enchantment, is interwoven with a new way of seeing oneself in the world. This is often described as a form of re-birth or a resurrection. In other words through re-vision there is a shift and a change in the disguise or persona and a realization that there is more than is seen on the surface.

The psychotherapist Neville Symington offers us an example of this level of change coming from within the person. He describes an experience from his work when he was interested in how some people who were drug addicts or recidivist prisoners recovered from their condition and got better. He writes:

> I came across a fellow who had been a serious alcoholic and drug addict, and he had been in and out of prison. I asked him one day . . . "what it was that had brought about the change." His experience was recounted like this, he was in the alcoholic ward . . . and they had a rule that if one of the patients went out and had a drink they weren't allowed back in. Also, his wife had thrown him out, and he was never to come near the door of the

---

18. Merton, *Seven Storey Mountain*, 107, 208–9.

19. Merton, *Sign of Jonas*, 281.

20. Merton, *Mystics and Zen Masters*, 111.

house again, or she would call the police. Anyway he went out of the ward, he went to the local off-licence, bought a couple of bottles of wine and drank them, and he came back and he sat on a bench at night in the grounds of the hospital, and it was pouring with rain. He had an empty bottle lying beside him, and he said to himself, "There are only two things I can do: Either I commit suicide, or I take this bottle and throw it through the windows" [of the alcoholic ward]. He was sitting there with rain pouring down, and he said that suddenly a very strange idea came to him. There was a vision. He said to himself, "Or I could decide to get better."[21]

The third thing-like thought was a decision, the first two were not decisions, and the new thought came unexpectedly. The difference in the third thought and the reason it could be described as a decision, was that it was a creative thought, a moral thought, an aware thought, closely related to conscience and so a spiritual thought. What does that mean? A creative thought is one generated from within—not just thoughts born out of previous and restrictive knowledge or alternatively an ingested and repeated thought that has been communicated by others. It is part of the awareness, a knowing from within, a vision that has the potential to emerge and so to offer a new way of seeing oneself in the world. The man was moved by a new vision of who he could become. He was changed in the depths by something and did in fact recover and not relapse. Using religious language one could say that this was a re-birth and a re-enchantment of what had been previously a half-dead way of being alive.

There is then a way out of the adult life of care and all those states of mind captivated by the disguise and caught in the shadow, and it seems to involve a break in the continuity of the habitual way of seeing the world. As Merton was later to describe it, this is the break in "the habitual, half-tied vision of things."[22]

Even in ordinary everyday work life there can be visionary moments of true freedom and inspiration. For the Russian theologian Nikolai Berdyaev it was only these that "infused significance, authenticity and nobility into a world of unmeaning, make-believe and degradation."[23] If it is possible to glimpse this "more than" or "other than" there is in all human beings a sense of hope of something else. It is a presentiment or intuition that imagination is more real and reality less real than they look. The Dominican priest

21. Symington, *Spirit of Sanity,* 26.

22. Merton, *Other Side of the Mountain,* 323.

23. Berdyaev, *Dream and Reality,* 217.

Donald Goergen describes it as feeling that the overwhelming violence of facts that oppress and repress is not the last word. It is once again linked to a suspicion that reality is more complicated and nuanced than realism and what contemporary culture wants us to believe. It is an alternative to materialism with the feeling that the frontiers of what might be possible are not limited by the boundaries of what is perceived. Furthermore that in a wonderful and unexpected way life is arranging the inspired events which will open the way to freedom and unforeseen rebirth.[24]

Is Re-enchantment Mysticism?

The French philosopher Rene Girard in his exploration of scapegoating uses the phrase "the moment of revealed discovery" to describe a third position that can be reached—a moment of revelation. This is when the moment of our desire to imitate others and the moment when the group unites to expel the person who is different can be transcended. Girard thought this could come about through

> the impact upon the human psyche of the revealed texts of scripture and the telling and the retelling of the story of Jesus, the one who accepted victimization inherent in his society. . . . Because of Jesus and his capacity to live completely within the freedom of God, human beings discover that they too can live simply and gratuitously, in total freedom.[25]

Melvyn Matthews describes how the recovery from a deeply divided and alienated life towards wholeness and peace is rooted in what he calls the incompleteness of the self and the re-enchantment of the self through loving attention to God and others. This he calls "the contemplative or the monastic, or properly speaking, the mystical life" where we wait for the arrival of Christ. The re-enchantment of life and so also the re-enchantment for the Church are about "a theology of participation in God, and the mystical way is that way which opens the doors towards this participation."[26]

The equation that seems to make a lot of sense is that placing our self at the center of a belief that humanity is in charge, leads and has led to dis-enchantment and a dis-spirited society. Placing God at the center and the mystical way returns us to the essentials of spirituality where God is affirmed as the source of being rather than an object weighted and smothered

24. Goergen, "Globalization of Hope," 9.

25. Matthews, *Both Alike to Thee*, 42–44.

26. Ibid., 137.

by our projections. Through participation with God through contemplation and prayer there is re-enchantment and a return to what has been referred to as that "starlit darkness" and to our "pristine and raw and uncomprehending beginnings"—a movement in other words towards the child mind.[27]

Despite the early enchantment that is covered over and suppressed by the later dis-enchantment there is something that moves in us that defines our very being and which remains free from all our activity and ego-knowing. This true self is the spirit of the child and there is an essential urge and desire to live out of this part of our self no matter how old and disillusioned we have become. Through a sense of presence and potential there is the realization of some sort of vague understanding that there may be meaning and hope, and if so then some prospective awareness of a destiny or an intention that each of us carries. This is another way of feeling real, and it is closely akin to the creativity that makes life feel worth living. In the spirit of the child it is about feeling alive and real, present and aware of the shared existence with others but also as oneself as different in a separate body. This is the possibility of re-enchantment.

27. Ibid., 138.

8

The Secret Life of the Wounded Child

And if I have prophetic powers, and understand all mysteries, and all knowledge, and if I have all faith, so as to remove mountains, but do not have love [caritas] I am nothing. (1 Cor 13:2)

For some people the very idea that childhood can be meaningfully associated with joy and so in any meaningful way carefree is unrealistic. A significant number of children have experiences of emotional, physical, and sexual abuse, and others are neglected. Some may have experienced a restrictive illness or disability, or been exposed to loss or upsetting situations by the adults or by friends or siblings in their lives. A difficult or damaged childhood will cast a long shadow and can lead to an inability to trust and problems in later relationships. The lack of trust can lead to a sense of reluctance to relinquish any control with others, and so in the context of religious experience it can mean it is hard to accept simplicity and dependence in any relationship with God.

In chapter 2, we discussed Donald Winnicott's idea of the mirror as the precursor of the mother's face. A similar sort of experience can happen in relationship with God. In his "Spiritual Canticle" St. John of the Cross (1542–1591) expresses this insight in the following way:

> When you looked at me;
> your eyes imprinted your grace in me;
> for this you loved me ardently;
> and thus my eyes deserved
> To adore what they beheld in you . . .
> and let us go forth to behold ourselves in your beauty.[1]

1 John of the Cross, *Collected Works*, 476.

As Richard Rohr expresses it, St. John of the Cross was far ahead of his time in the spiritual and psychological understanding of how love works and how true love changes us at a deep level. The mystic speaks of "divine love as the template and model for all human love, and human love as the necessary school and preparation for any transcendent encounter." Therefore if one has never experienced human love, Rohr believes it will be very hard for the person to access God as Love. He writes, "If you have never let God love you, you will not know how to love humanly in the deepest way. Of course, grace can overcome both of these limitations." In this contemporary adaptation and translation of a Canticle by John of the Cross the very process of love at its best is described:

> You give a piece of yourself *to* the other.
> You see a piece of yourself *in* the other (usually unconsciously).
> This allows the other to do the same in return.

You do not need or demand anything back from them, because you know you are both participating in a single Bigger Gazing and Loving—one that fully satisfies and creates an immense Inner Aliveness.

> (Simply to love is its own reward.)
> *You accept being accepted—for no reason and by no criteria whatsoever!*[2]

For the child who feels unacceptable and has been treated in an unacceptable way it can be hard to believe that they are fundamentally good. The twelfth-century Cistercian Bernard of Clairvaux understood this equally well and wrote about it in his treatise on the four steps of love. He could see that the first step was to love oneself and from there it was possible to move through a series of states of mind with the second about loving God for what he gives us, then to love God for who he is, and in the fourth and final step to love ourselves for God's sake.[3] In the next chapter psychological and spiritual healing is explored especially for those who feel that they cannot even reach the stage of self-love, in other words they hate themselves and find it hard to believe in their own redemption.

It has to be said, however, that most people have experienced issues of loss and separation, and feelings of anxiety and insecurity during their childhood; for in reality everyone knows about envy, anger, and fear. These are all experiences from early childhood. Such feelings are about being human because a certain amount of lack of care, frustration, pain, and even

---

2. Rohr, adapted from *Naked Now,* 140–41.
3. Gardner, *Four Steps of Love.*

torment is inevitable in the course of everyone's growing up. These are the wounds that unavoidably encroach on every child's innocence. For all the vision of beauty, paradise eventually becomes obscured and veiled. However for some children these universal experiences can become cumulative, and so be too much to cope with. For some children, especially those exposed to apparently wilful parental indifference or cruelty of sufficient intensity and regularity to be traumatic, the enchanted early childhood world of pure dreams can quickly become a nightmare.

While everyone has damaging experiences during childhood, some wounds are more extreme than others and so may need longer to be understood and partially healed. Over time the human need to love and to connect, and so learning to love and to love others, becomes part of the process of moving beyond the shadow of repressed feelings and the disguise of the person we present to the world into the freedom of the spirit of the child. To move beyond the shadow and the disguise is not possible until both have been recognized and explored. In this process the shadow will become partially integrated and the need for the disguise relaxed. In other words what has been kept in the confines of the cellar is brought up into the living room. The ways to do this through psychotherapy or spiritual direction or indeed through grace are explored in the next chapter.

A Secret Life

> All happy families resemble one another. Each unhappy family
> is unhappy in its own particular way.[4]

Many of the most damaged children lead a secret life, hiding their true self for protection, and this tendency is carried into adulthood so affecting all relationships. For those who have experienced trauma and trouble as small children the world becomes contaminated by their experiences, which remain in some form throughout adult life. Early childhood can go wrong for a number of reasons: there are unfulfilled longings, terrible frustrations, the ignorance, heartlessness, and cruelty of parents and adults, and experiences of cumulative indifference to sensitivity, beauty, and tenderness. This means that subsequent emotional development for children who have these experiences is profoundly negatively affected, and there may be a tendency to repeat aspects of the injurious past either within themselves or towards others. As has been said, children to whom these sorts of experiences happen often have a reluctance and wariness to trust others. This can make

---

4. Tolstoy, *Anna Karenina*, 13.

genuine trust in God difficult to maintain and the capacity to love others limited.

"Soul murde" is one way of describing how the child is left after damaging experiences early in life often feeling sad and perhaps less able to feel natural joy in being alive. It has been defined as the destruction of the love of life and as killing the capacity for joy in another human being. As a character in a play by Ibsen puts it:

> You have committed the one mortal sin! . . . You have killed the love of life in me. Do you understand what that means? The Bible speaks of a mysterious sin for which there is no forgiveness. I have never understood what it could be; but now I understand. The great unpardonable sin is to murder the love of life in a human soul. . . . You have killed all the joy of life in me.[5]

One of the other common effects of a traumatic childhood is a sort of brainwashing where the child needs to suppress awareness of what has happened in order to keep alive some ideal of good parenting. In other words to survive the child adopts the parents' propaganda and version of events, and will carry the guilt and responsibility for what took place. For example, the child might rationalize what has happened in this way: I was hit because *I was bad* and deserved it; I was neglected and rejected because *I am unlovable*, and so on. My parents have separated and divorced and it is *all my fault*. Taking on the guilt and responsibility for the difficult and bad things is also a way of managing and defending against all the mixed feelings including repressed rage about what has happened, and this can contribute to a deeply ingrained but unconscious need for punishment.

In religious life this might lead to an exaggerated feeling of great sin and worthlessness. This is a distorted and false type of humility because it lacks insight into the motives for the depths of such feelings. One example is found in Thomas Merton who writes at the start of the autobiography of his early life, "Free by nature, in the image of God, I was nevertheless the prisoner of my own violence and my own selfishness, in the image of the world into which I was born. That world was the picture of Hell . . . "[6]

Not being sufficiently cared about or recognized as a separate human being can mean being deprived of what we all really need, which is essential nourishment based on feeling accepted and loved by the mothering person. It is hard for a child to maintain any joy or much sense of identity in the face of not feeling cared about, or recognized as a person in their own right,

5. Ibsen, *John Gabriel Borkman*, 331.
6. Merton, *Seven Storey Mountain*, 11.

or even hated by their mother or father. Everything and everybody is then approached with some degree of fear and "such dread that children only can feel" to quote a line from the novel *Jane Eyre*.[7]

One example of a child who knew about this dread was the poet Rudyard Kipling. His experiences have been described as like being an occupant of one of God's concentration camps. The difficulty he discovered is that such feelings are not forgotten though they can be explained away or pushed to the back of the mind. After six years of parental love in India, Kipling was sent with his three-year-old sister to England and did not see his parents for a further six years. Kipling was disliked and persecuted by Auntie Rosa, the name of the foster carer in an establishment that he named "the house of desolation." He was regularly beaten, exposed to extreme physical cold and to arbitrary and unreasonable discipline, and repeatedly reminded of his parents' desertion. How do children explain such treatment? Often the parents cannot be blamed for what happened—often it is important that they stay as good figures. And if God is good then whose fault is it? In psychoanalysis this is known as splitting. Kipling later as an adult was still torn by this dilemma as he angrily defended (so holding on to a belief in the powerful adult figures who had let him down) Britain's imperialist past.[8] Despite this Kipling's writing also contains the child's view of relationships in the natural world, based on his early happy six years in India, and his stories describe a world full of liveliness with connection to all other creatures. The relational consciousness he remembered from his early childhood shines through his tales.

In circumstances involving abuse or neglect often the true self of the child has had to take on a secret life and become hidden. Beyond the normal bruising, the child can become estranged from the center of their being, finding a way of behaving or a compliance that is more acceptable to their circumstances. This then becomes the persona, discussed earlier, which is the polished defense of the disguise where all the feelings of anger, loss, and upset are repressed and become part of the shadow of the person. Such sadness, such wounded aspects of the child, whether distorted ways of feeling and behaving or hidden and repressed, can restrict and damage the adult, and there is often a longing for deep healing and integration. This is a place of critical hurt, a repository of deep damage, meaning that the child grows up partly at war with their basic self. The adult, even in old age, may need to reach back into their infancy to bring this part of their self into conscious awareness and back into the stream of life.

7. Bronte, *Jane Eyre*, 52.
8. Jarrell, "On Preparing," 146.

R. D. Laing, psychoanalyst and psychiatrist, aimed to make madness intelligible. He revolutionized mental health treatment by his belief that the seriously mentally ill had something important that they were trying to convey, and in the 1960s he set up Kingsley Hall in London as an alternative to the then standard treatment in mental hospitals, allowing patients to explore their madness and so rediscover themselves. His autobiography shows how he also drew on his own experiences from early childhood to understand the experiences of his patients and how therapeutic intervention might help. In particular he drew insights from his complex relationship with his over-possessive controlling mother. He wrote about deception, dissimulation, and compliance, and he thought he had been "deep-programmed . . . against *living.*" In reflecting on his own experience he hoped that in the future children might find someone sympathetic in whom he or she might honestly and openly confide. As he expressed it, "without having to worry that it would be held against one, in some way, if one told the truth quite candidly about how one felt about life." However Laing reflects on his own decision as an older child to keep out of trouble just for the sake of a quiet life at home. One of the prices he had to pay for this sense of suffocation was frequent bouts of asthma. There were also implications for his life as an adult. For example, he recounts going out for a walk with his father when Laing's oldest child was just beginning to walk:

> She toddled a few steps ahead of us on her own and fell down. I ran forward and picked her up. My father turned to me and said, "You know, your mother would have given you a good spanking for that."
>
> I do not remember those days myself, but my father's remark fits with my feeling that if I fall down, in any way, I've done something wrong, it's my fault and I will, or will deserve, to be punished for it. It's still my fault if I catch the flu; or it is to teach me something: maybe that it's not my fault.[9]

Laing explored how even the biological basics are deeply socially programmed and so also subject to disturbance.

> Sleeping and waking, eating, drinking, digesting, urinating, defecating, and breathing are biological basics. These basics are deeply socially programmed. . . . They are conditioned by injunctions made effective in many more ways than straight commands and prohibitions, rewards and punishments and more subtle quasi-hypnotic procedures. One need not be told to go to bed. One need not be told to be tired. One is told one *is* tired.

9. Laing, *Wisdom*, 46–47.

> Later one is tired when one was told one will be, without having
> to be told anymore.[10]

The psychoanalyst Alice Miller also wrote about how children are
trained and treated "for their own good." She acknowledges how often parents have experienced something similar in their own childhood and writes
from her own experience as a child about her parents:

> Since they were not allowed to feel or, consequently, understand
> what had once been done to them, they were unable to recog-
> nise the abuse as such and passed it on to me in turn, without
> even the trace of a bad conscience.

This is known as destructive entitlement—it didn't do me any harm! Thanks
to her own questioning of her childhood, Miller writes that she then grasped
what so many adults must ward off throughout their lives. She understood
that there were serious implications of failure to confront the truth of repressed feelings and that this affected society. She writes that such people
are:

> preferring instead to plan self-destruction on a gigantic atomic
> scale, without even recognising the absurdity of what they are
> doing. These are the same people who, like all of us, entered the
> world as innocent infants, with the primary goals of growing,
> living in peace, and loving—never of destroying life.[11]

Loss and Loneliness in Thomas Merton's Childhood

In his early autobiography *The Seven Storey Mountain*,[12] Thomas Merton
traces his infancy and childhood. It is an account of cumulative losses and
constant emotional and geographical upheaval. Some of these are given in
extracts and described below. His parents were artists, his mother American
and his father from New Zealand of Welsh descendants. Merton remembers
his mother as "mostly worried" with "great ambition after perfection." He
notes that the diary his mother kept of his infancy "reflects some astonishment at the stubborn and seemingly spontaneous development of completely unpredictable features in my character." This is perhaps a wry comment
and observation on the need for compliance. Many years later Merton wrote

10. Ibid., 25.

11. Miller, *Drama of Being a Child*, x–xi.

12. Merton, *Seven Storey Mountain*, extracts from 13, 20, 24–9, 65–66, 78, 91,
103, and 162.

that perhaps solitaries are made by severe mothers. Here could be an initial suggestion of the secret life of the child needing to protect the true self from both impingements and criticism.

A year after Merton's birth the family moved to America as it was no longer safe to be in Europe at a time of war. They stayed near Merton's grandparents, whom he called Pop and Bonnemaman. His grandparents remained a stable part of his life until adulthood. Two years later his brother was born, and so with his brother only a baby and no other children to play with, Merton remembered his own imaginary friend Jack with his imaginary dog Doolittle. Merton records that his mother was eager for him to learn to read and write and he remembered "one night I was sent to bed early for stubbornly spelling 'which' without the first 'h': 'w-i-c-h' I remember brooding about this as an injustice. 'What do they think I am anyway. After all, I was only five years old." A year later Merton's mother became seriously ill but Merton was not told.

> And since I was destined to grow up with a nice, clear, optimistic and well-balanced outlook on life, I was never even taken to the hospital to see Mother, after she went there. And this was entirely her own idea. . . . Her sickness probably accounts for my memory of her as thin and pale and rather severe.

The two boys went to live with the grandparents. Merton was one day given a letter by his father:

> My mother was informing me, by mail, that she was about to die, and would never see me again.
>
> I took the note out under the maple tree in the back yard, and worked over it until I had made it all out, and had gathered what it really meant. And a tremendous weight of sadness and depression settled on me. It was not the grief of a child with pangs of sorrow and many tears. It was something of the heavy perplexity and gloom of adult grief, and was therefore all the more of a burden because it was, to that extent, unnatural.

Merton writes about the day of the actual death. He was six years old and left in a hired car at the hospital while the adults went in:

> The car was parked in a yard entirely enclosed by black brick buildings, thick with soot. On one side was a long, low shed, and rain dripped from the eaves, as we sat in silence, and listened to the drops falling on the roof of the car. The sky was heavy with mist and smoke, and the sweet sick smell of hospital and gashouse mingled with the stuffy smell of the automobile.

> But when Father and Pop and Bonnemaman and my Uncle
> Harold came out of the hospital door, I did not need to ask any
> questions. They were all shattered by sorrow.

Merton in his memory emphasizes the rejection by his mother but at the time visits by children to the hospital were not allowed. On returning home Merton remembered his father weeping by the window and his grandmother weeping upstairs. Some months later he went to the coast with his father who as an artist wanted to paint for the summer. Later they went to Bermuda, while John Paul his brother stayed with the grandparents. This pattern of upheaval and travel with his father set the pattern for the next few years:

> It is almost impossible to make much sense out of the continual
> rearrangement of our lives and our plans from month to month
> in my childhood. . . . Sometimes Father and I were living to-
> gether, sometimes I was with strangers and only saw him from
> time to time. . . . Things were always changing.

Aged ten, Merton and his father returned to France after his father had suffered a strange illness that brought him close to death. They ended up in the South of France where eventually Merton went to a boarding school. Initially bullied and begging to leave, he found he got used to it:

> Nevertheless, when I lay awake at night in the huge dark dormi-
> tory and listened to the snoring of the little animals all around
> me, and heard through the darkness and the emptiness of the
> night the far screaming of the trains, or the mad iron cry of a
> bugle. . . . I knew for the first time in my life the pangs of desola-
> tion and emptiness and abandonment.

Writing in more detail about the school Merton wonders what happens to individuals who seem fine away from the group but:

> When they were all together there seemed to be some diabolical
> spirit of cruelty and viciousness and obscenity and blasphemy
> and envy and hatred that banded them together against all
> goodness and against one another in mockery and fierce cruelty
> and in vociferous, uninhibited filthiness.

In this extract it is possible to see the need for Merton as a child to protect his inner self from the unpredictable attacks from other people, especially from a community group. At least the state of abandonment is safer and more familiar to him. Finally, after two years at the French school, Merton's father decided to move to England and there he came to the school to tell his son, "How the light sang on the brick walls of the prison whose gates had just burst forth before me." Merton then lived in Ealing, West London, with a distant relative, and attended a preparatory boarding school before at the age of fourteen being sent to Oakham School in Rutland in central England where he remained until his schooling had ended. However before entering Oakham, Merton writes about events that had happened "to complicate and sadden my life still further." Merton's father was ill, and though they went in the summer to Scotland on holiday, once again Merton was left with comparative strangers when his father's health deteriorated, and he had to return to hospital in London. After a particularly distressing incident Merton writes:

> I sat there in the dark, unhappy room, unable to think, unable to move, with all the innumerable elements of my isolation crowding in upon me from every side: without a home, without a family, without a country, without a father, apparently without any friends, without any interior peace or confidence or light or understanding of my own—without God, too, without God, without heaven, without grace, without anything. And what was happening to father, there in London? I was unable to think of it.

Merton describes the pain of one visit to his father when his grandparents and brother came to Europe to visit:

> But the sorrow of his great helplessness suddenly fell on me like a mountain. I was crushed by it. The tears sprang to my eyes. Nobody said anything more.
> I hid my face in the blanket and cried. And poor Father wept, too. The others stood by. It was excruciatingly sad. We were completely helpless. There was nothing anyone could do.

The responsibility for Merton's welfare was taken on by his English godfather and wife who lived in London. While his father's death left him sad and depressed for some months Merton then recalls imagining he was free, and from his account of the six years leading to his conversion we read of his life of drinking and fun, and later of the disaster of his time at Cambridge where it has been suggested that he possibly fathered a child with a chambermaid. This, alongside his lack of academic progress, led to his godfather sending him back to the United States. Merton was left full of self-hatred, thinking that all that had seemed to promise much had left him, "vain, self-centred, dissolute, weak, irresolute, undisciplined, sensual, obscene and proud. I was a mess. Even the sight of my own face in a mirror was enough to disgust me." From an analytic point of view one might here see the projection of the critical mother as Merton looks at himself, and also the feelings of guilt and responsibility with the associated need for punishment.

So here is a childhood with cumulative trauma and serious loss. There is great upheaval and little stability. Others have attempted, in a somewhat unsatisfactory way, to analyze what took place and to wonder how someone with such experiences, especially of parental abandonment, could move to become such a great spiritual writer and director. The extracts above show that Merton, like all traumatized children, associated himself as the cause of the trauma, "a man with veins full of poison, living in death." His auto-biography, written a few years after entering the monastery contains little compassion or self-awareness for his pain as a child, but speaks with the fervour of the newly converted and as a man saved from further damage in and by the world.

All children develop ways of coping with the demands of the family and the world, and the idea of the development of the persona or false self in the child is central to analytical thinking. Later Thomas Merton wrote extensively about the need for awareness and a stripping away of the false self in developing spiritual maturity. While the persona enables the child to function in the world and present a managing front real feelings are masked. The self that the child and later the adult presents to the world can hide or protect the inner being or true self from further attack or trauma. Merton appreciated that in many ways the persona or disguise is a very transient form for our psyche. This understanding is echoed by the Jungian analyst Fay Pye who writes of the persona: "And in its arrogance it is an imperti-nence in the face of the cosmos and the Ultimate," a cheap substitute for the "pearl of great price."[13]

How Trauma can Affect the Spiritual Story

Carl Jung understood the supreme importance of acknowledging feel-ings. He sometimes used the term "affectivity" to describe our emotional states, and as the Jungian Donald Kalsched writes, "The essential basis of our personality is affectivity where thought and action are, as it were, only symptoms of affectivity."[14] He thought that affect was the central organizing principle of psychic life because it linked all sorts of other aspects of the mind by lending each of them a common feeling-tone. This means that if there is early trauma with strong affect it can become a central complex affecting all sorts of other later experiences. It has been said that severe

13. Pye, "Transformations of the Persona," in Tuby, *In the Wake*, 45.
14. Kalsched, *Inner World of Trauma*, 88.

trauma always leaves in its wake "a lifelong disturbance of affectivity" which feeds into unconscious fantasy.[15] So, for example, reflecting on the account from Merton's autobiography, it is possible to see traces of these feeling-tones recurring in later less traumatic times, some of which are noted above, and the way that specific emotions become differentiated, and gradually with the help of language become feelings that can be communicated both to oneself and to others.

There is often a reluctance to really think about childhood difficulties; sometimes people say: "I had a wonderful childhood, I was very happy," but their expression or the tone adopted suggests something different. Perhaps when people are a bit too insistent about what fun it all was there is resistance to thinking about the shadow side of their experiences. For many the past does not feel relevant to the present; this can either mean that there is a preoccupation—perhaps an unconscious preoccupation with the past, or that it is repressed from conscious awareness. However, whatever the rationalization, early experiences both good and bad tend to emerge in present relationships and in behavior.

Jung appreciated that all these sorts of feelings would also inevitably be linked to primal religious experience, which he saw as a defining aspect of the human and so present in everyone whether acknowledged or not. Looking at this insight in the context of Christianity it is clear that if this is about a relationship with a personal God who loves us and who can only be encountered personally, then all the dynamics, commitments, and risks associated with relating to other people will come to the fore. One possibility is that God can take on the attributes of the all-powerful tormentor who punishes at will. Through such distortion and projection of expectations there emerges a critical, punishing, vengeful God. Then the relationship may become based on compliance, with the false self to the fore, guilt the cornerstone, and self-punishment as primarily the means of control. In such a constructed spiritual narrative, God may become a split-off all-good being leaving the all-bad located in the believer. This level of belief links to an early childhood way of placating and controlling the all-powerful adult which is called "magic thinking," where if the child was very quiet and good, he or she might escape further trouble or pain. The personal effect of all this is that it is difficult to believe that one can be loved for who one is. While in this process the adult is reduced to nothing—extinguished for the benefit of God—this is a false humility and stripping of the self because the benefit is secretly of and for the traumatized child in the adult and the false self remains intact.

15. Ibid., 89.

For some adults, feelings have become dissociated or detached, and then a relationship with God may follow a habitual but totally non-reflective path. This would be a form of psychic numbing where emotions feel dangerous or overwhelming and God is felt to be far away and needs to be kept in that position at all costs. In this state God is also put in the position of being detached, calm, and demanding, unconnected to emotion and pain.[16]

One of the suggestions in this book is that no matter what has happened either in childhood or as an adult there remains hidden within each person the spirit of the child. There remains the potential "to become." Another suggestion is that in the relationship with God this spirit of the child is needed, for it brings inherent creativity, spontaneity, and the capacity to live in the moment without self-consciousness. Christ is an exemplar for what is being called in this book the child mind where the spirit of the child meets the adult experience to produce a new perception. We are asked to become like Christ, we are invited to step out of our prison and to become free. Part of leaving captivity is to release the hidden or secret life of the wounded child—there is an invitation to be born again. If the past can be repaired, at least in part, then there is freedom to live in the present.

16. Gardner, *Journeying Home.*

9

Finding Spiritual and Psychological Healing

The god of my childhood wears black robes, has horns on his
head and carries an ax in his hand. How in the world was I still
able to slip past him? All my life I have been creeping stealthily
through my landscape, under my arm the little bit of life I keep
thinking I have stolen.[1]

Frequently the person damaged in childhood yearns for some form of
healing; though it may not be clear what form that healing could take.
The part of the child that needs to be heard and recognized, and so to emerge
into the light, is the wounded child part whose feelings have been hidden as
a way of self-protection. It could be said that an invitation from the divine
child or the true self within each person encourages each person to step out
of the constraints of convention and expectation to explore and to be healed
both psychologically and spiritually. In this chapter the way in which such
healing might occur is separated into three somewhat arbitrary areas.

Grace

How easy it is to hate oneself! True grace is to forget. Yet if pride
could die in us, the supreme grace would be to love oneself in all
simplicity—as one would love any one of those who themselves
have suffered and loved in Christ.[2]

---

1. Mehr, "Steinzeit" (Stone Age) quoted in Miller, *Thou Shalt Not*, 45.
2. Bernanos, *Diary of a Country Priest*, 251.

Healing past pain can come spontaneously through grace, which is understood as in part the divine energy of the living God that can break through into consciousness. It is a gift. Such awareness of the divine presence

> liberates us from the exhausting effort to maintain the false, habitual, or socially constructed masks we wear. . . . The grace of discovering ourselves in Christ frees us to respond "in a full and living manner" to every human being, every tree, flower, and bird, even the lowliest objects, with the new eyes of faith.[3]

In other words an act of grace that breaks through into the human heart can allow both healing and transformation—a transformation into awareness and connection.

Thomas Merton writes about the change in perception through grace whereby the world is no longer seen as "merely material, hence as an obstacle that has to be grudgingly put up with. It is spiritual through and through. But grace has to work in and through us to enable us to carry out this real transformation . . ."[4] Christopher Pramuk, commenting on Merton's meeting in Asia with Chatral Rimpoche, a Nepalese Buddhist hermit, a meeting which Merton describes as a grace, writes, "Grace, it seems, is surprising like that, breaking through with 'simplicity and freedom,' and surely provoking in us a little less seriousness, and a great deal more joy, desire, spontaneity, creativity, and laughter."[5] From such a description grace sounds awfully like the child mind—the divine child. For Merton it is Christ's victory over death that is the source of the grace that empowers our free and creative participation in the dawning of a new creation. This is the same grace that can quite unexpectedly and most powerfully break through into darkness and despair offering a freedom and a new way of living. As Merton writes, "There is always this grace of God for which it suffices to seek, to ask for deep in one's heart. It is often given to us without our asking, without our knowing anything about it."[6]

Participating in the struggle to heal the past is both something that needs to be done but in itself is also a deeply profound grace. It is part of the life and light of grace within us, and it is part of becoming the person that God intends us to be. For Merton it is the figure of Sophia, the wise child who can be reborn within us, within each person no matter how damaged by what has happened to them. For, "Sophia is the mercy of God in us. She is

---

3. Pramuk, *Sophia*, 136.

4. Merton, *Introduction to Christian Mysticism*, 144.

5. Pramuk, *Sophia*, 173.

6. Merton, *Courage for Truth*, 210.

the tenderness with which the infinitely mysterious power of pardon turns the darkness of our sins into the light of grace."[7] The option to open to this grace is always there even though it may be hard to see or to believe in it. The leap of faith that is called for is a leap into love, into the spontaneity and unexpectedness of divine grace. It is a leap into rebirth and a new way of being.

One dramatic example of such a leap is given by the contemporary spiritual guru Eckhart Tolle who famously described his breakthrough into life as a rebirth, where he changed from living in a state of almost continuous anxiety interspersed with periods of suicidal depression into a state of liberation. The joy that emerges from the account is that this epiphany just happened—through grace. In the account Tolle describes how, aged twenty-nine, he woke early in the morning full of absolute dread. This was a familiar scenario but felt more intense than previously. In the room where he was lying the shape of the furniture, the distant noise of a train passing by, and the deep silence of the night all seemed to combine to make everything feel not only alien and hostile but also utterly meaningless. He felt at that moment such a "deep loathing of the world. The most loathsome thing of all, however, was my own existence."[8]

Tolle is, at this point, someone full of self-hatred, unsure of why to continue with such misery, who speaks of a longing for annihilation and for nonexistence that seemed even more powerful than the instinctive desire to stay alive. The recurring thought that triggers his epiphany is that he felt he could not live with himself at that point. Part of him is suddenly aware that the thought is itself an extraordinary paradox and he questions the part of him that is able to make the comment about another part of himself. It seemed there were then two parts: "the 'I' and the 'self' that 'I' cannot live with." The breakthrough insight he had was the possibility that only one of them was real. It is at this point he recounts the impact of this realization—it is as if his mind stopped and so while remaining conscious there was no more thinking going on.

> Then I felt drawn into what seemed like a vortex of energy. It was a slow movement at first and then accelerated. I was gripped by an intense fear and my body started to shake. I heard the words "resist nothing," as if spoken inside my chest. I could feel myself sucked into a void. It felt as if the void were inside myself rather than outside. Suddenly there was no more fear, and I let

---

7. Merton, "Hagia Sophia," in *Collected Poems*, 369.

8. Tolle, *Power of Now*, 1.

myself fall into that void. I have no recollection of what happened after that.

Sebastian Moore, reflecting on who spoke the inner words "resist nothing," believes this was the Holy Spirit.[9] The outcome for Tolle of taking that leap was to arrive in a new place. Tolle describes how he experienced the completely new sensations and perceptions of the world; it is as if he has been reborn into the mind of the small child who views everything clearly with a single focus and without the obscuration of the compulsive thought commentary. The description of this moment of rebirth is characterized by the clarity and the intensity of what he hears and what he sees:

> I was wakened by the chirping of a bird outside the window. I had never heard such a sound before. My eyes were still closed, and I saw the image of a precious diamond. Yes, if a diamond could make a sound, this is what it would be like.

As Tolle opens his eyes he sees the dawn light and intuitively realizes, "that there is infinitely more to light than we realize. That soft luminosity filtering through the curtains was love itself." In looking again at his room it as if it were being seen for the first time: "Everything was fresh and pristine, as if it had just come into existence." Everything that he picks up and looks at is beautiful and alive. "The next day I walked around the city in utter amazement at the miracle of life on earth, as if I had just been born into this world."[10]

In understanding his own experience Tolle was later able to suggest that the depth of his suffering forced his consciousness to withdraw from his troubled self, which, as he realized at that moment, was ultimately an illusion and affection of the mind, and so what was his false suffering self immediately collapsed. It seems that at the moment of grace there was a breakthrough into the true self. He later recounts that gradually the effects, to a certain extent, wore off but that he remained free and able to watch the suffering self. Physical suffering is inevitable in that it is what happens to us as a species but what Tolle calls the emotional pain body is a bit different. It can accompany us throughout much of our lives and is fundamentally a mental construction made up of the accumulated pain and negative energy which can occupy both our mind and body. Tolle learned to stop thinking other than when it was absolutely necessary—the endless repetition of the old compulsive negative thought pattern had ended. In other words he remained free enough to observe and witness in the present moment.

9. Moore, "True Terror."
10. Tolle, *Power of Now*, 2.

Spiritual Healing through Spiritual Direction

Spiritual healing of the past can also take place through spiritual direction. This is a way of exploring a person's relationship with God, and is not counselling, psychotherapy, or advice-giving, although it can include elements of each of these. The focus is on the relationship between God and the person being directed, wherein the person is encouraged to listen to and respond through dialogue with a self-communicating God. The emphasis in the relationship with the spiritual director is therefore on personal experience rather than intellectual ideas. Spiritual direction would usually begin where the person is most aware of difficulty in their spiritual life, and therefore for some people issues from childhood can begin to surface, especially when the experience of trusting God arises. The person would be encouraged to open up to past difficulties, but in the context of religious experience, so that healing comes from spiritual practices such as prayer, meditation, and following a rule of life such as commitment to saying the office and attending church services.

For others, past difficulties that need healing will only surface as they become more open to God's love and compassion. This may include people who felt they had dealt with the past. As one spiritual director notes, God may be inviting "a deeper engagement with what has emerged," and with a chance to look at the past from another perspective, through the light of Christ. She illustrates this with an example of her own issue, which was one of paternal identity as she did not know who her biological father was. Her distress about this had been tracked through a recurring dream that she had. In each dream a maternity nurse held up a newborn baby that no father would claim. The last version of the dream or waking fantasy she explains in this way:

> [It] occurred unexpectedly in my prayer time last year with a replay of the old dream, this time with Jesus present. As the maternity nurse entered the room, Jesus reached out and said quite clearly, "Give her to me. She's mine." My searching and longing for my birth father is being resolved—all I need to know is that I belong to Christ.[11]

All the painful issues from childhood, those that are apparently or partially resolved, or those that were entirely unresolved, can come to the surface as the relationship with God deepens and the person's sense of self becomes

---

11. Pickering, *Spiritual Direction,* 152.

stronger. "As they begin to believe they are loved by God, as they come to know that God is on their side, they are enabled to enter places of pain."[12]

The response of the spiritual director is not to interpret or to particularly work with past trauma, but rather to provide the listening space and acceptance of what is being said. The capacity to do this depends in a large part on the spiritual director's own strength, their awareness of their own past and their relationship with God. Responses that come from a place of contemplative prayer and listening to God will keep the relationship contained within the spiritual frame.

"Ideally speaking, the 'spiritual director' will help others to reach the heights of spiritual and mystical perfection."[13] With this rather elevated aim Thomas Merton wrote about the role of the spiritual director primarily drawing on the monastic tradition, and bringing to his reflections his own spiritual experiences and original thinking. By the time Merton published his short book *Spiritual Direction and Meditation* in 1960, his ideas on spiritual direction had been changing over almost twenty years. In August 1952 he reflected in his journal on the process:

> Spiritual direction cannot be really fruitful, ordinarily, unless there is a real spiritual affinity between the director and his penitent . . . [who] to merit direction . . . must live up to this grace and actually rely on the director. . . . The director . . . must be ready with untiring patience to listen and to observe and to advise and to guide the soul.[14]

Here there are some similarities with the therapist and patient relationship found in psychotherapeutic work and the development of what is called the working alliance. On spiritual direction Merton writes, "direction is sometimes an experiment in recognition: they recognise something new in themselves and I in myself: for God recognises Himself in us."[15]

For Merton spiritual direction in the monastic setting is not about "encouragements and admonitions" and "not mere ethical, social or psychological guidance." Above all "It is *spiritual*."[16] It is about going beyond the surface, and looking behind the egoic self to the underlying truth. For something real to happen in spiritual direction there needs to be a genuine relationship and a space for the person who is being directed to discover

---

12. Ibid., 152.

13. Merton, *Contemplation in a World of Action*, 269.

14. Merton, *Search for Solitude*, 8.

15. Ibid., 30.

16. Merton, *Spiritual Direction*, 14.

for themselves God's way for them. Merton writes of the director as God's usher leading directees as God wills and not in the way necessarily sought by the director.

Spiritual direction can lead to healing, because, as he writes, "a director will reveal to us things which we have hitherto been unable to see, though they were staring us in the face." This gives emphasis to the individuality of the work, "direction is, by its very nature, something personal."[17] For those "being directed must bring the director into contact with [their] real self, as best [they] can, and not fear to let him see what is false in [their] false self." In turn directors want to know this inmost real self and help the person "reintegrate their whole existence, as far as possible, on a simple, natural, and ordinary level on which they can be fully human."[18] Then God's grace can work on them. The work of healing is primarily through meditation and contemplative prayer which is about, "*awakening* our interior self and attuning ourselves inwardly to the Holy Spirit, so that we will be able to respond to His grace."[19]

Awakening to what is real and the gradual stripping away of the false self is central. Merton saw contemplation as a gift from God. He thought that it utterly transcends everything and yet at the same time is the only meaning for our existence. Merton understood contemplation as a knowledge and love that are experienced through grace and a process that entails a change of consciousness, a developing transformation. For Merton "the *archetypal* figure of the 'spiritual Father' as depicted in the literature of early monasticism"[20] and the source material found in the sayings of the Desert Fathers[21] over time became endowed with a general validity for everyone. They were intended to help the person, originally the hermit or monk, to discover their own rule of life, or God's will for him or herself in particular. A focus on listening and surrendering to God's will is a principal element and can apply to those inside and outside the monastic enclosure. One well-known example offers a central tenet of spiritual direction: "A certain brother went to Abba Moses in Scete, and asked him to speak a word; and the old man said, 'Get thee gone, and sit in thy cell, and thy cell shall teach thee all things.'" In other words there is no point rushing around asking for

---

17. Ibid., 31.
18. Ibid., 45.
19. Ibid., 107.
20. Merton, *Contemplation in a World of Action*, 270.
21. Merton, *Wisdom of the Desert*.

advice unless one is prepared to face one's own inner world, or as Merton puts it, "face his own solitude in all its naked reality."[22]

Merton offered spiritual direction in some of his correspondence as well as one to one with many of the novices and other monks. In this one example, which is a letter he writes to an interested but initially agnostic Devon school teacher, John Harris, Merton offers generous actions alongside powerful thoughts:

> Do not hesitate to write if there is anything I can do for you, or send you. . . . The important thing is that you are who you are: you are not a "man with a problem," or a person trying to figure something out, you are Harris, in Devonshire, and that means you are not and cannot be another in a series of objects, you are you and that is the important thing. For, you see, when "I" enters into a dialogue with "you" and each of us knows who is speaking, it turns out that we are both Christ. This, being seen in a very simple and "natural" light, is the beginning and almost the fullness of everything. Everything is in it somewhere.[23]

It is hardly surprising that this calibre of correspondence led to deep truths, healing, and transformation for Harris. Another example came from an ex-novice from Gethsemani who wrote about the face-to-face spiritual direction he had with Merton, noting that Merton gave each novice all the time that was needed to let out frustrations and desires and to seek help with meditation and monastic tensions.

> None of this instruction in prayer and monastic living was proffered by Fr. Louis [Merton's monastic name] in a direct way. He never openly instructed a novice in a "how to" mode regarding prayer, silence and monastic living in general. His teaching was subtle though completely centered and a novice hardly knew how very excellent his spiritual guidance was.[24]

The novice, who eventually left the monastery, experienced Merton as pointing ever "towards the truth and the need for understanding, compassion and love in the quest for meaning in our short lives. We have all been made richer having had him with us in this insane and wonderful universe."[25]

---

22. Merton, *Contemplation in a World of Action*, 281.

23. Merton, *Hidden Ground*, 387.

24. de Trinis, "Novice and his Master," 16.

25. Ibid., 27.

Psychological Healing through Psychotherapy

Depth psychotherapy offers one contemporary route to the promise of the breaking open of self seclusion and exile following a damaging childhood, and so a returning to the source of life. In Isa 49:8b there is the vision of the servant who saves, "To apportion the desolate heritages." Saying to the prisoners, "Come out," and to those who are in darkness, "Show yourselves." It is this ancient promise of psychological healing that is part of all spiritual journeying.

Those first involved in exploring the inner world understood that for everyone the disguise was only part of the psyche and that life was so much more than what was conscious. It was discovered that in the world of feelings and emotions a large part of what was experienced, especially from early childhood, was not available to conscious thought. All the early pioneers, including Sigmund Freud and Carl Jung, involved in what was known then as the scientific study of the mind, were as much concerned with what was mysterious and unknown and what lay behind rational conscious thought and human behavior as they were with monitoring specific events that lay in the visible world.

Psychoanalysis was one way to open up, like allegorical thought, the ability to see what was not apparent. People appreciated, by only looking on the surface of things, that much was missed. In a sense reality was only half present. Sigmund Freud thought that the ego told only part of the story and searched for a deeper realization of the nature of what "I" meant. This was some quality that might have resonance "with the 'I Am that I AM' of the Old Testament."[26]

Carl Jung, whose increasing interest lay in the spiritual aspects of people, was, from a young age, intrigued by what lay beneath the surface. He understood that as humans, we only partly direct and certainly do not control what happens in the psyche. He suggested the analogy that we are like a plant that lives on its rhizome where the true life is invisible and hidden in the root system:

> The part that appears above ground lasts only a single summer. Then it withers away—an ephemeral apparition. . . . Yet I have never lost a sense of something that lives and endures underneath the eternal flux. What we see is the blossom, which passes. The rhizome remains.[27]

26. Zeal, "Hazards to Desire," 184.
27. Jung, *Memories, Dreams, Reflections*, 18.

Jung understood that there are times when this imperishable world irrupts into the transitory one. These were interior happenings and encounters with what he referred to as the "other" reality. This way of understanding what goes on in each of us is counter-cultural in our contemporary Western world. It explores what is not known, what is mysterious and not rational. Carl Jung's method tended to emphasize the present and the future but again he understood that the person needed to relate what they considered relevant in their history and talk about difficulties as they saw it. This process acts rather as a confession or catharsis and tends to widen the person's perspective as the analyst's responses are heard and absorbed.

This in turn leads to elucidation that includes working out the transference between the analyst and the person being seen—the transference is the feelings that the patient (the term usually used in psychoanalysis for the person being seen) projects onto the analyst based on the patient's relations with earlier significant persons, especially parents. Through such understanding the person is educated to have insight about their interactions and this in turn can lead to change and transformation—part of Jung's process of individuation which is the journey towards becoming the person we are meant to be.[28]

Another approach in depth psychology is found in the example of the work of Harry Guntrip, a psychoanalyst who helped to establish the British school of object relations therapy. He understood that problems needed to become conscious so they could be understood, usually through interpretations made by the analyst. He thought that part of the process was to bring what is hidden into conscious awareness through the provision of

> a reliable and understanding human relationship of a kind that makes contact with the deeply repressed traumatised child that enables one to become steadily more able to live, in the security of a new real relationship, with the traumatic legacy of the earliest formative years, as it seeps through or erupts into consciousness.

Guntrip emphasized that the process involved is one of interaction, "a function of two variables, the personalities of two people working together towards free spontaneous growth . . . it is the meeting and interacting of two real people in all its complex possibilities."[29] Such an interaction can involve stages of dependence, regression, and unconscious communication as the damaged child part is brought into the light.

28. Adapted from Samuels, *Jung and the Post-Jungians.*
29. Guntrip, "Analysis," 366–68.

Repairing the hurts and wounds from the past through psychotherapy can also strengthen the process of spiritual transformation, where part of our self that perhaps had gone into cold storage or that was hidden just below the surface begins to become alive. The inner child or the secret life of the child begins to wake up. By becoming conscious of and relating to their secret inner child adults have a chance to integrate this aspect and so become healed. This is a process of beginning to think feelingly, in other words, to bring together the idea of what has happened with the accompanying feelings.

Knowing a bit more about ourselves can lead to moving closer to knowing and loving God. St. Augustine prayed that to know myself is to know You (God).[30] In a sense moving towards healing or wholeness is about acceptance of who one is, rather than striving for a state of perfection. It is about discovering one's place in the world not in the sense of achievement but of being loved and of great worth. Opening up this possibility can happen through the relationship with the psychotherapist, which in turn can help spiritual life.

Thomas Merton's Experiences of Spiritual and Psychological Healing

As a young adult Thomas Merton's attempts to keep the loss and trauma of his childhood suppressed and the shadow at bay proved ineffective, and he developed symptoms of dizziness, panic attacks, and gastritis. In his autobiography he describes a life dominated by fear, but attributes the cause to his refusal to follow moral laws, though it seems more likely that the effort of keeping feelings repressed might have some relevance here. It is at this point of emotional defeat that Merton's awareness is drawn to religion and his conversion to Catholicism begins. Often it is only when we are completely low and desperate that we become open to the "more than our selves." It is the anguish found in "the twilight and the mists of life" that drives people towards the transcendent.[31]

What is clear from Merton's journals is that rejection and abandonment continued to contribute to times of anxiety and depression. However, what Merton's conversion and later acceptance by the Trappists gave him was an attachment and a secure base from which to find out who he really was and to find a way of slowly and sufficiently integrating the pain and anger of his childhood. While Merton did have a few sessions with an analyst

30. Augustine, *Confessions.*
31. Berdyaev, *Dream and Reality,* 44.

who was also a psychiatrist (which went very badly) and did find ongoing counselling help from a local psychologist from 1960, it does seem that the religious life of silence and prayer became part of his route to healing, and to some extent a rebirth and re-parenting through the intimate relationship with God.

Sometimes Merton puts this re-parenting into words. For example following appendicitis as a young adult, shortly after his conversion, Merton writes:

> This lying in bed and being fed, so to speak, with a spoon was more than luxury: it was also full of meaning. I could not realise it at the time—and I did not need to; but a couple of years later I saw that this all expressed my spiritual life as it was then.
>
> For I was now, at last, born: but I was still only newborn. I was living: I had an interior life, real, but feeble and precarious. And I was still nursed and fed with spiritual milk . . .
>
> My eyes were beginning to open to the powerful and constant light of heaven and my will was at last learning to give in to the subtle and gentle and loving guidance of that love which is Life without end . . .

And as he convalesced a few weeks later in Cuba:

> It would be hard to believe that anyone was so well taken care of as I was; and no one has ever seen an earthly child guarded so closely and so efficiently and cherished and guided and watched and led with such attentive and prevenient care as surrounded me in those days. . . . I was walking in my new simplicity and hardly knew what it was all about, so solicitous were my surrounding angels.[32]

So gradually through developing trust in and believing in the grace and the love of God his re-parenting and healing began and continued for twenty-seven years through good and not so good times in the Trappist monastery of Gethsemani.

Interestingly in one of Merton's journals called *Learning to Love*, written between January 1966 and October 1967, he writes of the continuing monastic experience of learning to love God, self, and others but he also includes his unexpected experience of falling in love after twenty-four years as a monk and aged fifty-one with a woman, a student nurse in her mid-twenties. He wrote, "Now I see more and more that there is only one realistic answer: Love. I have got to dare to love, and to bear the anxiety of

---

32. Merton, *Seven Storey Mountain*, 332–33.

self-questioning that love arouses in me, until 'perfect love casts out fear.'"[33] Merton realized that within this love there was his true call to solitude.

One interesting aside is that Merton after this experience is able to note (while visiting the doctor) the "happiness at being loved" shown by a small child in the waiting room, "the delightfulness of her littleness" and "her love for her mother and grandmother."[34] Perhaps this observation confirms that further healing from childhood may have taken place for Merton through his experiences as an adult.

Merton understood depth psychology and psychoanalysis; he read Freud and Jung and was able to make use of analytic thought in his work as novice master. In the second half of 1956 Merton had several disturbing encounters with the noted psychiatrist and Freudian psychoanalyst Dr. Gregory Zilboorg. The meetings provoked intense reactions in both men and it would be disingenuous to suggest that the meetings led to any healing for Merton, though it may have led to some serious self-reflection. In Merton's journal, written while he attended psychiatric and psychoanalytic workshops at a conference with Dr. Zilboorg, he writes of his conscious and unconscious life:

> On the surface I have my confusion. On a deeper level desire and conflict. In the greatest depths, like a spring of pure water rising up in the flames of hell, is the smallness, the frailty of a hope that is, yet, never overwhelmed but continues strangely and inexplicably to nourish in the midst of apparent despair.[35]

Merton found Zilboorg highly judgmental. As recorded by Merton, Zilboorg, among other things, castigates Merton for an hour and a half about his neurosis; for his dependence on vows as substitutes for reality; for his megalomania and narcissism; for his pathological hermit trend; and for his lack of affectivity. As noted by Merton the quotes include, "You are a gadfly to your superiors," "Very stubborn," "You are afraid to be an ordinary monk in the community," and "you thought only of yourself." Despite the strength of these highly critical comments Merton does recognize some aspects of himself in the descriptions and so his reaction is ambivalent, full of mixed feelings. He reflects on some of what Zilboorg says but is also furious, stunned, and upset.[36]

---

33. Merton, *Learning to Love*, 44.
34. Ibid., 163.
35. Merton, *Search for Solitude*, 57–58.
36. Ibid., 59.

His pain emerges as an association in the next journal entry where he writes about the birds on the lake—the loons, and here it is no coincidence that he chooses to reflect on birds that carry the name of madness. "The loon, I think, is a very serious bird and I take him very seriously. To me it is not crazy but even, in a way, beautiful. It means: distances, wind, water, forests, the loneliness of the North."[37] The after effect of this meeting with Zilboorg is implicit in his description. Although not noted in Merton's journal, a second meeting apparently took place with Zilboorg in the presence of the Abbot Dom James, where Merton, horribly exposed, became furiously angry and deeply upset. There is one further meeting between Zilboorg and Merton which takes place on 27 December 1956, when Zilboorg visits Gethsemani, and once again there is an unpleasant confrontation as he warns Merton against psychoanalysis—at least with him. However, on hearing of Zilboorg's death in 1959 Merton writes to a correspondent "Wasn't it sad to hear that Gregory Zilboorg was dead? I just learned it yesterday. A great and good man and may God grant him rest and eternal life . . ." Whatever pain Zilboorg had caused three years earlier Merton had partially resolved.[38]

There are a number of reasons that can help explain the difficult dynamics between the two men.[39] Zilboorg's accusation to Merton, "You want a hermitage in Times Square with a large sign over it saying 'HERMIT'"[40] seemed particularly wounding; it would appear to reverberate with Merton's early experience of critical rejection. One can surmise that Merton might have been anxious about meeting Zilboorg but was also looking for some support and insight both for himself and for his novices. In a letter to Abbot James Fox some months before the meeting with Zilboorg, Merton writes:

> I am beginning to realize that I am something of a problem and that I need plenty of grace now. I am coming to a crucial point in my life in which I may make a complete mess of everything—or let Jesus make a complete success of everything. On the whole my nerves are not too good and I can't rely on my faculties as I used to—they play tricks on me, and I get into nervous depression and weakness. However I have to react by faith, by love of the cross, and work especially.[41]

37. Ibid., 61.
38. Merton, *School of Charity*, 123.
39. Gardner, "Thomas Merton."
40. Mott, *Seven Mountains of Thomas Merton*, 297.
41. Merton, *School of Charity*, 95.

He also demonstrates great insight about the mental strain experienced by those entering the enclosed order. In a letter to one of his correspondents Abbot Augustine Moore who understood monastic life, Merton wryly notes, amongst other observations, the dangers of perfectionism and the tendency to force sanctity by sheer strain. He recognizes the false notion of the monastic life, "In fact, we are *ordinary* people."[42] This has echoes of Merton's understanding that God penetrates all so contemplation is not a "special 'state' that removes one from the ordinary things going on."[43] Acceptance that one is ordinary is a relief from stress.

Four years later, after Zilboorg's death, Merton began to meet with Dr. James Wygal, a Louisville psychologist who actually had been recommended by Zilboorg. This proved a very different sort of experience but not without its own problems. The connection did give Merton support somewhere outside the monastery where difficulties could be aired.

"Out of the depths I cry to you, O Lord" (Ps 130:1). Both psychotherapy and spirituality can provide a framework and an environment that can help damaged children return to search for what they missed out on in their early years. This is the feeling of being alive and real, to express happiness at being loved and the capacity to return that love to others. It is the chance to repair soul murder and to experience joy and a love for life. It is a chance to experience the spirit of the child. Religion gives the idea of a God who holds us in being and heals; personal, spiritual, and psychological understanding puts that into practice. It is a form of participative knowing, as it is embodied experience. Where we are damaged and where weakness and vulnerability lie can be the points of entry for allowing us to turn to God. Fear, despair, and anxiety can be occasions for turning to somebody or something more than our selves. Jesus Christ, child and savior, stands as a symbol of the true self, rebounding from suffering and destructiveness and manifesting an eternal resilience to the worst that the world can do.

42. Ibid., 58.
43. Merton, *Thoughts in Solitude*, 96.

10

An Invitation to Look and Find Paradise

> Our life is a faint tracing on the surface of mystery, like the idle,
> curved tunnels of leaf miners on the face of the leaf. We must
> somehow take a wider view, look at the whole landscape, really
> see it, and describe what's going on here.[1]

Present-moment awareness is about creating a gap in the constant busy-
ness of the mind. This also means a break in the continuum between
what is past and what lies ahead. It is through such a clear space that new
and creative possibilities are born. The closing down of present-moment
awareness in the small child happens as the weight of the adult life of care
and rational thought gradually but relentlessly obscures the enchanted
world. The possibility of re-enchantment and sometimes the invitation to
move from the grown-up life of care can come from a child: from being in
the presence of a small child, or from the wounded child part of oneself,
or from the healing found through therapy or spiritual life, or from good
memories of childhood, or indeed from grace and the Christ child. There
may be an inner prompting in the midst of a busy life to take stock, perhaps
to stop and consider for, "the soul has an instinct, like animals, for where
water is to be found."[2]

The focus is then on the inner desire for that thirst-quenching water of
life. In other words to move to a place of renewal and rebirth, where there
may be glimpses in adulthood of life beyond the shadow and the disguise,
and experiences, even if fleeting, of the spirit of the child. One way to start
to shift out of the obscured false self way of living is to begin to develop

---

1. Dillard, *Annie Dillard Reader,* 287.
2. Raine, *India Seen Afar,* 7.

awareness, to awaken the senses, to look, listen, feel, and touch as the small child does—to return to one's senses.

Really Looking

A baby who has just learned to focus and able to keep her head up has no real idea of what is going on but there is a straightforward and unabashed way of looking. The infant is set to learn to explore where she is. She is really looking. As adults the way to begin to catch glimpses of paradise again is also about really looking: a question of trying to keep the eyes open and to move away from only seeing what is expected. This involves minimizing if possible the editing that goes on automatically in the brain, so what you see is in part about how it is seen.

If there is awareness when looking then more may be revealed. So what might be expected? Experiences by people who were previously blind, and, who then regain sight may offer one perspective. The accounts vary hugely with some describing how they felt oppressed by the light and associated concepts of space, and others delighting in sight and the visual world. For example one little girl, newly able to see, is taken to a garden: "She is greatly astonished . . . stands speechless in front of the tree, which she names on taking hold of it . . . as 'the tree with the lights in it.'" Another account is of a twenty-two-year-old woman blind from childhood who, following an operation,

> was dazzled by the world's brightness and kept her eyes shut for two weeks. When at the end of that time she opened her eyes again, she did not recognise any objects, but, the more she now directed her gaze upon everything about her, the more it could be seen how an expression of gratification and astonishment overspread her features; she repeatedly exclaimed: "Oh God! How beautiful!"[3]

The contemporary spiritual guide Eckhart Tolle, whose epiphany was described in the previous chapter, suggests when a child first looks at a leaf that the parent encourages them to look at the markings and the color and the shape of it rather than foreshorten the looking by saying this is just a leaf. The tendency as we grow older is to analyze and categorize, but the looking with the spirit of the child involves a letting go, an emptying so that the vision is seen *before* being assessed. This is surprisingly difficult to do.

3. Dillard, *Annie Dillard Reader*, 304.

Really looking and being aware is a spiritual teaching advocated by all the different traditions. There seems a consensus that the secret is to allow the inevitable and endless thoughts to flow on their way without becoming caught up or seduced by them. Such looking is to look beyond the concepts, "into the realm of the real, where subjects and objects act and rest purely, without utterance. 'Launch into the deep . . . and you shall see.'" For Annie Dillard this way of seeing is a gift and her own vision of "the tree with lights in it," the expression she adopts that was used earlier by the young girl, came to Dillard as an adult when it was unsought. She describes her experience in this way:

> Then one day I saw the tree with the lights in it. I saw the back-yard cedar where the mourning doves roost charged and trans-figured, each cell buzzing with flame. I stood on the grass with the lights in it, grass that was wholly fire, utterly focused and utterly dreamed. It was less like seeing than like being for the first time seen, knocked breathless by a powerful glance. . . . I have since only very rarely seen the tree with the lights in it. The vision comes and goes, mostly goes, but I live for it, for the moment when the mountains open and a new light roars in spate through the crack, and the mountains slam.[4]

The novelist Elizabeth Goudge understood the way in which the child part can break through and effect a transformation, if only for a short time:

> I became a child again. I recovered the lost piercing senses of childhood, those senses that can pierce through appearance to reality. And like a child I did not bother myself as to what it was to which my vivid apprehension of sound and scent and colour was admitting me; but like a child I breathed it unconsciously into my being, as a pine tree absorbs the sun and rain and air.[5]

Perhaps to really look one needs to be alone. The troubled poet Rilke expresses this when he writes in a letter:

> What is necessary, after all, is only this: solitude, vast inner soli-tude. To walk inside yourself and meet no one for hours—that is what you must be able to attain. To be solitary as you were when you were a child, when the grownups walked around involved with matters that seemed large and important because they

---

4. Ibid., 308.
5. Goudge, *Green Dolphin Country*, 286.

looked so busy and because you didn't understand a thing about what they were doing.[6]

His words are similar to many written by Merton, who echoes the same theme of the need for solitude as part of becoming aware. "I am not defending a phony 'hermit-mystique,' but some of us have to be alone to be ourselves. . . . We need time to do our job of meditation and creation."[7] Merton in his lectures to the novices presented some of Rilke's poems and also highlighted Rilke's poetic view of reality as an inseeing. This is about getting right to the center of what is being looked at and is a form of contemplation that involves, using Merton's words, an "inner event in the person who sees, and it takes place in this encounter with something else, it's not just a subjective thing."[8] Here Merton has grasped that really seeing, for an adult, is more than a return to an early way of focusing as in the small child but adds the adult experience to it to form a new way of seeing—this is the looking of the child mind.

A Change in Consciousness

If we really look then perhaps sometimes we can glimpse, as can often happen in childhood, the realization that there is another level of life beyond or beneath all external affairs. For many people this knowledge remains within them. The knowledge is that there is a sense of something other, something more than the everyday, but life seems to present obstacles and demands that prevent pursuing this inner knowledge.

Really looking implies beholding both the external world and the inner world, and this process of contemplation involves a change in consciousness and feeling. Moving from a life of care is in part a transformation of consciousness, and there are different ways for this to happen. The words used to describe these ways are the same as those used to describe what may happen to each person after death. This makes sense, as moving from a life of care involves a death of what Merton called the false illusory self. Merton writes how the false care-worn self can be sloughed off by a repeated process of letting go and then renewal. It is as if there is a continuous dying and resurrection with the restoration of the authentic part or true self that has been overshadowed by the false self. This is an experience similar to recovery from a serious illness when the body is fully restored to health,

---

6. Rilke, *Letters*, letter 6, 23.

7. Merton, *Contemplation in a World of Action*, 223.

8. Pearson, "Inseeing and Outgazing," 14.

with associated feelings of lightness, where priorities are seen to be different and the world seems imbued with a new light.

There are different ways of describing a change in consciousness: awareness, insight, rebirth, restoration, renewal, self-realization. Each time this change of consciousness happens, whether small or large, is a breakthrough from the conventional way of seeing things. In that sense each is part of the breaking through beyond the shadow and the disguise. This means the appreciation, even if only for a moment, of the insignificance of ego concerns in the face of the awesome power and light of God. The care-worn self is over-identified with the small self, the personal ego, and if something of the divine can break through, often unexpectedly, then there is a breakthrough into a wider realization of something that is more than ourselves.

A sense of renewal can arrive from dramatic experiences of awareness or from gradual and deepening spiritual practices. One example of the former is the experience of Eckhart Tolle, who as described in the last chapter "woke in the hell of self-hatred and cried 'I cannot live with myself any longer!'" and had to see and ask "does this make me two!" Tolle found himself in a terrifying vortex of energy but the moment he stopped resisting, fear stopped, and the void no longer sucked him in, he simply fell into it and woke up later to birdsong and a world in light. "Heard within, they summon into Presence . . . a new act of total *attention*."[9]

An example of awareness emerging from the spiritual practice of regular meditation is given by a Sufi master, who describes the change of consciousness that can happen as a process of recurrent rebirthing whereby:

> Of course it is God who is reborn as you each time. . . . It is only by rediscovering the immaculate condition of your being . . . that you can be reborn again, or that God can be reborn as you. That is the meaning of the virginity of Mary, the mother of Christ.

Rather than advocating a regression the Sufi master suggests, this is about attunement to that internal state. "It is very vulnerable, trusting, and defenseless." Through deep contemplation awareness of the spirit of the child is reached, but within the adult consciousness and perception:

> We are discovering the child within, discovering it is still there within its distortion. You will get the impression that you are wearing a mask: that not only your body, but your personality, is like a mask protecting your real being. Your real being is

9. Moore, "Presence."

defenseless and immaculate, and will, by dint of its encounter with the descent of the Holy Spirit—that is all the influences of the heavenly spheres—be able to transform the more peripheral elements of your personality. That is why you think you are reborn: because you are transformed.[10]

In other words awareness of the child mind is possible within the organized frame of meditation and contemplative prayer. The defenselessness described in the quote above is because the shadow and the disguise are temporarily lessened, and this allows for a quality of transparency where God's presence can shine through. As said above, there has to be metaphorical death of part of the identity for a rebirth to occur. Jesus guides us to this: "unless a grain of wheat falls into the earth and dies, it remains just a single grain; but if it dies it bears much fruit" (John 12:24). While Paul puts it even more directly: "Fool! What you sow does not come to life unless it dies" (1 Cor 15:36).

Carl Jung who explored psychological transformation through looking at the processes of what happened in alchemical studies noted that the conscious, intentional death of the old self was seen to lead to the conception of the *filius philosophorum*—the philosopher's child. In other words through transformation a new and a wiser being who is a child arises in us. He writes about the inner voice as the voice of a fuller life, of a wider, more comprehensive consciousness, which is why in mythology "the symbolic rebirth coincides with sunrise . . . the moment of birth of their greater personality is known as illumination."[11]

There are different ways of thinking about rebirth and so transformation. The first is resurrection which involves the restoration to life of a personality that has died. Another way is rebirth as self-realization where, as discussed above, we let go of the restricted view of who we are and accept that there is a more than our selves. Rebirth can also take the form of renewal, where the person who has let go of their old self lives afterwards in a state of heightened consciousness. Another way in which rebirth can be experienced is through the birth of the radiant child. This is about an awareness of the archetype of the divine or eternal child.

This, according to Jung, is the child who paves the way for a future change of personality and who symbolizes healing and wholeness. Sometimes, as explored earlier, a healing dream, vision or epiphany can include the form of a beautiful young child appearing in radiant light: an apparition

---

10. Khan, *That Which Transpires*, 63–64.

11. Jung, *Development of Personality*, 184, par 318.

of the divine child.[12] Here is the inner meeting of the numinous and the luminous, the radiant child, the Christ child, the center of paradise and the golden world.

Christ's message to become as small children is the invitation to a rebirth, to a change in consciousness, to a meeting with the radiant child. In letting go of the care-worn self we become open, vulnerable, and own our dependence on God. If we deny this dependence and rupture the umbilical cord that connects us to the source of life and the ground of our being then we are in exile. We are captives of the false illusory world and the shadow and the disguise. If we reconnect with this, the deepest relationship, then rebirth and healing can take place. Here is the connection with the kingdom of God, a sense of paradise and the spirit of the child.

The Golden String, The Golden World—Paradise

> I give you the end of a golden string;
> Only wind it into a ball,
> It will lead you in at heaven's gate,
> Built in Jerusalem's wall.[13]

William Blake described moments of grace as a golden string which can easily get hidden or lost unless we attend to what is happening to us, and follow the string emerging from the labyrinth of life as we know it into a deeper reality. The monastic and mystic Bede Griffiths begins his autobiography by quoting that verse by William Blake and recounting an experience that took place during his last term at school. He walked alone in the evening and became aware of the sound of the birds singing. "It seemed to me that I had never heard the birds singing before," and walking on he sees hawthorn trees in full bloom,

> and again I thought that I had never seen such a sight or experienced such sweetness before. If I had been brought suddenly among the trees of the Garden of Paradise and heard a choir of angels singing I could not have been more surprised.

Overcome by awe as a lark rose and sank and the sunset faded,

> I felt inclined to kneel on the ground, as though I had been standing in the presence of an angel; and I hardly dared to look

---

12. Tuby, *In the Wake of Jung*, 98.
13. Blake, *Complete Writings*, 716.

on the face of the sky, because it seemed as though it was but a veil before the face of God.

This experience he thought was one of the most decisive of his life as he had become aware "of another world of beauty and mystery such as I had never imagined to exist, except in poetry." He later saw this experience as one that many have in different contexts, where there is a break in the routine of daily life, the life full of care:

> But however it may be, it is as though a veil has been lifted and we see for the first time behind the façade which the world has built around us. Suddenly we know that we belong to another world, that there is another dimension to existence.

Such experiences take us out of time and space into a place of harmony with creation and confirming us as part of the eternal order. Whilst many certainly do have this insight it can quickly lose significance, and, as discussed, the life of care can reassert itself and so the vision fades. For some the golden string leads back to the beginning where for Bede Griffiths there is Christ who is both the beginning and the end of the journey. The golden string *is* Christ who leads us to the heart of meaning in the world. Thirty years after this experience as a schoolboy the monk recognized, "That mysterious presence which I felt in all the forms of nature has gradually disclosed itself as the infinite and eternal Being, of whose beauty all the forms of nature are but a passing reflection." Searching in the solitude of nature and in his own mind Griffiths found God in:

> the society of his Church and in the Spirit of Charity. And all this came to me not so much as a discovery but as a recognition. I felt that I had been wandering in a far country and had returned home; that I had been dead and was alive again; that I had been lost and was found.[14]

It seems that whatever words may be used—the golden string or the enchanted world or, as is described below, the golden world, there is in everyone the sense of the numinous. No matter what may have happened to us during or after infancy, a glimpse of the potential for a different dimension remains, often hidden, within the psyche. It could be said that everyone carries the nostalgia for an ecstatic experience of beauty, contentment and containment; nostalgia for the spirit of the child and for innocence. Falling in love recreates some sense of this again in adolescence, but any glimpse is

---

14. Griffiths, *Golden String,* 9–11, 16–17.

hard to hold onto as life becomes weighed down with duty and worry and the rational asserts its dominance.

This awareness of the numinous is for Robert Johnson, a Jungian analyst, the truest reality to which a human ever has access. He has described his lifelong searching for what he has called the golden world. He writes about the early experience in his life that brought to conscious awareness the existence of this heavenly or golden world. Over time he understood that what was required in life was to inhabit a middle place where both the heavenly and the earthly are honored. He understood that in this middle place lay a certain amount of safety but where too lay holiness. In balancing the two, the visible and the invisible world, it became clear to him that the two worlds are in fact one.

His realization of the heavenly or golden world came in strange circumstances following a car crash which pinned him, then aged eleven, between a car and a wall. He was taken to hospital where he was operated on and left that night to recover. In the middle of the night Johnson awoke feeling terribly unwell, not knowing that an artery in his damaged leg had opened loose and he was in fact bleeding to death. Johnson writes that he knew what was happening at a psychic dimension and initially was determined not to die until he found himself in a glorious world,

> it was pure light, gold, radiant, luminous, ecstatically happy, perfectly beautiful, purely tranquil, joy beyond bound. . . . I could only revel at what was before me. We have words for this side of reality but none to describe the other side.

Johnson did not die but this glimpse of the golden world figured profoundly throughout his life returning again on occasions, and so as he writes, "a curtain separating the two realms was for me forever parted."[15]

Johnson's phrase "the golden world" that he used for this experience, which reoccurred on two further memorable occasions in adulthood, was first used by Mircea Eliade who understood that such transcendental states of consciousness were available to everyone and at any time. As with Merton's understanding of a life free from care, Eliade also knew that worldly concerns lead to opaqueness, so the requirement for the breakthrough from the visible to the invisible, from the material to the spiritual is acute awareness, a cleared mind, a lack of egoic presence, openness, and grace. The world becomes golden in its clarity and transparency, the "golden green light" that he writes about. As an adult, Eliade referred to many of his childhood episodes in his writings, but often with poignancy. In one he writes:

---

15. Johnson, *Balancing Heaven and Earth*, 2–3.

I practiced for many years [the] exercise of recapturing that epiphanic moment, and I would always find again the same plenitude. I would slip into it as a fragment of time devoid of duration—without beginning, middle or end. During my last years of lycée, when I struggled with profound attacks of melancholy, I still succeeded at times in returning to the golden green light of that afternoon. . . . But even though the beatitude was the same, it was now impossible to bear because it aggravated my sadness too much. By this time I knew the world . . . was a world forever lost.[16]

The poet Kathleen Raine writes about the golden dawn as a state of being, and she believes that it is not lost but rather hidden and so can be found again. She describes this golden dawn also as the "India of the Imagination" which is "universal . . . the place of every arrival, the term of every spiritual quest . . . the frontier between this and other worlds." This is a frontier that is everywhere and in ourselves. She thinks that in the West we have lost our Orient and indeed are dis-oriented, for in the India of the Imagination Blake's "dread forms of certainty" melt away, instead "certainties are lost, rather than found." Interestingly Raine traces her ideas about India to Rudyard Kipling's writing about "that archetypal childhood where we all converse with the beautiful and untameable animals of the wild places." In Hindu teachings it is the forest dweller who in later years of life renounces the world returning instead to the forest to converse with creatures and so become wise. Raine asks:

Is there any child who does not wonder how human beings could ever wish to do otherwise than live in the forest with the creatures and the trees and flowers and sun and rain and winds and storms and clouds?[17]

Longing for a Return

The nostalgia for what has been lost remains long after childhood and can impel seekers to search both within themselves and out in the world for this lost place, time and state of mind. For Thomas Merton it is the nostalgia for, or intuition of, paradise, and is about a longing for a return or restoration to an original state of being which is Eden. For him it is about a reversal of the fall and the separation from God. It is the journey forward to the beginning,

16. Ellwood, *Politics of Myth*, 98–99.
17. Raine, *India Seen Afar*, 3, 5–6.

"the restoration of that primordial unity and harmony of all creation in God," and it is part of what it means to be authentic.

For him the journey begins within the self as the false self comprising the shadow and disguise that leads to division and alienation from reality, and so the paradise life becomes impossible. It is only through surrendering the false self and the death of the exterior, egotistical self that paradise can be regained. To be in paradise, Merton writes, is to recover one's true self. Many in their longing for a return to an original state of being have undertaken this journeying home and actually journeyed away from the norm of conventional living. They have taken a counter-cultural stance. One such group were the Desert Fathers and Mothers who in different groupings set out to be away from the world and wander into the desert places, far away into the wilderness.

In his book *The Wisdom of the Desert*, Merton writes about the search undertaken by the Desert Fathers for "their own true self, in Christ. And in order to do this, they had to reject completely the false, formal self, fabricated under social compulsion in 'the world.'"[18] Finding paradise then became both an internal and an external journey.

> The simple men who lived out their lives to a good old age among the rocks and sands only did so because they had come into the desert to be themselves, their ordinary selves, and to forget a world that divided them from themselves.[19]

Merton in his analysis of their path writes of the need for the Fathers to lose themselves in the "inner, hidden reality of a self that was transcendent, mysterious, half-known, and lost in Christ."[20] The purpose of the longing was purity of heart—innocence.

As Helen Waddell writes in her book, *The Desert Fathers*, the men left a negligible contribution to the philosophy of religion but they did find eternity. She quotes from a finding given in the book *The Life of St. Anthony*: "The spaces of our human life set over against eternity are most brief and poor." She writes how the Desert Fathers taught us "how man makes himself eternal. . . . Christianity came first to the world as a starlit darkness, into which a man steps and comes suddenly aware of a whole universe, except that part of it which is beneath his feet."[21]

---

18. Merton, *Wisdom of the Desert*, 5–6.
19. Ibid., 23.
20. Ibid., 7.
21. Matthews, *Both Alike to Thee*, 2.

Thomas Merton also wrote about another group of searchers who sought to separate themselves from the world and longed to find paradise. The Shaker community was a group of people that had branched off from the Quakers, and who lived their lives based on beliefs of simplicity, celibacy, pacifism, and equality. Their message was deeply Christian, as Merton writes they were "simple, joyous, optimistic people whose joy was rooted in the fact that Christ *had* come, and that the basic Christian experience was the discovery of Christ living in us all now," and the belief in "a redeemed cosmos in which war, hatred, tyranny, and greed had no place—a cosmos of creativity and worship."[22]

As Paul M. Pearson notes in Shaker woodwork, in creating furniture and everyday objects, "there is a certain Edenic innocence as each item that the craftsman makes is a participation in God's work of creation and the craftsman's ideal was to make each object to best fulfil its vocation."[23] Both Merton and the Shakers had an ultimate belief in the goodness of humanity and creation which they found through their search for paradise; Merton also thought that the Shaker movement had a lot in common with the Cistercian way of life. He wrote about the image of the paradise tree—the Shakers' Tree of Life which he said had come to the Shaker community as a spirit gift, and this suggested to Merton a symbol of hope to be taken seriously in the midst of darkness and deception.

Both of these communities of seekers—the Desert Fathers and the Shakers—offer examples of ways of simple living and perhaps through their austerity a glimpse of paradise. Once again it could be said then that what may be experienced as paradise is where coherence and transparency is not obscured by rational and conceptual mind games. This is akin to what has been understood so far as the spirit of the child, and where the child mind is present in the adult. In such a state of simplicity and conscious awareness there is an emptying of the self, and for Merton it is then possible that each person can become paradise and so be the dwelling-place of God with humanity. He wrote, "We are His new Paradise. And in the midst of that Paradise stands Christ Himself, the tree of life. . . . This, then, gives us a beginning of awareness of who we are."[24]

In his essay *The Recovery of Paradise,* Merton quotes from Staretz Zosima in *The Brothers Karamazov,* "We do not understand that life is paradise, for it suffices only to wish to understand it, and at once paradise will appear in front of us in its beauty." Merton sees this as an astonishing

---

22. Pearson, "Introduction," in *Thomas Merton, Seeking Paradise,* 44.

23. Ibid., 44.

24. Merton, *New Man,* 161.

statement given that the novel is set in the context of such violence and blasphemy, but Merton sees it also as basic to primitive Christianity. Paradise is a state belonging to earth, in the present rather than the future and is also conceived as an antechamber to heaven. For the Desert Fathers this was a place of unity, "within themselves, or rather above and beyond themselves." It was the recovery of the innocence of Adam in paradise and a purity of heart. For Merton, wishing for paradise involves a devotion to the recovery of innocence. He writes:

> The innocence and purity of heart which belong to paradise are a complete emptiness of self in which all is the work of God, the free and unpredictable expression of His love, the work of grace. In the purity of original innocence, all is done in us but without us.[25]

Merton understands that this is not what he calls the narcissistic ignorance of the baby but involves knowledge, the capacity for reflection and awareness. The recovery of paradise takes place for the adult in humility and in spiritual nakedness. In other words not self-consciously but as the small child who just *is* present and just *is* vulnerable. Merton realized that the recovery of paradise is always hidden in us as a possibility, and is a difficult struggle involving repeated cycles of deaths and resurrections within the psyche, so that the Christian on their journey is both in the wilderness of the desert and in the garden at the same time. Through acceptance of dependence, emptiness, vulnerability, and selflessness can come awareness that paradise is ever present. "Here *is* an unspeakable secret; paradise is all around us and we do not understand it. . . . 'Wisdom,' cries the dawn deacon, but we do not attend."[26]

One of the things that Merton highlights in his response to the Shaker movement is their gift of music and dance which Merton saw as "one more expression of their belief in the power of God among his believers, of paradise consciousness, of realized eschatology, of the presence of God's kingdom. . . . He added in a somewhat wistful tone, 'God, at least they had the sense to dance.'"[27]

25. Merton, "Recovery of Paradise," 56.

26. Merton, *Conjectures*, 132.

27. Pearson, *Thomas Merton*, 49.

PART THREE

BECOMING

II

Dancing in the Water of Life

We are the children of the Unknown. . . . No one can enter the
river wearing the garments of public and collective ideas. He
must feel the water on his skin. He must know that immediacy
is for naked minds only, and for the innocent.
Come, dervishes: here is the water of life. Dance in it.[1]

The theologian Dorothee Soelle thought that in the materialist West we
are "orphan-like in relation to nature,"[2] and that in earlier cultures visions and experiences of another reality were commonplace—especially in
early childhood. Even in our contemporary culture the small child does not
discriminate between aspects of creation through accepting one thing such
as the butterfly, and rejecting another such as the slug, until they are encouraged to do so. Anything and everything is amazing and is worthy of notice
and interest until judgement sets in and positive values are apportioned to
one thing and negative attributes to others.

Embodying this same open spirit of the child, Thomas Merton understood through his love of nature that all creation was sacramental, and,
because of its innate goodness, contributed in its own way to the cosmic
praise of the Creator. He wrote that barn animals, flowering trees, fish,
and water joined in the communion of saints, praising God by being their
unique selves and displaying the vestige of God. In the talk to the novices
discussed earlier in the book he talked about, "the rabbitness of God is shining through, in all these darn rabbits."[3] Through his environmental vision

1. Merton, *Raids on the Unspeakable*, 160–61.
2. Soelle, *Silent Cry*, 11.
3. Merton, "Life Free from Care," 71.

he saw a communion between all living things, writing about the celebration of the divine spark in nature, and showing how, buoyed by the exuberance of the moment of connection with nature, he felt enticed into the dance of life: "We are invited to forget ourselves on purpose, cast our awful solemnity to the winds and join in the general dance."[4]

Merton wrote how this sense of connection and oneness such as meditating in a field accompanied by fireflies was not "a manifestation of narcissistic regression." Rather, he knew that this was:

> a complete awakening of identity and of rapport! It implies an awareness and acceptance of one's place in the whole, first the whole of creation, then the whole plan of Redemption—to find oneself in the great mystery of fulfilment which is the Mystery of Christ.[5]

This is what has been called nature mysticism. Merton thought that following God in "his mysterious, cosmic dance" happened when "children . . . are really children."[6]

It has been said that Merton lived successfully on the "ecotone"—on the margin between two distinct environments that shares characteristics of each[7]—in this context a place of vulnerability and awareness of both the beauty in nature and the damage done to it where the destruction and suppression of nature is an attack on re-enchantment and ultimately on life.

Born to Dance

Dancing embodies one of our most primal relationships to the universe. It is pre-verbal, beginning in small children before words can be formed. It is innate in children before they possess command over language and is evoked when thoughts or emotions are too powerful for words to contain. Research studies show that babies and small children up to two years old are born to dance responding to the rhythm and tempo of music and finding it more engaging than speech. It is suggested that humans may be born with a predisposition to move rhythmically in response to music.[8] Small children move naturally to achieve mobility, but they also move to express a thought or feeling and above all they move because it is joyful and it feels wonderful. When the movement becomes consciously structured and it is

4. Merton, *New Seeds of Contemplation*, 192.

5. Merton, *Dancing in the Water of Life*, 250.6

6. Merton, *New Seeds of Contemplation*, 192.

7. Weis, *Thomas Merton's Gethsemani*, 133.

8. Zenther and Eerola, "Rhythmic Engagement."

performed with awareness for its own sake then it becomes more formal dance. Re-finding our ability to move and to dance reconnects our mind and body but it also reconnects our spirit to the spirit of the child and the universe.

Above all dance is about being embodied but it is not just movement of the body but rather movement that relates the dancer to the world. The world becomes present in a particular way through dance; children know that and understanding that as an adult can only really happen through taking part and dancing. As the person dances so space opens up and things are seen that would not have been perceived or experienced without the movement. In this way dance is a way of active bodily engagement that leads to heightened awareness and perception. It can be a spiritual practice, the truth of movement and our connection with creation.

The General Dance

The general dance is the title that Thomas Merton gives to his final chapter in *New Seeds of Contemplation*. He writes that God made the world as a garden in which God took delight with the human being as "the gardener of paradise." While Adam gave the animals their names, Merton writes that God gave them no names at all, and that this is the higher light. It is the light beyond the apparent light of intelligence and concepts, "but the dark light in which no names are given, in which God confronts us not through the medium of things, but in his own simplicity." In this simplicity—the simple light of God with the simple light of the spirit—there is a taking away of the names and forms and content, and what Merton calls a "disappearance of identities." This, for Merton, is contemplation and in this moment of silence and stillness is the child mind. In this realization, in this real inner self "we have been made one with him." Here is the mystery of the incarnation. Merton adds that the false alienated exterior self can be removed, like a mask or a disguise, and so in contemplation reveal not only our inner self but God "wandering as a pilgrim and exile in his own creation." Merton urges a letting go of the serious, which is often not relevant, and a joining in God with play: "the Lord plays and diverts himself in the garden of his creation" and Merton adds, "if we could let go of our own obsession with what we think is the meaning of it all, we might be able to hear his call and follow him in his mysterious cosmic dance."[9]

There is no need to travel far to take part in the general dance. In one letter about prayer Merton suggests just spending time in silence watching

9. Merton, *New Seeds of Contemplation*, 188–91.

nature. He asks his correspondent whether they have a garden or some-where just to walk on their own. "Take half an hour, or fifteen minutes a day and just walk up and down among the flowerbeds with the intention of offering this walk up as a meditation and a prayer to Our Lord."[10] Alterna-tively being alone under the stars, watching a flock of birds—these are all times of "awakening, the turning inside out of all values, the 'newness,' the emptiness and the purity of vision that make themselves evident, provide a glimpse of the cosmic dance." For Merton, "the world and time are the dance of the Lord in emptiness. The silence of the spheres is the music of the wedding feast." He thought that no matter how we misunderstand or try to rationalize and analyze away or dismiss it this reality remains "the cosmic dance that is always there." As Merton writes, "Indeed, we are in the midst of it, and it is in the midst of us, for it beats in our very blood, whether we want it to or not." It is an open invitation for everyone no matter what their age to join in.[11]

The contemporary writer, Joyce Rupp, also sees the invitation of the cosmic dance as the invitation to experience our connection with the living world. She writes of leaning back in memory and catching a hint of what she knew as a small child, "the melody of the cosmic dance playing in my soul since those early days, a song that has never stopped singing in me." She writes of three revelations that have changed her life for ever:

> The first of these is the amazing revelation that I am made up of stardust, that every part and parcel of who I am materially was once a piece of a star shining in the heavens. The second discov-ery is that the air I breathe is the air that has circled the globe and been drawn in and out by people, creatures and vegetation in lands and seas far away. But the most astounding discovery that both awakened and affirmed my early childhood awareness is the fact that I am part of a vast and marvellous dance that goes on unceasingly at every moment in the most minute particles of the universe. . . . I see that I am not a separate entity, and never could be, because the tiny particles of my body are dancing, in-termingling with the particles of life around me.[12]

In her realization Rupp echoes findings from ancient Vedic mythol-ogy and modern physics. These are the same findings that Fritjof Capra ob-serves at the start of his book *The Tao of Physics*, which he calls the cosmic dance of energy. He writes of vibrating atoms and molecules, and a vision of

---

10. Merton, *Road to Joy*, 195.

11. Merton, *New Seeds of Contemplation*, 192.

12. Rupp, *Cosmic Dance*, line 3, 6–16.

"cascades of energy coming down from outer space, in which particles were created and destroyed in rhythmic pulses." His body too was participating, "I felt its rhythm and I 'heard' its sound, and at that moment I knew that this was the Dance of Shiva, the Lord of Dancers worshipped by the Hindus."[13]

Nature Mysticism Experienced in Childhood—Seeing the Far Distances

Connection with the dance of creation takes place through nature mysticism. One of the visions experienced by a Native American Indian when he was about four or five is described in this way. He had previously heard voices whilst out playing, but on this occasion when preparing to shoot at a bird with a bow made by his grandfather he heard the bird speak,

> "The clouds all over are one-sided. . . . Listen! A voice is calling you!" Then I looked up at the clouds, and two men were coming there, headfirst like arrows slanting down; as they came they sang a sacred song and the thunder was drumming. . . . "Behold a sacred voice is calling you; all over the sky a sacred voice is calling." . . . But when they were very close to me, they wheeled about toward where the sun goes down, and suddenly they were gone.

Cultures such as that of the Native Americans include rituals and preparation for entering into visions which are seen as the center of religious life and ways in which the people are helped "to realize our oneness with all things."[14] These are the sorts of cultures that work with such experiences while other cultures, like that in the West, destroy them, whether consciously or unconsciously. Yet the experiences continue for all in one form or another. It has been said that children are born as nature mystics in that they approach the divine, and are approached and enveloped by the divine reality, through the natural world. Before experiences are interpreted or categorized nature is often the root of wisdom, value, and enthusiasm.[15]

Here is another experience from our own western culture. What is interesting is the way in which in this account, and indeed it occurs in other similar accounts, the young participants seem to adopt a somewhat defensive manner when recounting what happened to them when they were smaller. In this example, the little girl refers to it in later telling as

---

13. Capra, *Tao of Physics*, 11.
14. Soelle, *Silent Cry*, 10.
15. Teasdale, *Mystic Heart*.

"the thing," and as is noted, her language is toned down and a bit awkward. Unlike in the Native American culture there is no framework for speaking about such happenings:

> Suddenly the thing happened, and, as everybody knows, it cannot be described in words. The Bible phrase, I saw the heavens open, seems as good as any if not taken literally. I remember saying to myself in awe and rapture. . . . So it is like this; now I know what heaven is like, now I know what they mean in Church. . . . Soon it faded and I was alone in the meadow with the baby and the brook and the sweet-smelling lime trees. But though it passed and only the earthly beauty remained. I was filled with great gladness. I had seen the far distances.[16]

Specific research has also shown that especially for small children the first impact of the beauty of nature can be quite overwhelming. One participant in studies of religious experience writes about the profound effect between the ages of four and five years old of a walk over a stretch of land in Pangbourne, Berkshire in England. The child, now an adult, remembers seeing the mist and the flowers as shimmering and almost alive. The mist seemed like gossamer and the harebells as if on fire. Even as a small child she knew that this was life, a living tissue, appearing like a shining bundle of energy. The effect was to leave her feeling an intrinsic part of something universal, something "which was fragile yet immensely strong, and utterly good and beneficent." And in this whole she had her own space.

The writer goes on to say that the vison stayed with her all her life giving her a reservoir of strength which almost seemed to be fed from an unseen source, but which quite suddenly even in the midst of the very darkest times broke through as a bubble of pure joy. Clearly the experience was not expressed in such adult language but the power was such that "by whatever mysterious perception, the whole impression and its total meaning were apprehended in a single instant." Years later, after reading Thomas Traherne, Meister Eckhart, and St. Francis of Assisi, she recognized what had happened and that she was not alone. Another writes of being around five years old and seeing that the dew on the grass was sparkling as jewels and there was a powerful feeling of protection from the trees:

> In the heart of the child that I was there suddenly seemed to well up a deep and overwhelming sense of gratitude, a sense of unending peace and security which seemed to be part of the beauty of the morning, the love and protective and living

16. Soelle, *Silent Cry*, 12.

presence which included all that I had ever loved and yet there was something much more.

A third gives an account as a child of waiting for a firework display to begin.

> A breeze stirred the leaves of a group of poplars just to my right; stirred, they gave a fluttering sound. There, then, I knew or felt or experienced—what? Incommunicable now, but then much more so. The sensations were of awe or wonder, and a sense of astounding beauty—at that moment in dusk.

What is noted as significant about such experiences of nature mysticism is that it helped each person who described them to become the person that he or she had it in them to become. It also presaged a sense of something more than them which was a sense of the numinous. The assurance that arose from the experiences was of a religious kind with one of the participants saying that the recollection acted as a kind of tap-root to springs of life. It brought with it an assurance, a guarantee that remained constant. For some the assurance could be called on many years later. For one the memory of the epiphany became a great comfort following bereavement. One participant in the studies described how the early childhood experience did not lead to an ongoing belief in God following that experience and on into adulthood. Rather he describes himself as "one who believes again, after a long intermission. It is probably that, but for that event in childhood, there would have been no 'again.'"

For others there is a sense of great loss. Writing about an experience at the age of three one person writes of her joy and wonder at a group of dandelions:

> I was overcome by an extraordinary feeling of wonder and joy. It was as if I was part of the flowers, and stones, and dusty earth. . . . I knew something profound and eternal then. Now I am deeply conscious that my human failings have taken me far from my childhood understanding of a greater reality.[17]

Recapturing the Original Vision

While for some such visions in childhood remain accessible in some form, for others the experience, whilst never discarded, is lost to conscious thought. It has been suggested that in the second half of life similar

17. Robinson, *Original Vision*, 32–33 and 49.

perspectives of a sense of openness may open up: "I have reached the place at sixty-nine, where I know that it would be as easy to hold the sun in a teacup as fully to know and understand the all-powerful being we call God" and from another person in their fifties: "I think that I am only now coming to know what it means to be a human being."[18]

It is often poets who can access the nature mysticism of childhood spirituality where the natural revelation of the divine surrounds us and is experientially known without intellectual rationalization or conceptual thought. For such poets the child is still somewhere active within their psyche. One poet writes how if poets are to go on writing they need to keep something of the child alive in them. This is because for many the world as it becomes increasingly familiar also becomes "staler" and one sees it "fade into the common light of day." But the poet believes "I think I can recover the delight and wonder."[19]

This poem by Shelley (1792–1822) conveys the oneness and connection of nature mysticism, suggesting that for Shelley the childhood spirituality of nature mysticism remained a conscious experience from which to draw:

> I am the daughter of earth and water,
>   And the nursling of the sky;
>
> I pass through the pores of the ocean and shores;
>   I change, but I cannot die.
>
> For after the rain, when with never a stain
>   The pavilion of heaven is bare,
>
> And the winds and sunbeams with their convex gleams,
>   Build up the blue dome of air,
>
> I silently laugh at my own cenotaph,
>   And out of the caverns of rain,
>
> Like a child from the womb, like a ghost from the tomb
>   I arise and unbuild it again.[20]

Another poet who captures nature mysticism and the original vision was Thomas Traherne (1636–1674). Donald Allchin encouraged Thomas Merton to reread Traherne, whom Merton had previously discovered at Columbia University. In his reflections on the English mystics, Merton

18. Ibid., 45.
19. Ibid.
20. Shelley, "The Cloud," in *Poems of Shelley*, 190.

understands that Traherne was enlightened by an innocence and joy, seeing the world with simplicity and wisdom. Merton writes that Traherne is "not altogether a child" as he also speaks in theological symbols, with a love of the positive and of creation. Merton quotes directly Traherne's *Centuries of Meditations*:

> We infinitely wrong ourselves by Laziness and Confinement. All Creatures in all Nations and Tongues and Peoples Praise God infinitely; and the more for being your Sole and Perfect Treasures. You are never what you ought till you go out of yourself and walk among them.[21]

Traherne, like many poets, including Merton, sees God illuminated in nature, where God's infinity is revealed in infancy as in Eden,

> Those things which first his Eden did adorn
> > My infancy
> Did crown. Simplicity
> Was my protection when I first was born.
> > Mine eyes those treasures first did see
> Which God first made . . .[22]

In this way Traherne anticipates Blake, Wordsworth, C. S. Lewis, and the Romantic (and possibly rather English) idea that children's souls are closer to God than those of adults, and that imagination can bring us back to that secret garden we lost. For Traherne walking and meditating in nature can help us to move towards the child mind. In one of his sequences of meditations Traherne reflects on his experiences as a child with the glimpses of glory and innocence found in the original vision and his search after these glimpses are spoiled for what he calls felicity. He writes how the Savior's command to become as a small child is "deeper far than is generally believed." It is not only to do with dependence on divine providence or cultivating simplicity but in peace and purity through the freeing of the soul from worldly concerns and achievements.

> The first light which shined in my infancy in its primitive and innocent clarity was totally eclipsed, insomuch that I was fain to learn all again. If you ask me how it was eclipsed, truly by the customs and manners of men, which like contrary winds blew it out; by an innumerable company of other objects, rude, vulgar and worthless things that like so many loads of earth and dung did overwhelm and bury it. . . . And at last all the celestial, great

---

21. Merton, *Mystics and Zen Masters*, 133–34.
22. Traherne, *Selected Writings*, 23.

and stable treasures to which I was born, as wholly forgotten, as if they had never been.[23]

The turning point in Traherne's life was when he turned to the countryside; "I came into the country, and being seated among silent trees, had all my time in my own hands, I resolved to spend it all, whatever it cost me in search of happiness." From his meditations and in his poetry, Traherne is concerned to show how life is gift just as the creation is gift and that we are part of that gift and can live within it as part of it. He writes: "You never enjoy the world aright until the sea itself floweth in your veins, till you are clothed with the heavens and crowned with the stars." He recalls his childhood experiences in his poem "Wonder":

> How like an Angel came I down!
> How bright are all things here!
> When first among his works I did appear
> O how their glory did me crown!
> The world resembled his eternity,
> In which my soul did walk;
> And everything that I did see
> Did with me talk.

It is to this state of mind that Traherne seeks in his poem "The Return," and here is the understanding not of regression but rather towards to an integration and beyond to transcendence.

> To Infancy, O Lord, again I come.
> That I my Manhood may improve;
> My early tutor is the womb;
> I still my cradle love;
> 'Tis strange that I should wisest be,
> When least I could an error see.[24]

What attracts Traherne, and that he is earnest to convey, is the "different way of seeing everything . . . that everything communicates with, and in a real sense is part of, everything else. The result is a life of joy."[25] This is what Merton was trying to convey when he urges us to let go of our self-consciousness and seriousness and, as quoted above but worth quoting again, writes, "join in the general dance."[26]

23. Ibid., 86–87.

24. Ibid., 92, 75, 20–22, 47.

25. Matthews, *Awake to God,* 78–82.

26. Merton, *New Seeds of Contemplation,* 192.

Deepening the Connection with All Living Things

It is possible to see from his journals how Thomas Merton understood the need for silence and solitude and that this led to experiencing the supernatural within the natural. It was a way to return to a sense of childhood spirituality and a way beyond into the child mind.

> To gaze lucidly and attentively upon nature's signs to him—like those offered by "the speech that rain makes"—was a means for Merton to transcend his conflicted inner life by embedding himself in a larger world of "creeping and crawling things" that functioned like a chorus, beckoning him to appreciate his natural life. . . . Merton knew himself to be essentially uncomplicated as he gazed upon the natural world . . .[27]

Merton's early love of nature was noted by his mother in the book she kept of virtually everything he said or did in the first two years of his life. Ruth Merton notes that Tom seems conscious of everything, he wants to stand in his pram to look at the river; and, "Sometimes he throws himself on the ground to see the 'cunnin' little ants.'"[28]

Years later he could write this prayer of praise on behalf of all of nature, connected as children of God by the one creator:

> Today, Father, this blue sky lauds you. The delicate green and orange flowers of the tulip poplar tree praise you. The distant blue hills praise you, together with the sweet-smelling air that is full of brilliant light. The bickering flycatchers praise you with the lowing cattle and the quails that whistle over there. I too, Father, praise you, with all these my brothers, and they give voice to my own heart and to my own silence. We are all one silence, and a diversity of voices.[29]

Merton's nature writings are full of detail and delight and his long periods of silent meditation in the grounds of the monastery deepened his sense that he was not merely observing but rather accepting himself as part of the landscape and part of God's creation, and where the inner and outer landscapes seemed as one. His journal *Dancing in the Water of Life* was written as Merton began his full-time commitment to the solitary life as a hermit. Merton uses psychoanalytic language to describe what he is experiencing:

---

27. Weis, *Thomas Merton's Gethsemani*, 10.
28. Ibid., 28 and Shannon, "Tom's Book," 489.
29. Merton, *Conjectures*, 177.

All this is the geographical unconscious of my hermitage. Out in front the "conscious mind," the ordered fields, the wide valley, tame woods. Behind, the "unconscious"—this lush tangle of life and death, full of danger, yet where beautiful beings move, the deer, and where there is a spring of sweet pure water—buried!

Merton writes "the smallest and most ordinary things are made holy and great,"[30] and it is this insight that connects to Merton's writing on "le point vierge" (literally the virgin point and explored later). As Merton interacted more fully with nature so he allowed the very atmosphere around him such as the birds, trees, and creatures to permeate his inner being: "He allowed his prayer to blossom into an earth-based spirituality."[31] At times it could perhaps be said that there are hints of a return to those "cunnin' little ants"—anthropomorphism as found in small children. This is something that most children are exposed to through children's literature and films. The younger the child the stronger the anthropomorphism tends to be and the more it makes sense—for example, bears going to school, cats having birthday parties, dogs dressing up, horses sadly subject to human cruelty and so on. By seeing animals talking and feeling and living like small children a deep connection is engendered. Educationalists, scientists, and most academics almost uniformly criticize this tendency believing that it promotes fantasy and inhibits children learning the correct facts about other creatures. However one might suppose that the Native American whose experiences are described at the start of this chapter would see it as perfectly realistic within a religious frame. Indeed children themselves have no problems with it either.

This may partly connect to the observation as a small child that the animals and insects are not so different; identification develops and through that connection occurs. Writing about her childhood in Charleston, Sussex, Angelica Garnett writes:

> In front of the house there was a patch of gravel. . . . Numerous tiny creatures threaded their way among the boulders: spiders, beetles, ants, busy, intent and unaware of me, a female Gulliver in their midst. Giant though I was, I was perhaps less aware than they of our difference in scale. I was each ant, each beetle; I knew what it was to have six legs and swivel eyes, to hesitate, searching for information with trembling antennae, suspicious and fearful.[32]

30. Merton, *Dancing in the Water*, 224, 226.

31. Weis, *Thomas Merton's Gethsemani*, 131.

32. Garnett, *Deceived with Kindness*, 44.

However the suggestion in the context of this book is that rather than attributing human characteristics, emotions, and ways of behaving to living things, Merton is instead glimpsing with the child mind how all living things—animals, plants, water, and the land itself all reflect God's glory and sanctity: "Heaven is even now mirrored in created things."[33] This means that each is true to themselves. "The more a tree is like itself, the more it is like God." Merton explains: "The forms and individual characters of living and growing things, of inanimate beings, of animals and flowers and all nature, constitute their holiness in the sight of God." For all things, including human beings, "Their inscape is their sanctity. It is the imprint of God's wisdom and reality in them."[34]

In a wonderful hymn of confession to and communion with God and all of creation, Merton, as night watchman for the monastery, senses, as he looks out at the night and the stars, "animal eloquence, with the savage innocence of a million unknown creatures" where "the animals are the children of God." Here is a "huge chorus of living beings" that rises up, "life singing in the watercourses, throbbing in the creeks and the fields and the trees, choirs of millions and millions of jumping and flying and creeping things." In the midst of the might and power of divine creation he feels God's mercy and tenderness—God as parent to all of life, "There is no leaf that is not in Your care."[35] Here in the silent night time is the child mind where both the spirituality of the small child and the adult mind that has dimmed the original vision are included, and, then, transcended by the child mind which takes him beyond into the divine inscape.

Thomas Merton's insights into deep connection with nature led to some robust exchanges in his correspondence with Czeslaw Milosz, the poet and writer, who raised the issue of sentimentality towards nature. Merton strongly defended his stance and responded that "nature and I are very good friends, and console one another for the stupidity and infamy of the human race and its civilisation."[36] For Merton's relationship with nature came, as we have explored, not from sentimentality but instead from a sense of deep connection and oneness with all living things, and so, given Merton's strong sense of solidarity with all of nature, it was inevitable also that he would respond strongly to the early signs of the destruction of the environment. He understood our attitude to nature as in part a projection of our attitude to ourselves; and the destruction of habitats and wildlife linked to mate-

33. Merton, *No Man is an Island*, 101.
34. Merton, *New Seeds of Contemplation*, 30.
35. Merton, *Sign of Jonas*, 342, 352–53.
36. Merton, *Courage for Truth*, 65.

rialism and the "dominating attitude of scientistic and technical control." Wisdom was being replaced by technology. He saw it as "all part of the same sickness" that led to "the great spiritual problem of the profound disturbances of ecology all over the world, the tragic waste and spoilage of natural resources etc."[37] In correspondence with Rachel Carson, the conservationist and author of *Silent Spring* first published in 1962, Merton picked up on the irresponsibility with which "we scorn the smallest values" as linked to the way that "titanic power" is used to "threaten not only civilisation but life itself."[38] Linked to Merton's stance against nuclear weapons he understood that despite apparent affluence there was a hatred for life itself and a profound alienation from creation and the connectedness with all of life. He acknowledged his own propensity when he linked dumping chemicals on anthills to try to get the insects to move elsewhere. Merton describes how one day there is the lovely sound of small songbirds and then finding one of them lying dead on the grass the next day. Reflecting on what might have happened Merton castigates himself: "What a miserable bunch of foolish idiots we are! We kill everything around us even when we think we love and respect nature and life." The capacity to end life so carelessly and almost as if in ignorance means, as he notes, the huge numbers of species that have become extinct within living memory. Just by the way that we live there is damage caused to the ecological balance.[39]

Merton took up with interest the concept of ecological conscience which he saw as based on harmony with and an understanding of the reverence of all creation. He identified what he saw as the crucial issue facing humankind: "that the savagery that the Puritans projected 'out there' onto the wilderness is in reality savagery within the human heart." Merton "challenges us to come to terms with the deep conflict imposed by our patriarchal and oppressive culture, that is, the tension between the wilderness mystique and the mystique of exploitation and power in the name of freedom and creativity."[40]

37. Merton, *Turning Towards the World*, 274 and 330.
38. Merton, *Witness to Freedom*, 70.
39. Merton, *Turning Towards the World*, 312.
40. Weis, *Environmental Vision*, 147–48.

12

Poetry

The Language of the Child Mind

Poets and poetry have been drawn on already throughout this book for certain poets seem able to articulate so well aspects of the child mind. This chapter explores why this might be and focuses on the characteristics of the language of poetry. For as a form of expression poetry usually communicates authenticity. Poets speak and write of a way of looking at the everyday with a sensitivity that can take the hearer and reader beyond that everyday into another level of consciousness. Perhaps there are ways that some poetry can tap directly into the unconscious of the reader or hearer and reach spiritual depths previously hidden. Some poetry can offer a way of feeling or understanding something with few words. There can be a transparency, "clear air and dazzling light" where the poet is:

> capable of penetrating to a secret world and of receiving the dictation of a transcendental inner voice. . . . What is it then, the secret world to which the poet penetrates, the world discovered by the poet-seer?—Paradise![1]

It is suggested that sometimes the very words of a poem can reflect language that could be associated with the child mind, the spirit of the child. These are when words are pared, refined, and chosen in simplicity by the poet—the paradise-hearer—to express an essential state. Some poetry can cut through the shadow and the disguise of the reader by reaching to the heart or the essence of the subject. The poet has a single aim to express the feeling, the expectation or the observation. The poem *is* the feeling, the expectation or the observation—all else falls away in this single focus.

1. Gascoyne, *Holderlin's Madness*, 10–11.

Some Words from the Spirit of the Child

Visions of the golden world, of paradise, are, like any experience of the numinous almost, impossible to describe. Poetry often comes closest to the
experience of verbalizing what could be called paradise intuition or consciousness and so capturing the spirit of the child. This was an intuition
that Merton thought united the poet and the contemplative. "All really valid
poetry (poetry that is fully alive and asserts its reality by its power to generate imaginative life) is a kind of recovery of paradise. . . . Here the world
gets another chance." Merton writes about the poet as a paradise hearer.[2] He
sees the poet as attempting through their creative work to recover contact
with their inner world; it is a recapturing of an inner and deeper truth. This
is then a reaction to the alienation and to the distortion brought about by
the age of science and technology that has led to a sense of bewilderment
and disorientation. The poet, as does the contemplative, seeks more, and
both aim to go beyond the limited world of objects; poetry can stimulate
contemplation, and contemplation can inspire poetry; for "the true poet is
always akin to the mystic."[3]

Poetry is about transcending the limits of conventional discourse.
Merton demonstrates this in some of his own poetry, and in some of his
translations of, and reflections on, the works of other poets. One example of
this is found in his essay, first published in 1967, on the poet Louis Zukofsky,
where Merton notes how Zukofsky, in his simple use of childlike phrases
and with childlike feeling, writes sparingly almost as if using the language of
childhood in the sense that the language of the everyday becomes charged
with expectations and simplicity.

For Merton this language is then the language of paradise. The poems
are the essence of a conversation with a child, but not baby talk and certainly
not cliché. "To talk to a child is to participate in the study of language, to
say words for the first time, thus recognizing their immensity. Baby talk is
for adults only." Merton appreciates that Zukofsky's poetry springs from a
ground of immense silence and love; this can be heard with a paradise ear.
The words are framed as part of the whole creation, where, as with the child
mind, "every small thing becomes necessary, for when All is gratuitous every small thing is seen to be wanted, to be important, to have its own unique
part in the big gift of all things to each other."[4]

2. Merton, "Louis Zukofsky," 128.

3. Merton, "Poetry and Contemplation," 339–40, 345.

4. Merton, "Louis Zukofsky," 128–29, 131.

The poet has the patience and good sense to listen. This is contemplative awareness. The nineteenth-century American poet and philosopher Henry David Thoreau, in his poem "Inspiration" describes well the peculiarity of the senses of the paradise ear and eyes of the poet with his lines:

> I hearing get who had but ears,
> And sight who had but eyes before,
> . . .
> I hear beyond the range of sound,
> I see beyond the range of sight.[5]

Merton notes that similarly the speech of the child is paradise speech for it familiarly addresses all things, not yet knowing them as alien and anticipating nothing from them but joy: hence it is, for him, also Franciscan. This is the relational consciousness discussed earlier as found in childhood spirituality. The small child addresses creation without judgement or hierarchy—until told otherwise.

In Thomas Merton's own poem "Grace's House,"[6] he writes about a drawing of a house on a hill that had been sent to him by a four-year-old girl called Grace. Merton uses the picture of a largely pre-verbal and unselfconscious world to locate his contemplative understanding and spiritual experience of the inner life and the spirit of the child. For Merton the drawing can be seen as a reminder of perhaps a long forgotten sense of paradise—an Edenic landscape epitomized in terms of plant and animal life where the grass is alive, the animals aware, and each blade of grass matters. The poem offers an adult commentary on the painting, but with layers of meaning reaching back to a state of child mind simplicity. It has been suggested that this is one of the best of Merton's poems of sacramental awareness. Grace's drawing suggests a holistic vision grasped intuitively in a way that adults lose and forget because it is inaccessible to the analytic mind . . . the adult mind of verbal conceptual thought. The poem tells of experience that, "can be known only from within, through love and wisdom, relational and participatory knowledge,"[7] all aspects found in the spirituality of children.

It was St. Thérèse of Lisieux who said, "to write is nothing—nothing at all. . . . One must be in it to know."[8] Grace draws what she knows, she is in it. Merton writes poetically about the drawing from a place of contemplative awareness and experience. The poem is about recognition of an inward

---

5. Thoreau, "Inspiration."

6. Merton, "Grace's House," in *Collected Poems,* 330.

7. O'Connell, *Cross Currents Public.*

8. Thérèse of Lisieux, *Story of a Soul,* 18.

journeying home, "somewhere I had been as a child . . . a reunion." For Merton the inner self remains a child—a dweller in paradise but we lose our path to this inner self. In one line, he writes:

Alas, there is no road to Grace's house!

In this poem, Merton offers each reader a reminder and recognition of this universal state of the spirit of the child, a state of paradise consciousness and grace, the Eden where Adam too was an infant. This consciousness, as happened with Adam, is lost to us inevitably by precocity, or as the early Fathers described it through an act of immodest maturity or growing up too quickly. The Christ child reveals not simply the childhood we have lost, but a new childhood in and through him. It is a state of connectedness and a movement towards ultimate unity.

Merton's poem is about the relational consciousness found in childhood spirituality, where relational refers to the importance of God, other people and creatures together with the self. It is the quality of such suggest change line break to inter-dependent interactions from a spiritual perspective that Merton focuses on in the poem.

O paradise, O child's world!
Where all the grass lives
And all the animals are aware!

It has been noted earlier that very young children appear naturally to have relational and conscious intuitions at a very young age; they seem to be aware of, and have an implicit understanding of, their relationship to their environment long before they can name it, and as has been noted they have experiences that "transcended the human, pointing to something beyond." One parent writes of her very young son calling excitedly to her. "When I hurried over he pointed triumphantly out of the window and ecstatically cried out 'Grass!'"[9]

As noted earlier the consciousness part of relational consciousness emphasizes awareness, mystery, and value-sensing. Awareness-sensing is being in the here-and-now, a state of mind which is characteristically vivid.

The huge sun, bigger than the house
Stands and streams with life in the east
While in the west, a thunder cloud
Moves away forever.

---

9. Hay and Nye, *Spirit of the Child*, 61.

What really stands out is the intensity and immediacy of awareness. Things just are and seem to be outside of time. There is no past or future— just the present moment and what is there in that moment. This is pure consciousness—we might call this mindfulness. However once the experience is fitted into the language and the culture it already becomes diluted.

Another quality that emerges in such poems is value-sensing. Children readily express emotion and the value of what is happening in their everyday experience. There is often an animistic tendency to attribute or project their own emotion and thoughts onto animals and things. In one of Zukofsky's poems, Merton describes how the poet writes of the red fox crying from the pain of porcupine quills in his paw who in turns brings tears to the watching child. And in Merton's poem there is a similar acknowledgment of the feeling state of the dog in the picture:

> Important: hidden in the foreground
> Most carefully drawn
> The dog smiles, his foreleg curled, his eye like an aster.
> Nose and collar are made with great attention:
> This dog is loved by Grace.

In Merton's understanding of the poet as mystic, he sees there is in both an innocence: "in the sense that they see God everywhere in His creation and in His mysteries, and behold the created world as filled with signs and symbols of God."[10] Merton writes that the poet's art depends on "an ingrained innocence" which would be lost in "business, in politics, or in too organized a form of academic life." The poet points "beyond all objects into the silence where nothing can be said. . . . We [poets] are the children of the Unknown." Merton sets the poets with their immediacy and innocence outside the confines of the established political system,

> As for the technological Platos who think they now run the world we live in, they imagine they can tempt us with banalities and abstractions. But we can elude them merely by stepping into the Heraklitean* river which is never crossed twice. When the poet puts his foot in that ever-moving river, poetry itself is born out of the flashing water. In that unique instant, the truth is manifest to all who are able to receive it. . . . No one can enter the river wearing the garments of public and collective ideas. He must feel the water on his skin . . . immediacy is for naked minds only and for the innocent.[11] (*Heraklitus Greek poet and philosopher (*c.* 540–480 BCE) asserted there was no perma-

10. Merton, "Poetry and Contemplation," 345.

11. Merton, "Message to Poets," in *Literary Essays,* 371–74.

nent reality except the reality of change; permanence is but an illusion of the senses.)

In his later thinking on the theory of poetry Merton wrote about the immediacy of everyday life where, for the poet, the everyday can be seen as sacramental. It is the poet who may intuit the inner spiritual dimension of ordinary events and objects, "to recapture the freshness and truth of their own subjectivity."[12]

One of the poets whom Merton translated was Raissa Maritain. Maritain was a writer whose poetry arose from her deeply contemplative lifestyle. She rejected the idea that poetry arose from the imagination but thought rather that it emerged from depth and purity born from silence. In the preface to Raissa Maritain's "Journal" her husband Jacques, the Thomist theologian, wrote about the place where "all sources join within the soul, and where the creative experience of the poet is only the pure mirror of his spiritual experience."

Similarly Rowan Williams notes how poetry and contemplation both identify, sketch, or point "to what it might be for God to find words in the world." Both "alike challenge other kinds of words for God" including old, safe, lazy, and useful words.[13]

In her essay "Poetry as Spiritual Experience" Raissa Maritain wrote about the passive absorption required in the poet, similar it seems to the absorption of the small child in something. It is not for her about the activity of working at the imagination but rather about contact "with reality in itself ineffable . . . God. Poetry. An absolutely straight and pure inner activity goes to the one and to the other—goes, sometimes, *from* the one *to* the other."[14] She saw poetry as a musical language that can awaken spiritual activity, and her style was to pare down her language to the purely reflective. She saw the beauty of the natural world as a dim foretaste of another reality which is the supernatural. Her poetry also highlights the joy and pain she found in contemplative prayer, where a certain obscurity allied with intimations of knowledge forged in spiritual experience is expressed. This sort of poetry where there is a genuine light that shines through she called Poetry with a capital letter. Here, Poetry is a divine gift that reveals the essence, the one and the highest.

Poets and other artists, great creators and saints are all she wrote, "imitators of God" but the results of their contemplation and reverence lead to different outcomes. For all there is a deep connection with all creation,

12. Merton, "Poetry and Contemplation" in *Literary Essays*, 25.

13. Williams, "New Words," 50.

14. Maritain, *Raissa's Journal,* 5, 374–75.

where, as Raissa Maritain observes there is a "voice that envelops and speaks the whole planet. . . . And calls animals by their name."[15] One biographer writes that Raissa Maritain in her writing and in her prayer "learned to intercede for all her kind . . . joining in the great collective sigh of creation"[16] where through awareness and true looking it could be seen that the creator's concern for the cosmos is also the poet's concern with words and images.

In the same way that the small child is totally involved with what it is they are looking at, so for the poet such deep absorption seems to almost lead them to become the poem. One reader writing about a friend's poetry found that "strangely the poetry was itself you . . . vital with tenderness and speed and power." He thought her poetry was her ever-living child that would live on long after her death: "eternally young."[17]

Poetry on Innocence and Experience

The subject of the innocence of childhood was especially written about by the Romantic poets and also later in the Victorian era. It is worth commenting that this was an innocence often eulogized at a time when the actual treatment of many children was both abusive and exploitative.

One example from this period would be Alice Meynell (1847–1922) and her "Poems and Essays on Children" exemplify the genre. Perhaps these essays on childhood might now be seen as sentimental, with some even verging upon a "children do the cutest things" genre, but nonetheless they still highlight aspects and insights that can also be seen as relevant for thinking about the spirit of the child within the adult. In one contribution, Alice Meynell writes about the child's look of intelligence which is "outward . . . without inner restlessness . . . [with] few second thoughts to divide the image of his momentary feelings." She likens the child who is "the last and lowest of rational creatures" with an animal in terms of their shared "singleness. . . . The simplicity, the integrity, the one thing at a time."

In her poetry, Alice Meynell also touches on aspects of the spirit of the child that linger on in the adult, and in one poem equates the poet with a quiet child who is told the secrets of the "leaves and grains, All things shy and wild" the small but basic things in life. In "Sonnet" she writes of "the golden hour" of youth so carelessly left behind. In another poem, "In Early

---

15. Suther, *Raissa Maritain,* 86.

16. Ibid.

17. Stapledon, *Opening of the Eyes,* 7.

Spring," she weighs the innocence in "the young child's eyes" with the experience of age that knows what lies ahead, "I have it all by heart."[18]

An early twentieth-century poet who writes of the point of origin in the child, and who saw childhood as a place of renewal is Charles Péguy. Merton wrote that in his depths he thought that he "had more of Péguy in me . . . than even I have realised."[19] Péguy was a friend of Raissa and Jacques Maritain and he writes in his poetry about his own childhood and the lives of his own children. "All that is young is the loveliest and greatest of all." Péguy felt he recaptured the rejuvenating power of childhood in his adulthood through his own children and believed that the sacrament of baptism, the sacrament of the little ones could when conferred on the adult lead back to infancy and that through such reconnection there could be a wellspring of renewal.

> In the child, in childhood, there is a unique grace,
> A wholeness, a firstness,
> Something total, An origin, a secret, source, a point of origin.[20]

There are similarities here with Merton's use of the phrase "le point vierge" as an untouched essence, as the embryo of the eternal child within each of us (discussed fully in chapter 15). Péguy understood that the initial naturalness can never be entirely recaptured and saw adult wickedness and dissipation as causing the loss of innocence. In his work "The Mystery of the Holy Innocents"[21] the spirit of the child as the place of grace and of God's favor is fully explored. Whilst the style is of its time and there are undoubtedly aspects of sentimentality, his long poem gives a sense of the desire to regain simplicity and openness. He writes of nostalgia for childhood, but alongside there is the longing for a similar spirit in the adult. For Charles Péguy it is holding on to this spirit as an adult which is everything.

> Happy is he who remains like a child
> And who like a child keeps
> His first innocence.

He writes that "it is the children who know" and in contrast it is the "grown-up people who know nothing." For innocence is full, and in contrast, although it is thought to be the opposite, experience is empty. Childhood contains a secret which is that it is the favor of God's grace. Charles

---

18. Meynell, *Poems and Essays*, 87 and 14.

19. Merton, *Courage for Truth*, 74.

20. Péguy quoted in Saward, *Way of the Lamb*, 61.

21. Péguy, "Mystery."

Péguy expresses the longing in the adult to find again that state of childhood but then:

> You realise that you no longer remember it.
> And not only that, but you cannot find it again. It has vanished
> from your memory.
> It is too pure a water and has fled from your muddy memory,
> your stained memory.
> And it wanted to flee, it did not want to remain . . .

In another long poem, "The Portal of the Mystery of Hope" he writes that hope can only be received from God; it reconnects the hopeless person "to the source, to a reawakening in him of the child." In the poem, hope is portrayed as a little child, but a child of greater immediate urgency than her serious older sisters—faith and charity.

Innocence is usually contrasted with the corrupting world of the adult. This insidious process is well recognized (and discussed earlier in the book), as in for example William Wordsworth's great poem "Ode: Intimations of Immortality from Recollections of Early Childhood" quoted earlier. In this poem Wordsworth encapsulates the move from a state of childhood innocence to the dark prison and sleep of the world of experience. In the post-Enlightenment world of experience, fact and reason have sway and so there is a single vision with little tolerance of the creative imagination. For the poet Wordsworth what is lost is a form of knowledge which we then spend the rest of our lives trying to recover. The search to recapture the "glory and the freshness" is fruitless: "The things which I have seen I now can see no more." Early childhood is a place of insight, where the infant is addressed as "thou best philosopher."[22]

William Blake's Organized Innocence and His Influence on Thomas Merton—"A Love that has Never Died"

William Blake's "Songs of Innocence and of Experience" contrast the pastoral carefree world of childhood with the careworn adult world of corruption and repression. In the engravings that accompany his poetry, William Blake uses the image of the bird of paradise to represent innocence and creative freedom. Experience is represented by a dark forest where the adults reveal "marks of weakness, marks of woe" separated from paradise by "the mind-forg'd manacles."[23] In his collection the "Songs of Innocence," Blake draws

22. Wordsworth, "Ode," 71–77.
23. Blake, *Complete Writings*, 216, 263, 480.

attention to the positive aspects of natural human understanding prior to the corruption and distortion of experience, but also sees that innocence can be blind, a state of blissful ignorance and it is here that experience can compensate. What children lose is the freedom to be themselves, at home in the world.

For William Blake the splitting between good innocence and bad experience needs to be surmounted and he saw that from such apparently contrary states of the human soul something infinitely richer could be comprised from a synthesis of the two positions. This is similar to what Carl Jung called the transcendent function. For both Blake and Jung it was the idea that a third position can emerge from often two different places, and in a sense the third position is a combination or mixture of the two but also includes something more than both.

William Blake's poems in "Songs of Innocence" show a simplicity and vulnerability but include some desperation in the joy, because of the knowledge that the joys depicted are exclusive to infancy and so very short-lived. As he is aware of the danger of mawkish sentimentality Blake often includes the shadow of experience so that what seems apparently carefree carries a deeper sense of something different. The poet may be in touch with childhood, but only as an adult:

> In the very act of celebrating childish innocence, the poet corrupts it through his inability to prevent the shadow of his own experience falling over the scene. This drives away the very spontaneity he is seeking to express, as the scientist can never observe how creatures behave when they are not being observed.[24]

Inevitably the projection of the adult experience effects even the words used and what they represent; this is similar to paintings of scenes of the nativity that include intimations of the crucifixion that is to come.

In two long poems, "Vala or the Four Zoas" and "Milton," William Blake did envisage a land, "Beulah," where adults can return to permanent childlike innocence. It is a place without shadow where no negative experiences mar, in other words, a place of delusion or disguise, stuck in what seems like a regressive sentimentality. Thinking about the spirit of the child in the adult is a more complex and nuanced vision—Blake wrote about the fourfold vision that includes imagery, symbols, dreams, and the imagination together with the deep unconscious levels of the mind. What has to be avoided above all else is the one dimensional view of the rational scientist.

24. Sagar, "William Blake," 2.

In other words what Blake understood was that it is not the either/ or of innocence/experience. Rather it is a movement from the despair of the reductive single vision that then releases creativity. This means the possibility of a very different, mature, adult, strong innocence possible only on the far side of experience, William Blake calls this "organiz'd innocence." This he thought only possible when the "mind-forg'd manacles" have been cast aside, when the adult has dispensed with the Newtonian blinkers, and through this cleansed the doors of perception, transformed the warring energies within (the "reptiles of the mind"), and finally reconciled the contraries in selfless love. Perhaps Blake achieved this as one of his biographer's wrote of him: "He was a man without a mask, his aim single, his path straight forwards, and his wants few; so he was free, noble, and happy."[25]

The works of Blake were known by Merton from his childhood, and there are references to his close rereading of Blake over the next forty years. Blake's philosophy affected Merton in many ways, and it may be suggested that Merton's thinking on the child mind has similarities to Blake's idea on organized innocence. In his autobiography Merton writes that his father Owen read Blake's poems on innocence to Merton when he was ten years old and tried to explain to him what was good about Blake. Six years later, after his father's death, Merton began to read Blake for himself. "I think my love for William Blake had something in it of God's grace. It is a love that has never died, and which has entered very deeply into the development of my life." On a walk up a nearby hill at his boarding school in England, Merton, aged sixteen, wrote that he reflected on Blake wondering what sort of person he was, and what did he believe:

> How incapable I was of understanding anything of the ideals of
> a William Blake! How could I possibly realize that his rebellion,
> for all its strange heterodoxies, was fundamentally the rebel-
> lion of the saints. It was the rebellion of the lover of the living
> God . . .[26]

Deepening his interest and love of Blake, Merton wrote his MA thesis on Blake's mystical vision and as he wrote, immersing himself in Blake's work, he included his thoughts on the contemplative way and the Roman Catholic Church as a place of forgiveness and liberty.[27] The great significance of all this is that the year before the thesis on Blake was completed, Merton was converted to Catholicism, and among the few possessions that

---

25. Raine, *William Blake,* 22.

26. Merton, *Seven Storey Mountain,* 107–9.

27. Merton, "Nature and Art."

Merton later took with him to the Abbey of Gethsemani was his copy of Blake. He wrote,

> He has done his work for me: and he did it very thoroughly. I hope that I will see him in heaven.
>
> But, oh, what a thing it was to live in contact with the genius and holiness of William Blake that year, that summer, writing the thesis.[28]

Merton's first novel *My Argument with the Gestapo* written before entering the monastery and only published after his death in 1969, ends with the author ready to start a new work:

> I think suddenly of Blake, filling paper with words, so that the words flew about the room for the angels to read, and after that, what if the paper was lost or destroyed?
>
> That is the only reason for wanting to write, Blake's reason.[29]

In his article on "Poetry and Contemplation" revised in the late 1950s, Merton writes about the union between the aesthetic and the mystical and links this to William Blake. When visiting Shakertown during the last decade of his life Merton finds himself thinking of Blake, a contemporary of the first Shakers, who believed that Christ *had* come so "that the true Christian is the one who lives and behaves as a 'Child of the Resurrection.'" Merton was reminded of Blake by the quality of the wooden furniture that conveyed a human but visionary and clear atmosphere—this is what Merton called paradise consciousness, and an original blessing, and this is surely also a link with the simplicity and lack of self-consciousness encapsulated in the child mind. He returns to this in a preface to a book on Shaker furniture where he writes that he has brought in quite a lot about William Blake. At his first visit Merton comments on "something young about the old buildings," of the creative imagination and later of the humility practiced by the Shakers.[30]

In 1968 Merton reviewed Thomas Altizer's book, *The New Apocalypse: The Radical Christian Vision of William Blake* agreeing that Blake was a prophet and against, "a *narrowing* of vision, a foreclosure of experience and of future expansion, a locking up and securing of the doors of perception."[31]

---

28. Merton, *Seven Storey Mountain*, 229.

29. Merton, *My Argument*, 259.

30. Pearson, *Thomas Merton*, 17.

31. Merton, "Blake," 3, 6.

The same acknowledgment of the weight of experience suppressing the spirit of the child is captured in the twentieth century by T. S. Eliot. Again Merton was introduced to Eliot's writing in childhood while at school. His influence is detected in Merton's early novel and also in one of Merton's own poems "Elias—Variations on a Theme," a meditation on spiritual freedom, which the commentator also links to a similarity with William Blake:

> Where the fields end
> Thou shalt be My friend
> Where the bird is gone
> Thou shalt be My son.[32]

Merton later lectured the novices on the poetry of T. S. Eliot, which includes verses on the state of mind needed to return to innocence following experience and the obscuration of learning and convention.

Merton's Late Antipoetry and the Language of Infancy

It could be said that some of the experimental poetry of the 1960s reflected an unconscious adoption of the child mind with an emphasis on and excitement about playing with recovering a reality behind or beyond the usual manipulation of words. This alternative movement took words outside what was seen as a fraudulent and cruel culture, that was seduced by trivia and non-sense represented by mass culture, mass-media, and advertisements. Instead of "agonizing under imposed and calculated forms of knowledge and freezing rationalism,"[33] or the usual poetics of rhythms, melody, and pictures, Merton suggests in some of his late poetry the spirit of the child— openness, spontaneity, rebellion, and playfulness in thought and action:

> I think poetry must,
> I think it must
> Stay open all night
> In beautiful cellars

In his last two long works "Cables to the Ace" and "The Geography of Lograire," sometimes referred to as antipoetry; Merton sets aside the usual conventions. Experimenting with form and style, much of the work is parodying and contemptuous of modern culture yet includes sadness at contemporary spiritual impoverishment. These works have been described as a

---

32. Merton, "Elias," in *Collected Poems*, 239–45. Commentary in Woodcock, *Thomas Merton, Monk and Poet*, 75.

33. Petisco, "Thomas Merton's Antipoetry," 30.

"discontinuous mosaic . . . the reader is led to make his own connections," but with echoes of "the Blake who wrote the Prophetic Books."[34] The work demands that the reader let go of old ways of thinking and lazy, adult assumptions. Listening to Merton reading from "The Geography of Lograire" with the sound and the rhythm and the cadence of the words it is clear that the language is up for experiencing:

> Should Wales dark Wales slow ways sea coal tar
> Green tar sea stronghold is Wales my grand
> Dark my Wales land father it was green
> With all harps played over and bells
> Should Wales slow Wales dark maps home
> Come go green slow dark maps green late home
> Should long beach death night ever come
> And welcome to dark father-mother land.[35]

The way that Merton writes here brings to mind the term "chora" used by the psychoanalyst and linguist Julia Kristeva. This is used by her to describe the burblings of infancy and the pre-verbal child before the adoption of the symbolic order when language and structure prevail. In her work on the language of poetry she sees poetry and the sounds made by the small child as outside the usual logical constraints, fed only by unmediated experiences.[36] In other words the babbling language of this pre-lingual stage of development is spoken *before* the shadow and the disguise has been established and she saw it as feminine and unconstrained. Here there is no distinction of self from that of the mothering person or even the world around you. Instead everything that is experienced as pleasurable is taken in without any recognition of boundaries. This is the stage when, she believes, we were nearest to the purity of existence or what Jacques Lacan called "the Real." Kristeva writes of some poetry's willingness to similarly play with grammar, metaphor, and sense by taking words outside the structural constraints of their usual meaning. Words become sound before meaning: musical, rhythmic, and undifferentiated—words that represent the spirit of the child. In other words the experience that seems to dull the innocence can be further honed and stripped to regain the melody and playfulness of earlier language.

Perhaps, too, Merton in his late poetry is asking the reader and listener to lay aside the usual ways and conventions of reading and listening

---

34. Woodcock, *Thomas Merton, Monk and Poet*, 174.

35. Merton, "Cables to the Ace, 53" and "Geography of Lograire," in *Collected Poems*, 431 and 459.

36. Kristeva, "Revolution," 93.

to poetry; to renew a sense of wonder at the delights and power of sound and language beyond the conceptual meaning. The essence of the meaning may be conveyed in surprising ways that can lead on to further associations and so there are no limits to what can be felt. It involves a receptiveness and a toleration of what the poet Keats called "negative capability" a state of managing uncertainty without needing to know.[37]

---

37. Keats, "On Negative Capability," 19.

13

The Divine Play of God

Play and Creativity

> The old man finally dies, worn out by loneliness and life-long worries. After death he shuffles tiredly through a house where all the rooms are darkened, cluttered, and dusty, but at the far end of a corridor he sees a glimmer of light around the door frame. He opens this door and there is a garden full of sunlight, space, and birdsong. He breathes in deeply the scent of flowers and sees in front of him a small radiant child who looks up and says, "Hello, have you come to play?"

This contemporary tale (origin unknown) contains the care worn adult whose vision and senses are blunted. As all these are stripped away the light begins to return and the image of God returns as a small child ready to play. Play, creativity, and the imagination are not only aspects of childhood but are characteristics of the spirit of the child that remain still potentially available in the adult. In absorbed play and concentrated creativity self-consciousness can be forgotten and the disguise or the false self is left behind. Play can also be a way to integrate the shadow and all the parts of ourselves that we would rather not think about. After all a good kick at a ball is a great way of getting rid of angry feelings, and painting a creative way of expressing feelings that are barely conscious.

Creativity can be seen also as a way of connecting with God, the creative act can be seen as a way of breaking through to eternity as it is "a movement of self-transcendence, reaching out to what is higher than oneself." In that sense creativity is a form of rebirth, and the act, unlike the works, takes one beyond time, beyond the shadow and the disguise, "it is wholly within, subjective, prior to all objectification."[1]

At his first retreat at the Abbey of Gethsemani Thomas Merton wrote about the abbey as an earthly paradise and he explained it in the context of manual work:

> However hard it is, it is still a form of play. Even the strictest penance is play, too. The liturgy, too . . . To be as little children, we must play like them, do things not because they are physically necessary, but freely, as if arbitrarily, almost: for love. . . . This use of work as play . . . results, indirectly in the Abbey being an earthly paradise.[2]

He understood even before joining the Trappists the importance of Jesus' command and how this could be integrated into adult life.

Playing is for Children and for Adults

> Man only plays when he is in the fullest sense of the word a human being, and *he is only completely a man when he plays*.[3]

In a letter written on the subject of aesthetics the poet, philosopher, and playwright Friedrich Schiller celebrates play as the cure for the alienation and fragmentation caused by the split between reason and nature and freedom and necessity. He is actually writing about playing in adulthood, as it is often assumed that play is the serious and immensely enjoyable business that belongs only in childhood.

Certainly play is about being alive and inventive and it not only transcends culture, it is much older than culture and indeed than humanity—as all mammals do it, especially when young. It is part of our relational consciousness and our connection with other created beings. This has been noted in observations of young animals where all the characteristics of human play have been noted:

> They invite one another to play by a certain ceremoniousness of attitude and gesture. They keep to the rule that you shall not bite, or bite hard, your brother's ear. They pretend to get terribly angry. And—what is most important—in all these things they plainly experience tremendous fun and enjoyment. . . . In play

1. Berdyaev, *Dream and Reality,* 210, 220.
2. Merton, *Run to the Mountain,* 336.
3. Schiller, "Letters," letter xv, 9, lines 1–2.

there is something "at play" which transcends the immediate
needs of life.[4]

Play involves creativity and imagination, and it can complement the
realities or compensate for the deficiencies of everyday existence. Children
who are absorbed by play are not caught up in being compliant, acting or
responding to please someone else. They may be trying to work something
out, but they are also very much in the present moment. Play can be introverted where fantasy situations are explored, or play can be extroverted.
Often both are happening at the same time in the game that begins with the
words "let's pretend." Sadly such childlike intensity of imagination tends to
be lost in adulthood alongside the capacity to wonder and exclaim.

Playing is often seen as something that we grow out of. Yet Plato in
The Laws wrote that, "Man is made as God's plaything and this is the best
part of him. And, therefore, he should be of another mind than what he is at
present and live life accordingly. Life should be lived as play."[5] Adults can
feel disapproval about such an attitude, a disapproval which would seem to
be linked to envy of pleasure and fun, of youth, or of experiences that the
adults did not have. Some adults take the attitude of destructive entitlement,
in other words what happened to them (no matter how negative) has to be
repeated: "I didn't have fun like that so why should others"; some adults may
feel threatened or disturbed by the fantasies involved.

One adult after participating in adult play therapy describes how from
the age of twelve or thirteen she was told it was no longer appropriate to play
in certain ways, instead she was to be serious:

> "You must worry and you must take care and think about se-
> curity" . . . so we grow up absurd . . . it's sinful to play. . . . I was
> an only child and much of my existence was creating my own
> scenes and playing in them. I always had this thing laid on me of
> "Oh, Marion, you don't understand reality. Why don't you grow
> up?" . . . I still get it and both my daughters are in their twenties.[6]

Rowan Williams has written about the profound impatience by adults
for children to move out of what he calls "the child's indeterminate world,"
characterized by "irresponsible talking" and where fantasy can hold sway.
He writes about fiction, and about imaginative writing, where children can
be transported to "a magical or mythological level within the familiar world

---

4. Stevens, *On Jung*, 87.
5. Quoted in Rush, *Getting Clear*, 257.
6. Ibid., 262–63.

now grown strange or to a parallel and normally hidden world."[7] He believes that play, the imagination and creativity—being a child!—are being undermined by the contemporary definition of a child as a consumer and an economic subject. In this disguise the child becomes a pseudo-adult pressurized also into becoming a sexual subject, and so Wordsworth's "shades of the prison house" just take on another form, but with the same closing down of play and the imagination.

Yet nothing is ever completely lost, and in his account of playing as an adult the psychologist Carl Jung describes how he consciously submitted himself to the impulses of the unconscious, and what surfaced was a memory of playing when he was aged ten or eleven with building blocks. He remembered how he had built little houses and castles and then later moved to use ordinary stones with mud for mortar. As he remembered the past he felt a good deal of emotion and realized that, "There is still life in these things. The small boy is still around, and possesses a creative life which I lack. But how can I make my way to it?" He writes that it was a painfully humiliating experience to realize that there was nothing to be done but to play childish games and so he gathered stones from the lake shore and began to build a small village.

> I went on with my building game after the noon meal every day, whenever the weather permitted. As soon as I was through eating, I began playing, and continued to do so until the patients arrived; and if I was finished with my work early enough in the evening, I went back to building.[8]

The playing helped him to clarify his thinking and also released fantasies for further exploration and so he returned to playing, sometimes hewing stones or painting a picture whenever he felt stuck in his life or work.

Similarly Merton embodies in many ways the spirit of the child and later he sometimes mentions in his journals that children have visited with their parents or he has come across some whilst out of the monastery. One example is given in 1967 whilst living at the hermitage. He notes quite a crowd turning up for a picnic organized by his friends the O'Callaghans (it is worth noting the playful trick that Merton then follows with the pretend fly in the library):

> Pleasant, bewildering, all this movement and brightness and multiplicity—fishing, pogo-sticks, softball, a frisbee, other games the names of which I never knew—children filling my

7. Williams, *Lost Icons*, 15 and 18.

8. Jung, *Memories, Dreams, Reflections*, 197–99.

hands with rubber crabs and flies they made at school (I put a large black fly on the open dictionary in the library). Questions. Coming and going. "Now I'm going to sit there next to you. Keep my place for me. Don't let anybody take it while I get my plate. That's my plate there, you watch it, don't let anybody take it . . ." The kids are so beautiful though. Their eyes and their smiles. And very nice kids too.[9]

There is a good example of playful fun in a short letter Thomas Merton wrote to Arthur the young son of one of his correspondents. He sent some stamps and this message:

Since, as you realize, I conduct an immense and sinister traffic in hallucinogenic drugs and Argentinian soccer players and since this traffic has ramifications in five continents and many large and small islands, my secret agents everywhere keep me well provided with STAMPS.

. . . some are still impregnated with opiates, others scrawled with secret information concerning future interplanetary wars . . .[10]

The letter was signed "X127," which was Merton's laundry number in the monastery.

Art is the result of play and this can be seen where Thomas Merton expressed playful creativity in his drawings, and in his journals he writes of trying out new styles "abstract-looking art" which later became what he called "abstract calligraphies" or "strange blobs of ink." There is a sense of playfulness in Merton's approach to this art work: "These abstractions—one might almost call them graffiti rather than calligraphies—are simple signs and ciphers of energy, acts or movements intended to be propitious." They "simply came to life when they did" as "notes of harmony" and "summonses to awareness."[11]

Playing and Transitional Space

As we play as small children we learn about life, and play can also be seen as the route into the world of culture, language, and creativity. This can include religious and spiritual experiences. If we are able to play we can inhabit magical and different places and become different people. In other

---

9. Merton, *Learning to Love*, 246.

10. Merton, *Hidden Ground of Love*, 400.

11. Bochen, "Calligraphies," 39–40.

words play allows us to move out of the constraints of ourselves and our circumstances.

The child psychoanalyst and paediatrician Donald Winnicott wrote about watching babies as they began to hold and to suck and explore. He was intrigued by their attachment to what he termed a transitional object. This might be a piece of blanket or a teddy bear or any object that attracted the infant. From his observations he built up a theory which has relevance for the spiritual life. Donald Winnicott understood that in these very early months of life this transitional object is experienced as neither internal nor external. In other words the baby has no conception of what is part of them or not, but as they develop they see that the piece of blanket or the teddy bear is connected with them, but at the same time not actually part of them. In some way the piece of blanket has a life of its own—he described this transitional object as the first "not-Me possession."[12] The object can be picked up and sucked or thrown away so the baby can do things to it and it can also represent the mothering person and stand in for her if she goes away. In this way the blanket or teddy can be a symbol for the parent and it is the first experience of play. It offers a space where creativity can happen.

Winnicott thought it crucial that those in charge of looking after the baby respected and tolerated this early experience, so that the experience was allowed to become part of the child and so provide the foundation for later imagining. The deprived or damaged infant may then need help later to begin to experience this intermediate space and the creativity that comes from play. This help can come from psychotherapy or from aspects of the spiritual life. Learning to play in this way gives a space for the living transforming experience of being in the world. We all need, no matter what our age, space for play and creativity. Through play, creativity is manifested, and from this cultural experience develops. Children are drawn to make meaning through play and imagination, and some adults are too.

The thinking about how play contributes to spiritual life is linked to the idea that our conception of God belongs in the same space as the transitional object. In other words this is the space between inner and outer reality, between the personal and the material, between the subjective and objective realities, a space to which both contribute. It is in this space that we can emotionally and spiritually play with our experience and thinking about God.

When we play, we are part of and are contained within a larger framework than just ourselves. In play there is potential space. If we are part of something that includes space and the more than ourselves, then there is

---

12. Winnicott, *Playing and Reality*, 2.

the opportunity for something new to arrive and this irruption could be creative and healing. This is why play is such a helpful way of understanding spiritual experiences. If we allow ourselves to let go of some control then we allow the possibility of something that is outside us to affect us. In genuine spiritual experiences there is allowing God to take charge. There can be both relief and energy to this abandonment to God. In the passage that follows God can be substituted for the word "play":

> In play, if we are game enough, we are seized and both find our-selves and lose ourselves in a larger whole which plays through us if we no longer insist of being rulers of it. That which reigns [Play] is neither inside nor underneath what goes on, but is in-deed at its very heart, the guarantor of its place and significance. It is fully present to those who are graced with the ability in any given moment to be open to it. The healing renewal which we experience in play is not gained by any simple human willing or intention.[13]

Play is not just a human invention that we can look at dispassionately or think about conceptually. To deconstruct or overly examine it may prove some theory or other, but destroys the spirit and the experience. The essence of play is all about being in it and being part of it. For example, in the same way that the true being of music is not found in the notes that are laid out on the sheet of paper but rather in the sound, experience, and presentation, so the linguistic use of play such as in expressions such as "the play of light" or "the play of the waves" indicates that:

> The movement which is play has no goal which brings it to an end; rather it renews itself in constant repetition. The movement backwards and forwards is obviously so central for the defini-tion of a game that it is not important who or what performs this movement.[14]

There is a description of a child playing by standing in the water at the beach moving back and forth with the motion of the waves. When her father had asked her what she was doing (note the adult emphasis on doing rather than being) she had stated simply she *was* the water. She was unable to explain it in any other way. The child had experienced total openness and involvement becoming one with the Other. This could be seen as playing

---

13. Friedman, "Therpaeia," 65.

14. Gadamer, *Truth and Method*, 93.

and as a spiritual experience; the child knew that the spiritual, the other world is embedded in play and in the here and now.[15]

Playing Creatively with God

The creation story in Genesis is one of imagination and wonder where the creation itself in every moment can be seen as God's play. The whole of creation is an expression of God's presence in the world. Everything is in a space for becoming and God continues making things new and making new things. In Hindu mythology this creative activity of God is called *lila*, the play of God and the world and all creatures are part of this divine play. Thomas Merton writes about the Wisdom-child of Proverbs as playing in the world and as part of every person. "I . . . suddenly saw that everybody was Proverb . . . And they did not know their real identity as the Child so dear to God who from before the beginning, was playing in His sight all days, playing in the world."[16]

Playing is part of our nature and part of our relationship with a loving God. Play deriving from the earliest games of "peek a boo" and hide and seek evolve in adult spirituality into a childlike playing with the absence and presence of God. It has been suggested that poets and mystics are the best and most articulate players of this game.

> Perhaps their love for and artful use of metaphor is a kind of compressed game of hide and seek in itself, which makes them more comfortable with such play. The poets also make it quite clear that this game is not trivial.[17]

Playing can be seen as a deep metaphor for our relationship with God. The tradition of the Holy Fool found in St. Francis and his followers, discussed earlier, exemplified this creative and lively aspect. Mechthild of Magdeburg, the thirteenth-century spiritual writer and mystic used the image of play as the language to describe the relationship with God.

> I God am your playmate!
> I will lead the child in you in wonderful ways for I have chosen you.
> Then I shall leap into love—from love into knowledge—from knowledge into enjoyment
> —from enjoyment beyond all human sensation.[18]

15. Hart, *Secret Spiritual World.*

16. Merton, *Courage for Truth,* 90.

17. Berryman, "Children" 27.

18. Privett, "I God," 17.

Playing in the relationship with God involves imagination, and our imagination can give a space to play with the idea of becoming the small child who God wants us to become. In this way, "it is the imagination which governs our experience of God."[19] Playing with the image of God inevitably involves some subjective projections, coming from inside us, otherwise God would not feel real to us, and this explains the idea of the punishing destructive God alongside the comforting and loving God. If we can understand how our past can affect our image of God then there is a freeing of this. Perhaps then it is to break through such images to the God who disrupts all our expectations.

Rather than getting stuck with one set image of God, spiritually playing offers us the ongoing space to explore our relationship with God. This is about some creative movement between the inner imagination and the external. In this way our relationship with God is founded on playing creatively with our experiential sense of God aligned with the more objective images from religious traditions. Using theological language this would be the God who is immanent and the transcendent God: "The space in between reveals itself as the space of meeting."[20]

As Thomas Merton showed in the earlier description of work as play, play for adults can become an attitude towards life and involve a total acceptance of where one is at any particular point in time. This is about naturalness, freedom, and the ability to drop the rigid roles that get adopted so early in life. With that playful carefree attitude it is understood that the mask that we wear is in itself a form of playing, where we play at being a parent, playing at being a banker or working in a shop. The art is to understand the disguise for what it is and that beyond the persona or the mask is the imaginative spirit of the child. The breakthrough would be to see that indeed in one sense we are God's plaything created from his imagination, and that the very universe itself is play. In his book *Zen Catholicism* Dom Aelred Graham explores the adult's frequent need to play God and how this could be changed into letting God play. He quotes Ananda Coomaraswamy: "As regards the best in us, we are really God's toys" and sees as part of the Christian revelation that we let God play. A reminder is given:

> We who play the game of life so desperately for temporal stakes might be playing at love with God for higher stakes—our selves, and his. We play against one another for possessions, who might be playing with the King who stakes his throne and what is his

19. Schneiders, *Women and the Word*, 70.
20. Ulanov, *Finding Space*, 36.

against our lives and all we are: a game in which the more is lost,
the more is won.
   To allow God to play is to let go of the self-conscious me.[21]

For Thomas Merton creativity is understood as participation with the creative power and activity of God. This is when creativity is grounded in the divine in contrast to when creativity is used to bolster the accomplishments of the ego or the false self. He thought that true creativity is linked to the dismantling of the false self and the task of becoming one's true self and so participating in the on-going creation of the world. Given this then the small child is already deeply involved with true creativity in all his or her activity.

For adults the task is to return to recognition of their dependence on God as the ground of their being. In his essay on "Theology of Creativity" Merton warns against the clichéd use of the word creative which can lead to a secular caricature, "a futile and demonic attempt to squeeze divine powers out of man."[22] For Merton the creativity that counts is linked to the renunciation of the false self, an emptying into the likeness of Christ, the divine child, so that God's creativity can work through us. For Thomas Merton, as for William Blake, true creativity and imagination is then the action of the divine presence within.

Imagination, Dreaming and the Child Mind

Early sense impressions can lay dormant only to surface years later. We can be reminded of some aesthetic moment, if not in detail but through a feeling. This is well described by the theologian C. S. Lewis who writes of the beauty of a toy garden, some moss and twigs, made by his brother on the lid of a biscuit tin, "it made me aware of nature . . . as something cool, dewy, fresh, exuberant." The impression of that creation from early childhood later became important in memory. "As long as I live my imagination of Paradise will retain something of my brother's toy garden." He writes that it later evoked in memory a sense of longing, a longing for a longing that took him out of the commonplace.

The imaginative experiences of childhood give a foundation for later creativity, and sometimes there can be direct connections. For example, Lewis's own imaginative creativity when he was aged six, seven, or eight has some links to *The Chronicles of Narnia*. He acknowledges that "at this

---

21. Graham, *Zen Catholicism*, 126.
22. Merton, "Theology of Creativity," 367.

time . . . I was living almost entirely in my imagination" as he mapped and chronicled Animal-Land, an island with "dressed animals" and "knights in armour." Lewis writes that whilst this prepared him for his later career as a novelist, the only thing that Animal-Land had in common with Narnia was "the anthropomorphic beasts" as Animal-Land was "astonishingly prosaic" whilst Narnia contained wonder.[23]

For the poet Kathleen Raine true imagination is a supernatural gift, something of the divine, and thus is in many ways an alien presence in any society. Whilst appreciating its presence in childhood she saw that "the imagination, whose 'kingdom is not of this world,' must wage a bitter struggle against 'adaptation,' compromise, and ultimate forgetfulness." Given that adaptation to environment is seen as a virtue in the world this means that the imagination tends to get pushed to one side as we gradually leave childhood until it is ultimately relegated to a past memory. Writing about the poet David Gascoyne and quoting from his novel, *Opening Day*, written at the age of sixteen, Kathleen Raine states:

> The poet, who in infancy "lived in the strange and antique solemnity of semi-consciousness, through the bright dreams of which only those things that were especially pleasing, beautiful or new, unpleasant, horrible or terrifying could penetrate," called such adaptation by another name—spiritual death, "the gradual sinking of his individuality, his thwarted talents, to the drab level of this mundane suburb that for ever sprawled beneath an ashen sky"; a death many have had to die, compelled by necessity to join that long procession of black-coated city workers of whom Eliot in Dante's words exclaimed: "I had not known death had undone so many."

The hero from David Gascoyne's novel discovers beauty where he can and especially in nature—even the unpromising nature found in the London suburbs. For this character whatever is seen as dispossessed and unheeded beauty can still stir his imagination to a sense of paradise. Even the coarse grass, sticks, and weeds that he describes as: "Tatters of leaf and scorched pods," remnants "On the far edge of Being" can still appear redeeming. He wrote how that even on the least promising and busiest of days the sun can sometimes offer the possibility that the Kingdom of Heaven can come to earth.[24]

---

23. Lewis, *Surprised by Joy*, 4 and 10–11.

24. Raine, *Defending Ancient Springs*, 36 and extract from Gascoyne, "Fragments" quoted in Raine, 39.

Imagining when awake can lead to the introverted playing found in fantasies and the extroverted playing shown in creativity. Dreaming is the activity of imagining when asleep. In one sense dreaming can be seen as also the activity of the spirit of the child because dreams are innocent in that they lack the disguise adopted by the waking mind and are unaffected by the conscious will. In dreaming there is huge creative potential both in understanding the inner world and the shadow part of the psyche, and, also, from sometimes apparently spontaneous and unwilled reorganization of information made available to the unconscious.

In his account of his own experiences Carl Jung describes setting out on an exploration using both his dreams and also what he termed "active imagination" encouraging fantasies when he was awake.

> It was during Advent . . . that I resolved on the decisive step. I was sitting at my desk once more, thinking over my fears. Then I let myself drop. Suddenly it was as though the ground literally gave way beneath my feet, and I plunged down into the dark depths . . .
>
> In order to seize hold of the fantasies, I frequently imagined a steep descent. I even made several attempts to get to the very bottom. . . . The atmosphere was that of the other world.[25]

In the course of these fantasies Jung encountered various figures; one of the personages Jung called Philemon and with him he conversed and learnt a great deal. He represented a superior insight and Philemon taught Jung the meaning of psychic objectivity and the reality of the psyche. In some ways this relationship has echoes of the imaginary friend met with in childhood; a fantasy experience which feels hugely real and is developed by children who may be especially isolated. Similarly in adulthood when we might need a wise figure to help us there may be a need for space to imaginatively spend time with Jesus Christ seeking guidance and strength. Some traditional spiritual practices encourage this use of imaginative spirituality as a way of breaking through where religious life has become stuck and deadened. It is a creative use of our inner world, an imaginative playfulness in our relationship with God.

Both dreaming and imagination have the power to translate what was previously unconscious or consciously hidden into images that are available and can be understood and thought about. This can vary usually but intense experiences can become visionary experience where the active imagination and religious encounter merge. The theological writer Evelyn Underhill's work on visions, first published over a century ago in 1911, still helps with

25. Jung, *Memories, Dreams, Reflections*, 203, 205.

understanding the experiences of so many of what she refers to as "an exalted and uncontrolled imaginative power."[26] She weighs up the rational, the psychological, and the mystical stances in her analysis of what she calls "supersensual intuitions." She also raises the place of the dream imagination and the power of some messages projected from without, noting that, for some, such experiences will transform lives. She sees these as contact between the visionary and "transcendental beauty or truth" which draws on deep activity within the spiritual self.

Carl Jung understood this, from his own experiences, as contact with the collective unconscious, the deep stratum that lies below the personal consciousness. Writing in the 1950s about the increasing number of visions of the Virgin Mary, Jung linked this to a deep longing amongst ordinary people for the glorification of the feminine. He noted that it was largely children who had the visions, and suggested this might have given pause for thought, as he believed that widespread visions reported by children showed that "in such cases the collective unconscious is always at work."[27] He saw all such visions as surfacing from deep unconscious sources. He also understood that changes in the Catholic Church, such as the acceptance of the dogma of the Assumption of the Virgin Mary, was a counterbalance to the overly masculine, historic, and rationalist views that had for some time dominated the church. Such shifts Jung saw as the result of the movements of the Holy Spirit.

Thomas Merton also recognized the need for the feminine and records waking from a dream, woken by the gentle voice of a nurse whilst he was staying in hospital:

> It was like awakening for the first time from all the dreams of my life—as if the Blessed Virgin herself, as if Wisdom had awakened me. We do not hear the soft voice, the gentle voice, the feminine voice, the voice of the Mother: yet she speaks everywhere and in everything. Wisdom cries out in the market place—"if anyone is little let him come to me."[28]

26. Underhill, *Mysticism*, 266.

27. Jung, *Psychology and Religion*, 461.

28. Merton, *Turning Towards the World*. 17.

14

The Internal Landscape of the Child Mind
and Models of Spiritual Maturity

Thomas Merton was constantly struggling with the question of identity, and in his search for spiritual integrity and thereby maturity he engaged in a continual struggle to be free from an imprisoning and distorting self-consciousness that plagued him and, he believed, all human beings to a greater or lesser extent. He included in this searching both grace and psychology and he saw that these could work together, sometimes being in conflict. Merton was searching for full identity in Christ and for what spiritual maturity might mean, and from glimpses of his work the suggestion in this book is that he appreciated that spiritual maturity could be seen as the child mind.

The analytical framework for exploring the internal landscape of the child mind is provided by Carl Jung and his thinking on a mechanism that he called the transcendent function.[1] It is the core of Jung's theory of psychological growth and what he called individuation, which is seen as the way in which each person is guided in a teleological way to become the person that he or she is meant to be. The transcendent function is a central metaphor for psychological growth and it involves a dialogue between consciousness and the unconscious—between the grown-up ideas of self-determination through ego development, and the unprovable and unscientific concepts like intuition, imagination, dreams, and emotions, often the very qualities known in early childhood. Jung believed that though experienced as incompatible with the rational ego honed through conceptual thought, the disowned and the apparently unnecessary parts of human consciousness

1. Jung, *Structure and Dynamics*, 69.

which had been relegated to the unconscious had to be reclaimed as part of individuation.

Jung believed that every idea, attitude, and image in consciousness had its opposite, or was compensated for by another in the unconscious and that the two "struggled with each other in a kind of polarized dance. If these opposites were held in swaying tension, he posited, a new, third thing would emerge that was not a mixture of the two but qualitatively different."[2] Jung writes:

> The confrontation of the two positions generates a tension charged with energy and creates a living, third thing—not a logical stillbirth . . . but a movement out of the suspension between the opposites, a living birth that leads to a new level of being . . .[3]

For Jung the aim of the transcendent function which emerges from the psyche is the realization in all its aspects "of the personality originally hidden away in the embryonic germplasm; the production and unfolding of the original potential wholeness."[4]

The transcendent function can be used as a way to consider a conversation between what apparently seem opposite states of mind as explored earlier in different chapters in the book: one is the spirit of the child and the other the adult emphasis on conceptual thought and rationalisation. The transcendent function is about a way of holding in a state of tension the enchanted world and the disenchanted world; also holding the opposites of spontaneous creativity and thoughtful reflection; containing the opposites of a lack of self-consciousness with the centrality of the self, and finally an awareness of both the shadow and the disguise.

What will emerge through the transcendent function is the child mind. For the transcendent function has been implicitly used throughout this book in the sense that often opposing experiences or states of mind have been discussed and the child mind has been suggested as both a synthesis of, and a more than, the two combined. One example would be the apparently opposing states of innocence and experience leading to the organized innocence described by William Blake. Another would be the state of dependence known to us all in early infancy and the apparent opposite which is the adult state of independence: the third position achieved through the transcendent function is that of the adult being-in-dependence

2. Miller, *Transcendent Function*, xi.

3. Jung, *Structure and Dynamics*, 90.

4. Miller, *Transcendent Function*, 5.

with God. The enchantment found in looking at the world through the eyes of the small child has been placed in opposition to the disenchantment that seems so present in adult consciousness; here the synthesis and the 'more than' leads to re-enchantment. Similarly, the inner landscape of the child mind includes the hinterland of actual childhood experiences and the repression and obscuring of this through the adult mind. The child mind absorbs and transcends both of these to reach a re-awakening and rebirth, for there has been a birth and a death which synthesized and transcended leads to a grace-filled state which is resurrection consciousness.

"Who is this 'I' that you imagine yourself to be?"[5]

Thomas Merton struggled in his writing with the idea of what the adult self is, what the spiritual self might be, and how what he calls the false self with all its seductive illusion could be stripped away to uncover the true self. In this he joined the ranks of many psychoanalysts and psychotherapists who have, over the last century and more, wrestled with how to understand what identity and selfhood might genuinely mean.

As has been highlighted in this book, Merton thought that the adult self as it is known is usually inconsistent, frequently strange, and often deceptive. In particular Merton acknowledges the duplicity of the self, the disguise that is presented to the world. He saw this exterior "I" as caught up in temporal plans and projects, looking for achievements and recognitions and so foreign to the interior self where there are no plans or demands for achievements. In contrast Merton writes that this interior "I" looks only to be and to move, as this is a dynamic part "according to the secret laws of Being itself and according to the promptings of a Superior Freedom (that is, of God), rather than to plan and to achieve according to his own desires."[6] It has to be said that Merton's understanding of the false self sometimes focuses on the completely superficial aspects and sometimes takes in deeper and more complex strata. It is not a fixed but rather a dynamic entity in his thinking. Generally, Merton understood that each of us is shadowed by an illusory person and this becomes an obstruction, a barrier to some sense of truth in personal identity. The emotions associated with the false self are all based on the whim of our desires and bolstered by accomplishments and achievements and usually the approval of others.

The analytic perspective, as was explored earlier, offers further psychological understanding to the concept of the false self and how it is organized

5. Merton, *Inner Experience*, 4.
6. Ibid., 5.

and perhaps also a helpful approach about how and why the false self develops and originates in early childhood. In his book *The Inner Experience,* Merton does not limit the false self to the realm of the conscious. He takes it to a far deeper level and he includes various recesses of the unconscious, where neurosis and psychotic derangement can often hold sway. At its deepest level the false self for Merton is the self that is limited by both time and space and to time and space. It has a biography and a history, both of which we write by the actions we perform and the roles that we play, and both of which are destined to cease with death. The false self honed in adulthood looks endlessly for arrival, achievement, and completion while in contrast the inner landscape of the true self, the child mind, is about becoming, open to exploring the ever possible and so always incomplete. It is the ego-self, the self as object that keeps us at the very surface of reality, it is the disguise and it also includes the shadow. Simone Weil is one of many who understood that there was a need to get below and beyond this barrier.

Simone Weil's Notion of Decreation

Simone Weil thought that in order to fully love God and our neighbor the self needed to be decreated. There's no clear definition of what this means though in her essay "Decreation" she defines it as to "make something created pass into the uncreated."[7] She believed that aspects of the self cluttered and obscured the relationship with God, and like Merton saw the self as in part a shadow that obscured the light of God: "every time that we raise the ego (the social *ego,* the psychological *ego* etc.) as high as we raise it, we degrade ourselves to an infinite degree by confining ourselves to being no more than that."[8]

For Weil we can be co-creators with God but our part is to decreate ourselves. "We possess nothing in this world other than the power to say 'I.' This is what we must yield up to God—in other words, to destroy."[9] So for Weil the "I" is the false self and whatever has contributed to this needs to be withdrawn to make space for God. Her reading of the self as illusory has links with Lacan's understanding of the small child, discussed in an earlier chapter, seeing the seductive whole image in the mirror though feeling differently from what he or she sees, in other words inside the child is in bits and pieces.

---

7. Weil, *Gravity and Grace,* 32.

8. Ibid., 33.

9. Ibid., 26.

However Weil's decreation takes such thinking much further and indeed seems to preclude all those childhood experiences that it is suggested in this book are absorbed into the child mind, and indeed she precludes even her relationships with other living beings. For her, self-effacement leaves God free to be with creation with no person around: "If only I knew how to disappear there would be a perfect union of love between God and the earth I tread, the sea I hear."[10]

If there is thought of the child mind Weil finds it only at the moments of birth and of death. She writes, "There are only two instants of perfect nudity and purity in human life: birth and death. It is only when newly-born or on our death bed that we can adore God in human form without sullying the divinity."[11] Here there are echoes of the writing of Georges Bernanos whose character, the country priest, looks on the arrival of his own death in the same way as he looked at small children, adding that at the moment of death: "Alas, one would need also to become as a small child."[12]

For Weil it was from infancy that what she called the great affliction began. Weil's longing for union with God is expressed through the purest of perceptions—in other words without any self-consciousness of the "I" who is doing the looking. My suggestion is that Weil's longing is the longing "to become." It is the potential to look as the small child looks without the recognition of the act taking place. In other words, "To see a landscape as it is when I am not there."[13] When the mind is completely focussed on the object, there is no space for awareness of the feeling. She writes: "Perfect joy excludes even the very feeling of joy, for in the soul filled by the object no corner is left for saying 'I.'"[14] Simone Weil thought from her experiences that the only way to be with God was to go through the self to the very inside of being.

There are clearly similarities between her thinking about decreating and Merton's phrase self-naughting which he thought could happen through contemplative prayer. This is likened to one aspect of becoming as a small child as it is fundamentally about humility. It is the emptying out of the false self that for Merton is akin to a process of rebirth and fuelled by a deep spiritual instinct: a demand that each of us is faithful to the original potential with which we were born. Merton allows for the possibility that a recovery of this authenticity and independence can be gained through psychological

10. Ibid., 42.

11. Ibid., 37.

12. Bernanos, *Diary of a Country Priest*, 248.

13. Weil, *Gravity and Grace*, 42.

14. Ibid., 31.

breakthrough and liberation, though he adds the proviso that it would be for someone who would need "a great deal of money and can afford a long analysis—and can find an especially good psychoanalyst." The risk is that it might instead lead to adjustment rather than change and growth, so rather than born again "we simply learn to put up with ourselves."[15] Merton is at pains to emphasize that any rebirth is not a single event but:

> . . . a continuous dynamic of inner renewal . . . growth in the life of the Spirit, a deepening of new life, a continuous rebirth, in which the exterior and superficial life of the ego-self is discarded like an old snake skin and the mysterious, invisible self of the Spirit becomes more present and more active.[16]

He continues that to be born again is to become ourselves through the unpredictable and often unexpected spirit that moves constantly over the face of the whole earth.

The Internal Landscape of the Child Mind

In this book the idea of the child mind has similarities with the idea of the true self and the potential within each person for authentic living with which we are born and that remains present into adulthood—the potential for creativity, freedom, and self-realization: " . . . it is, like the music of the spheres, absolutely personal. It belongs to being alive."[17] The contemporary psychoanalyst Christopher Bollas writes, "The life of the true self is to be found in the person's experiencing of the world." He extends the psychoanalyst Winnicott's idea of the true self as aliveness itself, and posits that this core self is, "the unique presence of being that each of us is; the idiom of our personality."[18] He suggests the true self is within us as a potential before object relating—in other words it lies at a deeper level than the ego. Here there is connection with the idea of becoming—the potential inherent in Jesus' command "unless you become . . ."

Winnicott himself understood the depth of the true self, with recognition of the person as a three or four dimensional being. He wrote about the true self as being in a state of immanence and the place that gives rise to the spontaneous gesture. He implied that this state was about being found and

---

15. Merton, *Love and Living*, 196–97.
16. Ibid., 199.
17. Cohen, *Private Life*, 192.
18. Bollas, *Forces of Destiny*, 9.

yet inviolate and his use of the word "immanence" evokes divine presence.[19] For in this book it is suggested that in the adult the inner landscape of the child mind has a strong relational aspect and this characteristic is of course also the central part of the life of the actual infant. Winnicott famously said "There is no such thing as a baby . . . if you set out to describe a baby, you will find you are describing a baby and someone."[20] For of course actual babies need loving carers and demand total attention certainly whilst awake.

Therefore Jesus' command implies a willing God eagerly involved in relationship when we are awake to him, for the child mind is a call to divine intimacy—to being found without being violated, and we are invited to call God *Abba*. Merton writes:

> The basic truth is our dependence on God in a realm where so terribly much is completely unknown and in a way unknowable. What we must do is to keep that fact in mind and turn frequently to God in simple faith without expecting to "see" Him or to understand too much about His ways, but anyway to follow the principles of the Gospel and to live for truth above all.[21]

In this extract Merton holds in tension the apparent opposites of, firstly, the small child's experience of total dependence and vulnerability where there is no understanding, and secondly, the encouragement and advice to the adult part to hold that negative capability in mind, and, in faith, appreciate the mysterious nature of discipleship.

The journey towards union with the Christ child is above all a relational experience. The experience takes us on a dynamic journey that involves a moving in and out from being unconsciously independent—where we are not giving the idea of a relationship with God a second thought. We may move then into an awareness of our somewhat defensive holding onto our so-called adult independence. If there is movement towards a sense of inner intimacy with God or Christ, then this could be a glimpse of conscious dependency—the relationship starts to matter and this inner relationship begins to affect our external relationships. The fourth part of this dynamic movement involves a deeply felt intimacy; this is a state of unconscious dependence. The dance of separation and intimacy is an endless process of becoming. This potential to become is the internal journeying across the landscape of the child mind. We are becoming in our relationship a being-in-dependence with Being Itself. This is a living relationship and a

---

19. Rodman, *Winnicott*, 213.
20. Winnicott, *Maturational Process*, 38 fn.
21. Merton, *Road to Joy*, 63.

movement towards God in a love that is always moving towards oneness: towards the Being that is all-embracing. The capacity for self-transcendence becomes possible when we fall in love with God. It is like any falling in love where one's being becomes a being-in-love.

In its deepest manifestation the child mind involves some recognition of qualities from infancy and childhood but it transcends known experiences both as child and as adult. In the same way that one has to go beyond the humanity of Jesus to reach his divinity so there is a need to go beyond the recognition and retrieval of the humanity of the small child that we once were to reach the divinity of the Christ child—the eternal child who lives in the deepest part of our being where it is a communion of mind with mind. Beyond the reality we can apprehend is the mystery whereby the small child we were is united with the Christ child and, through playing and relating together, so divinized.

Inevitably it also has to be stated that the child mind is not a thing or an entity. While the phrase the child mind has been used throughout this book as if it is in itself a concept it is rather more an idea, and to use an analogy favored by many it is instead like the finger pointing towards the moon. "There is no mystical experience without symbolism. Words and letters, it is true, are no more than a finger pointing to the moon, but without that finger who will see the moon?"[22] So clearly the idea of the child mind is neither the finger nor in itself the moon but offers a vision or an image that can help in imagining and reflecting on change. In other words it is a sign that points beyond itself, a signalling of what might be. It is an image of a new and different reality that involves awakening from the myopia and listlessness of much of what it means to be an adult and to open up the potential—in other words to become.

Merton on Final Integration and Spiritual Maturity

In his extended review and essay of Dr. A. Reza Arasteh's book *Final Integration in the Adult Personality*, which was written towards the end of his life, Merton places the idea of rebirth and life in Christ in the spirit as fundamental to Christian theology and practice; he reminds us that it is after all the whole meaning of baptism but also an idea central to monastic vocation. He also confirms that this notion of rebirth is found in many other religious or spiritual traditions including Zen Buddhism and in the Sufi tradition. The rebirth is in fact the command by Jesus, "unless you become":

22. Johnston, *"Arise My Love,"* 159.

... emphasis is placed on the call to fulfill certain obscure yet urgent potentialities in the ground of one's being, to "become someone" that one already (potentially) is, the person one is truly meant to be.[23]

For Merton this is about transformation to a new and more complete identity. The reason Merton finds Arasteh's book important is that the author used ideas from depth psychology: humanistic psychoanalysis, existential psychotherapy, and logo therapy, and incorporated material from the mystical tradition of Persian Sufism. Rejecting psychoanalysis when it merely leads to adaptation, Arasteh understands existential anxiety as "a summons to growth and to painful development." Arasteh draws on Jung's thinking on the development of the person to full spiritual maturity and ripeness. However, despite the fact that Arasteh does not acknowledge specifically Jung's transcendent function it seems that the transcendent function is undoubtedly at work here. It is where the anxiety that blocks vital energies is in opposition to conventions, and the opposition is then seen to generate the necessary strength for psychic rebirth into a new transcultural identity. "This new being is entirely personal, original, creative, unique, and it transcends the limits imposed by social convention and prejudice. Birth on this higher level is an imperative necessity for man."[24]

In his review Merton traces the need for the infant immersed "in a symbiotic relationship with the rest of nature" to move out of what he describes as "sensual self-centredness" into acquiring an identity to being "a responsible member of society." Once this has happened there is still another birth to be undergone, and in the book that Merton reviewed this final integration is traced through the lives of three exceptional individuals: Rumi the Persian mystic and poet, Goethe, and one of Arasteh's patients. Interestingly, in a later book *Rumi, The Persian, The Sufi* which Arasteh sent to Merton, Arasteh describes that to become a fully integrated personality there must be completion of the circle of existence and that to achieve maturity the person "must be born again and again and experience numerous spiritual rebirths."[25] The description given of how this affected Rumi showed that he had "achieved a rebirth into a conscious inner state of unity with all beings."[26] Here again Arasteh cites Carl Jung and the humanistic psychotherapist Erich Fromm who both explained how conventional life and conformity act as a barrier to full realization. Arasteh's description from the

23. Merton, "Final Integration," 452–62.

24. Ibid., 457.

25. Arasteh, *Rumi The Persian*, 25.

26. Montaldo, "Thomas Merton," 18.

Sufi perspective reiterates the illusory nature of the self and how our self-consciousness and clinging to a sense of self obscures the potential implicit in Jesus' command "unless you become . . ." Failure to listen to the inner voice leads to a situation where

> fiction becomes real and falsity appears as truth. What the individual calls personality is really that which shadows his potential personality and deprives him of maturing. That which he calls self is really that which fails his self, and what to him is "I" is only a barrier to his becoming "I."[27]

Merton comments, using phrases taken from the book, that final integration or maturity involves a person fully born with an entirely "inner experience of life." This is something more in terms of identity than the limited ego-self: an attainment to a deep inner freedom where guidance is through "spontaneous behavior subject to dynamic insight." For Merton there is an openness, and an emptiness, a poverty such as is found in the early Franciscans, in St. John of the Cross and many others. There is no longer limitation from the culture in which the person has grown up because they have passed beyond its limiting forms while retaining its best and most universal ones. Merton quotes the phrase "finally giving birth to a fully comprehensive self," where there is "a unified vision and experience of the one truth shining out in all its various manifestations," this brings "perspective, liberty, and spontaneity."[28] Although Merton does not use the specific term the child mind it seems that he is speaking of the breakthrough into something very similar.

While Merton links the rebirth that precedes final integration as something like the dark night described by St. John of the Cross, he notes that Arasteh uses the language of Sufism and the idea of the loss of self, a spiritual death that is followed by reintegration and new life on a totally different level. Merton reframes the full meaning of final integration in the Christian context where he sees it also as eschatological and "a rebirth into the transformed and redeemed time, the time of the Kingdom, the time of the Spirit . . . the reintegration of that self in Christ."[29]

---

27. Arasteh, *Rumi The Persian*, 27
28. Merton, "Final Integration," 458.
29. Ibid., 461.

Oth er Models of Spiritual Maturity: The Second Naïveté, James Fowler's Stages of Faith, and William Johnston on One-Pointedness

Paul Ricoeur the French philosopher was interested in seeing if he could establish a dialectic between views that are generally taken to be polar opposites. Over a lifetime he believed that philosophy was always a reflection on experience which is already there: philosophy starts nothing and is not foundational. "Its task is to adjudicate among conflicting interpretations— each of which claims to be absolute."[30]

Among other subjects, he wrote about the second naïveté as a way to engage in faith and especially as a way to engage with reading and understanding the Bible. The first naïveté, which is mentioned by Ricoeur only in passing, refers to religious belief or specifically the interpretation of Scripture where everything is taken at face value—it is experienced literally. There could be some equivalence here with the way that the young child views the world. There is at this stage no distinction between metaphor and what is actually seen. For Ricoeur the opposite position to the first naïveté is a state of critical distance where rational forces and rational inspection leads to the literal meanings of religion being rejected. Once the step is taken back from religious belief and the whole subject is critically evaluated the person cannot believe the simple naive concepts. This too has equivalence with some of the ideas discussed in this book where the cares of the world and the state of disenchantment obscures any vision of what might be called original participation. Ricoeur suggests that following this distancing and disillusionment there is a way to re-engage in faith through what he called a second naïveté. He evocatively writes, "Beyond the desert (Rational stage) of criticism, we wish to be called again."[31] In this second naïveté, Scripture and religious concepts are seen as symbols, (i.e., metaphorical constructs) that we now interpret "in the full responsibility of autonomous thought."[32] There are similarities here with the mechanism of the transcendent function where the myths experienced as truth in the first naïveté are judged in fact as myths, but having experienced the critical distance these concepts are then able to be re-engaged with again but at a different level. There is a move towards recognition of the concepts as symbols of something greater than what the words or teachings imply in their literal sense. Perhaps there

---

30. Reagan, "Paul Ricoeur," 536.

31. Ricoeur, *Symbolism of Evil*, 349.

32. Ibid., 350.

is some equivalence with the child mind and spiritual maturity where both the earlier states are included, integrated, and transcended.

In his book *Stages of Faith* James Fowler explores the psychology of human development and the quest for meaning, offering six stages that culminate in what he calls universalizing faith. Fowler precedes his analysis of the six stages with a section on "infancy and undifferentiated faith," in which he describes what happens between a very young baby and the mother. He concludes that "we all begin the pilgrimage of faith as infants." He rightly observes that our first pre-images of God have their origins in early infancy composed "from our first experiences of mutuality, in which we form the rudimentary awareness of self as separate from and dependent upon the immensely powerful others."[33] So here the seeds of trust, courage, hope, and love are, as he writes, "fused in an undifferentiated way and contend with sense threats of abandonment, inconsistencies, and deprivations in an infant's environment." Fowler takes us then through the first five stages to stage six where he describes persons exhibiting qualities that "shake our usual criteria of normalcy. . . . Their heedlessness to self-preservation and the vividness of their taste and feel for transcendent moral and religious actuality give their actions and words an extraordinary and often unpredictable quality." He writes about their devotion to universalizing compassion and their enlarged visions of universal community. He sees this stage as exceedingly rare where the person's environment is inclusive of all being and where they live with "felt participation in a power that unifies and transforms the world." They have "a special grace that makes them seem more lucid, more simple, and yet somehow more fully human than the rest of us." Fowler points to Thomas Merton as someone whose life exhibited these qualities. He sees that those who come to embody universalizing faith are drawn into those patterns of commitment and leadership by the providence of God and what he calls "the exigencies of history."[34]

So how far do the qualities outlined by Fowler correspond to what it is suggested is to be found in the internal landscape of child mind. Certainly the enlarged and universal vision and the special grace seem to correspond; however, the position of leadership is not usually coterminous with Jesus' command. Fowler does acknowledge this, and comments on the need for humility and the necessary desire found in those who reach stage six, for inclusiveness and a selfless passion for a transformed world made over not in their image, but in accordance with an intentionality that is both divine and transcendent.

33. Fowler, *Stages of Faith*, 119, 121.
34. Ibid., 121, 200–202.

Scripture tells us that the person who is awakened in this way has "the mind of Christ" (1 Cor 2:10–16). That does not mean the human person is psychologically or morally perfect, but such a transformed person does henceforth see things in a much more expanded and compassionate way. In Ephesians it is called "a spiritual revolution of the mind" (Eph 4:23).

While the models suggest a hierarchy of spiritual development, the whole human race is called to divinization where no categories are relevant. William Johnston calls this coming to a state of one-pointedness: "in this process there is no discursive thinking. One lets go of all reasoning and imagining in order to enter into a new world of silence where with great joy one discovers one's original face, one's true self." He quotes Jeremiah who heard the interior words (Jer 1:5): "Before I formed you in the womb I knew you." In this moment Johnston writes, the prophet found his true self, his unconditioned self, his original face to quote Zen "before his father and mother were born."[35]

For most mystical writers such experiences are an incomprehensible mystery and in that way place those who are able to be open to such happenings in the same state as that known in infancy where nothing made sense and all was unfathomable—indeed then as now we had not the capacity to understand it. A great number of religious and philosophical systems speak of the return, or returning home—we come from God and return to God. For example Lao Tzu whose work is discussed earlier speaks of returning to the root. "This root is seen by Lao Tzu as the mother of all creatures. The return to the root is the natural return of children to their mother" where there are echoes from Job 1: 21 "Naked I came from my mother's womb and naked shall I return there."[36]

35. Johnston, *"Arise My Love,"* 154 and 184.
36. Ibid., 142.

15

Epiphanies of the Child Mind

Our awareness of our inner self can at least theoretically be the fruit of a purely natural and psychological purification. Our awareness of God is a supernatural participation in the light by which He reveals Himself interiorly as dwelling in our inmost self.

When the veils are removed, then one can touch, or rather be touched by God in the mystical darkness.[1]

Thomas Merton's vocation was to live what he discovered about himself, in that way he was always open to becoming and there was always potential for change. For the adult Merton the child mind is linked to the experiential, to a theology of feeling and a condition of simplicity. This means to be without artifice, unpretentious, aware of the unconscious and so awake to the illusory nature of the world—and so able to speak truth to power. The foundation for this is a dependence on God framed within the concept of mercy exemplified in God's relationship with his creation and with each one of us. Writing on mercy Merton sees this as what binds us in relationship to God, and highlights that it does not depend on our perfection.

I have always overshadowed Jonas with My mercy, and cruelty I know not at all. Have you had sight of Me, Jonas, My child? Mercy within mercy within mercy . . .

What was fragile has become powerful. I loved what was most frail. I looked upon what was nothing. I touched what was without substance and within what was not, I am.[2]

1. Merton, *Inner Experience,* 12 and 70.
2. Merton, *Sign of Jonas,* 354

The child mind is another way in which Merton is speaking about the true self, and a state of spiritual maturity. It is a state where the person can at times move beyond the self-consciousness of the persona. As explored earlier, the child mind is not a regression to an infantile state of mind, known *before* the shadow and the disguise obscure it, but rather a state that takes us *beyond* the shadow and the disguise. It is ending the sense of separateness from God and accepting our being-in-dependency with the Being—"Him in Whom is hidden our original face before we are born."[3]

Thomas Merton writes, "Our knowledge of God is paradoxically, a knowledge not of him as the object of our scrutiny, but of ourselves as utterly dependent on his saving and merciful knowledge of us."[4] Existing within this dependence we are carried by God, and in a letter to Jacques Maritain, that links us back to the earlier chapters on play and joining in the general dance, Merton says that then all we do becomes play which is "the only genuine seriousness. . . . All life is in reality the playing and dancing of the Child-God in His world, and we, alas, have not seen it and known it."[5]

For Thomas Merton spiritual maturity is a process of increasing dependency, intimacy, and union with Christ. However he believed it can also be found in other quite diverse religious traditions. He saw no difficulty with this broadening of the frame, understanding creation as a manifestation of the epiphany of wisdom. This he termed sophianic, and returned repeatedly to the figure of Wisdom found in Proverbs at play. Wisdom speaks: "I was daily his delight, rejoicing before him always, rejoicing in his inhabited world and delighting in the human race" (Prov 8:30b–31). Wisdom is associated with play and with the feminine and a contrast with the heavy more masculine seriousness of purpose and reasoning.

Overall there is a sense that when through the transcendent function the duality found in both the shadow and the disguise can be, even if only briefly, overcome, there is a sense of wholeness and present moment awareness. In the gospel of Thomas, Jesus lays down for his disciples the following conditions for entry into the kingdom of heaven:

> Jesus saw children who were being suckled. He said to his disciples: These children who are being suckled are like those who enter the Kingdom. They said to him: Shall we then, being children, enter the Kingdom? Jesus said to them: When you make the two One, and when you make the inner as the outer and the outer as the inner, and the above as the below, so that you will

3. Merton, *Hidden Ground of Love,* 624.

4. Merton, *Contemplative Prayer,* 103–4.

5. Merton, *Courage for Truth,* 38.

make the male and the female into a single One . . . then shall you enter the Kingdom.[6]

This, then, is about becoming integrated, and through the transcendent function moving beyond the accepted dualistic mindset of conceptual consciousness. The image is of connection with the breast of God, as an infant nursing, where the person is less and less conscious of self as a separate thing. "Liberation is the dawning awareness of our true selves already living in Christ, which is to say, resting in the womb of God, in creation, and in one another."[7]

This dawning insight can be found in contemplative prayer, "where we discover our own deepest reality from which we have strayed like runaway children becoming strangers to ourselves."[8] Once experienced, Merton writes of the "infinite fragility of the divine life in us" where self-affirmations might destroy "His weakness and littleness in me—fortunately indestructible." He calls this a mustard seed, "the struggle of the very small to survive."[9] Similarly he sees the true self like a "shy wild animal" that can only emerge when "all is peaceful, in silence . . . alone."[10] The struggle is to become open to the process of rebirth, despite the fear of what we might find within us and the death of our attachments.

This is presented in a particularly evocative way in Merton's readings of the translation of "When a hideous man . . ." in *The Way of Chuang Tzu*.[11]

When a hideous man becomes a father
And a son is born to him
In the middle of the night
He trembles and lights a lamp
And runs to look in anguish
On that child's face
To see whom he resembles.

Commenting on this poem, James Finley, who was a novice monk at the Abbey of Gethsemani with Merton, writes that each day we hope to discover within us the face of the child born anew. "But left to our own devices we discover only the old man of misguided self-seeking." The answer is found in childlike abandonment, where we come to God "the way a child

6. Ross, *Jesus Untouched*, 81.

7. Pramuk, *Sophia*, 136.

8. Finley, *Merton's Palace of Nowhere*, 19.

9. Merton, *Turning Toward the World*, 167.

10. Merton, *Inner Experience*, 5.

11. Merton, "When a Hideous Man," in *Way of Chuang Tzu*, 77.

takes a drink of water." He writes, "Our guru is the child within—small and simple and without pretence, who would have us reach out in a tender healing touch without our left hand knowing what our right hand is doing."[12]

There are many instances in Merton's writings that suggest epiphanies of the child mind, the three selected in this chapter stand as examples of such breakthroughs in his self-realization and are taken from different stages in his life.

The Epiphany at Mass—I am the Child who is God

The first epiphany is in June 1949 where Merton writes of his experience when taking mass. There is a process that develops through the months that precede this which begins in February 1949 when Merton reflects on the martyred innocents who confessed through their dying. He takes this idea and begins to look at what vocation might mean in the light of innocence. His reflection leads to the following insight:

> Inside me, I quickly come to the barrier, the limit of what I am, beyond which I cannot go by myself. It is such a narrow limit and yet for years I thought it was the universe. Now I see it is nothing. Shall I go on being content with this restriction? . . . Desire always what is beyond and all around you, you poor sap! Want to progress and escape and expand and be emptied and vanish into God.[13]

Here he begins again the serious business of understanding his identity and the process of continual conversion through becoming. He sees his conventional limits as offering insight into his nothingness, but expresses the frustration of not being able to go beyond. The very process of reflection seems to exacerbate the problem. However once the conceptual thinking is laid aside, Merton writes, "I forget to reflect any more," and with the self-consciousness of rational thought lessened he is surprized to experience what he calls "a little escape, at least to the threshold, and love moves in darkness just enough to tell a man that there is freedom."[14]

There are a number of instances recorded by Merton after that where he notes the importance of the mass and what he describes as closer union with the whole mystical body. The experience recounted over the months is a process of deeper and deeper immersion in the mass with an awareness of

12. Finley, *Merton's Palace*, 26 and 81.

13. Merton, *Entering the Silence*, 275.

14. Ibid.

the need to die to self and this culminates in the child of God epiphany. This takes place in the context of what it means for Merton to become part of the diaconate, and, on Ascension Day 1949, to be ordained as a priest, so he is naturally deeply involved in his responses to the sacraments. In commenting on receiving his newly published book *Seeds of Contemplation* Merton writes that there is too little in the book about the passion and the precious blood of Christ, he feels he's only hinted at it and that therefore the book is cold and cerebral.[15] In a period of quiet whilst in preparation for becoming a priest Merton writes of finding a new center which was not anything he could grasp or understand but that had left him "dazzled."[16]

As the days pass and the ordination date comes nearer Merton notes his increasing dependency on the Virgin Mary—he sees himself abandoning any techniques, throwing himself on her mercy, dependent on her guidance and certain that she alone through God's dispensation can help his helplessness.[17] Merton, at this time, is becoming increasingly immersed in the mass—in the prayers and the ceremonies which he sees as so easy and simple and happy, but he wonders what the mass will do to his interior life, perhaps holding the key to what he sees as his inadequacy.

> I cannot explain more at the moment, except that Christ the High Priest is awakening in the depths of my soul. . . . Instead of *myself* and *my* Christ and *my* love and *my* prayer, there is the might of a prayer stronger than thunder and milder than the flight of doves rising up from the Priest Who is the center of the soul of every priest . . .[18]

The mass is becoming an encounter with "the Living God" with the desire to be absorbed in "purity"—"lost in God."[19] Merton, always aware of what he saw as his many failings and his wrongdoing is led to throw himself on the mercy of God. In writing about the ordination he feels he has been transformed through the labor and the happiness of the three days of ceremony and that from this there has been a new birth within him and that through him a new world has been brought into being: "For this I came into the world" and the love and mercy together "makes me truly the child of Our Lady"—a mysterious fulfilment.[20] Such glimpses continue

---

15. Ibid., 287.
16. Ibid., 295.
17. Ibid., 308.
18. Ibid., 311–12.
19. Ibid., 314–15.
20. Ibid., 317–19.

in the days after the ordination; described as a lucidity and peace about which there is no coherent thing to say, rather a grace leading to a dark and deep radiance. It is for Merton about the action of the mass and the whole experience returns to him at odd hours "seizes me and envelops me," a state that emphasizes "the joy there is in being nothing and in depending on Our Lady for everything . . . to rely entirely on her love and protection."[21]

Here is the voicing of deep dependency with echoes of the powerlessness known to very small children. This is the poverty of spirit implicitly included in Jesus' command. Interestingly in this account there are echoes from the writing of Georges Bernanos where in *The Diary of a Country Priest* the narrator understands his lack of strength: "Though I have judged myself severely at times, I have always known that I possessed the spirit of poverty. The spirit of childhood is much akin. No doubt they are really one and the same thing."[22] Earlier in the same book there is an account of how powerlessness is the main-spring of a child's joy because everything is left to the mother: "Present, past, future—his whole life is caught up in one look, and that look as a smile," the character continues with his belief that if the church had only been able to give that comfort then "man would have known he was the son of God; and therein lies your miracle" for with that belief there would be no sense of loneliness.[23]

The great epiphany is described in Merton's account on 19 June 1949. He describes the experience as a "beautiful mixture of happiness and lucidity and inarticulateness" that fills him with great health. He writes, "I am forced to be simple at the altar" feeling that the indescribably pure light of God fills him with "what can only be described as the innocence of childhood." Here in this moment Merton is healed; he becomes unwounded as he receives mass. It is best read in his own words:

> Day after day I am more and more aware how little I am my everyday self at the altar: this consciousness of innocence is really a replacement. Another has taken over my identity, and this other is a tremendous infancy. And I stand at the altar—excuse the language, these words should not be extraordinary—but I stand at the altar with my eyes washed in the light that is eternity, as if I am one who is agelessly reborn. I am sorry for this language. There are no words I know of simple enough to describe such a thing, except that every day I am a day old, and at the altar I am the Child Who is God . . .

21. Ibid., 322.

22. Bernanos, *Diary of a Country Priest*, 237.

23. Ibid., 19–20.

> I swim in seas of joy that almost heave me off my moorings at the altar.[24]

While such an epiphany cannot be maintained for long, for those moments there was for Thomas Merton a deep connection with purity of being and the spirit of the child mind.

The Epiphany at Fourth and Walnut: That Innocence is in Everyone—Proverb and "Le Point Vierge"

The second epiphany selected takes place nearly ten years later. Earlier in this book, in chapter 3, Merton's dream of Proverb, the young Jewish girl, and his response to that was explored. Two weeks after the dream, on 18 March 1958, the experience of Proverb comes to Merton in a completely different context. This is on the busy roads of Fourth and Walnut in Louisville. This is far from the private individual epiphany at the altar; instead there is an awe-inspiring experience of God in all of humanity.

Merton gives us two accounts of what happened. One in his journal entry written the next day and the second with some alterations is found in *Conjectures of a Guilty Bystander*. In the journal Merton describes how the epiphany feels:

> . . . suddenly realized that I loved all the people and that none of them were, or, could be totally alien to me. As if waking from a dream—the dream of my separateness, of the "special" vocation to be different. . . . I am still a member of the human race.

Merton writes of the women he sees each as Wisdom and Sophia and Our Lady—"my delights are to be with the children of men!"[25] Incidentally in the second account in *Conjectures of a Guilty Bystander* this has extended to all persons.

In the journal account Merton writes again to dear Proverb, "I shall never forget our meeting yesterday. The touch of your hand makes me a different person. To be with you is rest and truth. Only with you are these things found, dear child sent to me by God." Looking at the pictures in the book Merton had picked up whilst in the town, *The Family of Man*; he sees that the whole book is a picture of Christ:

> There, there is Christ in my own Kind, my own Kind—"Kind" which means "likeness" and which means "love" and which

24. Merton, *Entering the Silence*, 326–27.
25. Merton, *Search for Solitude*, 182.

means "child." Mankind. Like one another, the dear "Kind" of sinners united and embraced in only one heart, one only Kindness, which is the Heart and Kindness of Christ.[26]

In the second account in his book *Conjectures* Merton describes this epiphany as the realization that we all belong to God and that:

> It is a glorious destiny to be a member of the human race. . . . I have the immense joy of being *man*, a member of a race in which God Himself became incarnate. . . . And if only everybody could realize this! But it cannot be explained. There is no way of telling people that they are all walking around shining like the sun.

The epiphany was possible because of his experiences in solitude. Such clarity would be both impossible and meaningless to "anyone completely immersed in the other cares, the other illusions, and all the automatisms of a tightly collective existence." In his moment of truth Merton could see the innocence, the unwounded center of each person, "where neither sin nor desire nor self-knowledge can reach, the core of their reality, the person that each one is in God's eyes."[27] If only, if only, Merton says, we could all see ourselves as we really are, and, if only, we could see each other in this way. The world would be completely different.

Merton follows his account immediately with his thoughts about the core of a person's reality. This absolute center point is the kernel, the embryo of the eternal child eternally present within each person. Merton took the term "le point vierge" from Louis Massignon, the French Catholic scholar of Islam and the Islamic world who derived the term from the mystical psychology of Islam.[28] Merton used it to describe the:

> . . . point of nothingness which is untouched by sin and by illusion, a point of pure truth, a point or spark which belongs entirely to God, which is never at our disposal. . . . This little point of nothingness and of absolute poverty is the pure glory of God in us. It is so to speak His name written in us as our poverty, as our indigence, as our dependence, as our sonship. It is like a pure diamond, blazing with the invisible light of heaven.[29]

In this reflection on his epiphany Merton takes the spark as being about our dependence and our relationship as children of God. Here we

---

26. Ibid., 183.

27. Merton, *Conjectures*, 158.

28. Bochen, "Le Point Vierge," 363.

29. Merton, *Conjectures*, 158.

become brothers and sisters with the Christ child at the heart of divinity and of God's creation. When Merton uses the phrase two years later it is about our connection with all other living things, where the birds are also children of God and all creation is permeated by the child mind. It is paradise regained:

> The first chirps of the waking birds—*le point vierge* of the dawn, a moment of awe and inexpressible innocence, when the Father in silence opens their eyes and they speak to Him, wondering if it is time to "be?" And He tells them "Yes." Then they one by one wake and begin to sing. . . . With my hair almost on end and the eyes of the soul wide open I am present, without knowing it at all, in this unspeakable Paradise.[30]

This is another epiphany of the child mind.

The Epiphany Beyond the Shadow and the Disguise

The third account is Merton's experience at Polonnaruwa, in what is now Sri Lanka. In the autumn of 1968 Merton was travelling in Asia before attending a conference in Bangkok. While in Dharamsala he met with Sonam Kazi a lay monk of the Nyingmapa tradition of Tibetan Buddhism and on 2 November Merton notes the following in his journal,

> I talked to Sonam Kazi about the "child mind," which is recovered *after* experience. Innocence—to experience—to innocence. Milarepa, angry, guilty of revenge, murder and black arts, was purified by his master Marpa, the translator, who several times made him build a house many stories high and then tear it down again. After which he was "no longer the slave of his own psyche but its lord." So too, a desert father came to freedom by weaving baskets and then, at the end of each year, burning all the baskets he had woven.

Here Merton writes of the child mind as a form of enlightenment leading to the realization that the life of the persona with the accompanying search for achievement and perfection is an illusion and disguise. Merton continues noting that,

> Sonam Kazi spoke of acting with no desire for gain, even spiritual—whether merit or attainment. A white butterfly appears in the sun, then vanishes again. Another passes in the distance. No gain for them—or for me.

30. Merton, *Turning Towards the World*, 7.

Down in the valley a bird sings, a boy whistles. The white butterfly zigzags across the top left hand corner of the view.[31]

This is the awareness sensing of childhood spirituality with present
moment observance, but it has an added depth this time around as it is a
renewed way of seeing. The innocence of what Merton sees emerges from
experience, and his recognition that before this it has been often obscured
by the false self with its needs for recognition and self-consciousness. Merton over these days writes in several journal entries of observing white but-
terflies and it is worth noting the white butterfly is often understood as a
symbol of rebirth and renewal, for powerful change and transformation. It
is sometimes seen as the world of the soul or the psyche and the lightness
and playfulness of being—all characteristics of the spirit of the child.

Merton takes from the book that he is reading, Giuseppe Tucci's *The
Theory and Practice of the Mandala*, many thoughts about the mandala,[32]
and this too now seems significant in the context of the epiphany he was
about to have. In Sanskrit the word mandala means circle and this circular
image often contains a quaternity or a multiple of four. In Tibetan Buddhism the purpose of the figure is to assist meditation. Jung wrote extensively on the mandala as one of the oldest religious symbols of humanity
where "they signify nothing less than a psychic center of the personality
not to be identified with the ego."[33] He saw the mandala as indicative of
the archetype of wholeness where four parts are held together in the idea of
the squaring of the circle. For Jung the object of the mandala is to express
"the *self* in contradistinction to the *ego*, which is only the point of reference
for consciousness, whereas the self comprises the totality of the psyche altogether, i.e., conscious *and* unconscious."[34] In this way the mandala could
be seen as an image of the integrated self, which is the integration of the
shadow and awareness of the illusory nature of the disguise, an organized
innocence beyond experience, the state of spiritual maturity.

From his reading about the mandala, Merton highlights the realization
that "the mystic knows that the principle of salvation is within . . ." The work
is to search for this principle and through will-power and vigilance to understand that it is the forces of the psyche that both binds (i.e., restricts) but
that can also provide "the means of salvation provided that he knows how
to penetrate into his psyche and subdue it." This is the recognition of the
power of the shadow and the disguise, and of the deep archetypal patterns

31. Merton, *Other Side of the Mountain*, 240–41.

32. Tucci, *Theory and Practice*.

33. Jung, *Psychology and Alchemy*, 99.

34. Jung, *Archetypes*, 389.

such as the child archetype that can both inhibit and lead to release. On 3 November 1968 Merton confirms that it is not liberation from the body but liberation from the mind that is important. "We are not entangled in our own body but entangled in our own mind."[35]

These insights took place in the weeks before Merton's visit to the ancient site at Polonnaruwa with its ruins of palaces and temples, and four huge figures of Buddha and one of his disciples. He writes that it "was such an experience that I could not write hastily of it and cannot write now, or not at all adequately."[36] What we read is then a diluted account of this vivid, immediate here-and-now glimpse of God.

It was an experience which in a strange way seemed to prefigure the totally unexpected event which took place in Bangkok nine days later when Merton's chance encounter with a faulty electric fan caused a major heart attack from which he died. What on 2 December was spiritual awareness became on 10 December spiritual reality. "Merton's transitory experience of Divinity at the feet of the great Buddhas was transformed into full communion with God. Insight became sight. Prophetic hint became Eternal Vision."[37]

In Merton's journal account, from which extracts are given below, there are examples of the characteristics of childhood spirituality but filtered through the adult spiritual maturity of his twenty-seven years in the monastery at Gethsemani. The two positions or states are integrated and through the mechanism of the transcendent function there arises the epiphanic moment of the child mind. Merton writes of his ability (and this is not merely about physical ability) "to approach the Buddhas barefoot and undisturbed." Whilst the very taking off of shoes is reminiscent of biblical admonitions of walking on holy ground, it can also stand as a metaphor for the necessary stripping away of the superficial self (the disguise). Here barefoot and undisturbed implies in the right frame of mind, free from the past and future egoic concerns. For Merton's long journey of integration of the past (the shadow), is part of what allows him to approach the statues unencumbered. Merton is standing freely no longer tied to roles, structures, institutions, but conscious and alive.

He seems completely in the moment and tuned in to feeling at one with nature and any heightened aesthetic experience when he writes, "I don't know when in my life I have ever had such a sense of beauty and spiritual validity running together in one aesthetic illumination." There is a

35. Merton, *Other Side of the Mountain*, 244.

36. Ibid., 322–24.

37. Weis, "The Birds Ask," 11.

sense of the uninterrupted flow of experience when concentrated attention gives way to a liberating feeling and action and awareness become merged. There is a sense of the activity almost managing itself or being managed by an outside influence, the whole thing transformed into a single flow. "Looking at those figures [here is the effort-filled attentiveness] I was suddenly, almost forcibly, jerked clean out of the habitual, half-tied vision of things, and an inner clearness, clarity, as if exploding from the rocks themselves, became evident and obvious [something transcending the self takes on the activity of looking]."

Part of Merton's awareness is of the mystery and the sense that part of the experience is incomprehensible. He writes in the same journal entry:

> . . . the peace not of emotional resignation but of Madhyamika, of *sunyata*, that has seen through every question without trying to discredit anyone or anything—without refutation—without establishing some other argument. For the doctrinaire, the mind that needs well-established positions, such peace, such silence, can be frightening.

His experience was of: "The queer evidence of the reclining figure, the smile, the sad smile of Ananda standing with arms folded." And from this looking came the epiphany:

> The thing about all this is that there is no puzzle, no problem, and really no "mystery." All problems are resolved and everything is clear, simply because what matters is clear. The rock, all matter, all life, is charged with dharmakaya—everything is emptiness and everything is compassion. I don't know when in my life I have ever had such a sense of beauty and spiritual validity running together in one aesthetic illumination. Surely, . . . my Asian pilgrimage has come clear and purified itself. I mean, I know and have seen what I was obscurely looking for. I don't know what else remains but I have now seen and have pierced through the surface and got beyond the shadow and the disguise.[38]

The evocative passage describing this vision offers a frame to explore the idea of spiritual maturity. For those moments Merton was able to get beyond the shadow and the disguise and experience the Reality: the clarity and simplicity of the emptiness and compassion. Merton glimpsed the deep union with God and it was at this moment that his thinking on the false and true self was actualized in his own inner world and in the child mind. As

---

38. Merton, *Other Side of the Mountain*, 322–23.

an aside there is an interesting resonance in this experience of clarity and purity with the Quaker, George Fox who on his death bed said: "Now I am clear, I am fully clear."[39]

For Merton, the inward vision was also deeply personal and the culmination of the personal searching and struggle in relationship with God. At the end of his talk on "A Life without Care," discussed earlier in the book, Merton says that our vocation is the same vocation as the disciples on the road to Emmaus. "This is what we are all here for. We are all here to see the Lord, and to see with the eyes of faith."[40] Merton in a state of relational consciousness experienced in front of those statues the innocence of his true self, the spirit of the eternal child, and glimpsed the divine. There is a biblical injunction to behold, which can be seen in this context as meaning the sense of awareness of inward vision and where "behold" is appropriate "only to the invisible kingdom of heaven within you and that kingdom is beholding."[41] Merton *beheld* these figures.

> We become the One we gaze upon. We are, eventually, just like the God we worship. This reciprocal gaze is the True Self, perfectly given to us, and always waiting to be perfectly received. It is so dear and so precious that it needs no external payoffs whatsoever. The True Self is abundantly content as it is.[42]

39. Fox, *Christian Faith*, 12.

40. Merton, "Life Free from Care," in *Essential Writings*, 72.

41. Ross, *Writing the Icon*, 11.

42. Rohr, adapted from *Jesus and Buddha*.

Afterword

O ne of the things that happened when writing this book is that more and more examples have leapt out at me of people who had experienced the idea of the child mind and so as adults exemplified the spirit of the child. For example, watching the 1928 film made by Carl Dreyer of the trial of Joan of Arc I was moved when she confessed before her martyrdom: "Yes, I am His child." Another find was dipping into the life of the poet Francis Thompson and reading his words where he said to look for him in the nurseries of Heaven. I remembered that Philip Toynbee wrote about the goal of life, "if there is one; if I ever reach it—will certainly be seen, then as something marvellously simple. Not a child's simplicity, but the simplicity of childhood regained. So many accretions to be cut out or planed away."[1] And the French priest Jean Sulivan, I discovered, thought the only way to be a disciple is "to grow young again" where there is an "unlearning" of things: "Spiritual sanity resides in a youthfulness which spontaneously rejects everything that is static."[2]

Another occurrence was that Bible passages seemed to offer further insights into Jesus' command. So, for example, if the Lord is Alpha and Omega (Rev 1:8)—the beginning and the end—then He is also in the becoming. If "in the becoming is the Word" then it is only through His power that the transformation can occur: "he gave power to become children of God, who were born, not of blood or of the will of the flesh or of the will of man, but of God" (John 1:12b–13). As children of God we have life in all its fullness. "I came that they may have life, and have it abundantly" (John 10:10).

I described Merton in the preface as a theologian of experience. I would now add to this that he is also a theologian of feeling. It is the very human and real way in which Merton spoke about his emotions that attracts so many. As a psychoanalytic psychotherapist and spiritual director it

1. Toynbee, *Part of a Journey,* 65.

2. Sulivan, *Morning Light,* 51 and 121.

was Merton's ability to understand both the psychological and spiritual and the connections and differences between them that so appealed to me. And dotted here and there in his writings is reference to what it might mean to restore the spirit of the child. Often in his writings is the idea of potential, new beginnings, growth, and becoming, and a realization that it is there for the having—a gift and a grace.

Often theologians and spiritual writers are supposed to know and to understand but most spiritual experiences remain a sort of supposition, a possibility that something that seemed unknowable has miraculously appeared and this has happened both within and perhaps around oneself. George Fox wrote about his conversion, "And this I knew experimentally" meaning experientially. Similarly Merton's realization, his knowing about his experience and his awareness of the need to get beyond the shadow and the disguise helps the reader to contemplate this opportunity.

The way of the child mind becomes an openness and acceptance of the mystery that connects everything living on earth. The suggestion made in this book is that Jesus' command "unless you become" is to send us back to ourselves at a deeper and earlier level, and together with adult wisdom move us towards a sense of a wholeness that can be called the child mind. It is a call to inner upheaval and a link to awakening, to awareness of the vertical instant, where Jesus invites us to re-birth in the spirit.

Donald Allchin wrote, "the life of humanity in time is constantly touched by moments of eternity and . . . these moments in which time and eternity meet are moments of redemption."[3] Each such moment is about being in a state of immanence, a proclamation of birth and a coming into life.

> See what love the father has given us, that we should be called children of God; and that is what we are. . . . Beloved, we are God's children now; what we will be has not yet been revealed. What we do know is this: when he is revealed we will be like him, for we will see him as he is. (1 John 3:1a and 2)

To follow Christ's command and to become as small children in our spiritual life requires a great leap of the imagination. The model is ultimately the Christ child who is smaller than small and bigger than big where wholeness is of immeasurable extent, older and younger than consciousness and enfolding it in terms of time and space. The spirit of the child is an awakening, an annunciation of something we can become. The ultimate is the incarnation of the Christ child—the moment of consciousness when in our

---

3. Allchin, *Joy of All Creation*, 184.

own child mind, glimpsing beyond the shadow and the disguise we fulfil our vocation and can say "I have seen the Lord."

Richard Rohr sees the final stage of spiritual development as akin to that of the very small child that we once were running naked into the room of life. I am who I am who I am. God has accepted me in that naked being, and I can happily give myself back to God exactly as I am. I am ready for death, because I have done it now many times, and it has only led me into Larger Worlds.[4]

"The child in us is always there, you know, and it's the best part of us, the winged part that travels furthest."[5]

---

4. Rohr, adapted from, *Where You Are*.
5. Goudge, *Green Dolphin Country*, 484.

Bibiliography

Allchin, A. M. *The Joy of All Creation.* London: New City, 1993.

———. "Foreword." In *Beyond the Shadow and the Disguise* by Monica Weis, et al., 5–9. Stratton-on-the-Fosse, UK: The Thomas Merton Society of Great Britain and Ireland, 2006.

Andrewes, Lancelot. *Ninety-Six Sermons.* Library of Anglo-Catholic Theology, 2001. Online: http://anglicanhistory.org/lact/andrewes/v1/sermon11.html.

Arasteh, A. Reza. *Rumi The Persian, The Sufi.* London: Routledge, 1972.

Augustine. *Confessions.* London: Penguin, 1961.

Barker, Culver. "Healing the Child Within." In *In the Wake of Jung,* edited by Molly Tuby, 48–52. London: Coventure, 1983.

Bauman, Zygmunt. *Intimations of Postmodernity.* London: Routledge, 1992.

Benjamin, Walter. *Berlin Childhood around 1900.* Cambridge, MA: Belknap of Harvard University Press, 2006.

Berdyaev, Nicolas. *Dream and Reality, An Essay in Autobiography.* London: Geoffrey Bles, 1950.

———. *Slavery and Freedom.* London: Geoffrey Bles, 1943.

Bernanos, Georges. *The Diary of a Country Priest.* Glasgow: Collins Fount, 1937.

Bernard of Clairvaux. *On the Song of Songs* 1. Translated by Kiliam Walsh. Cistercian Fathers Series 4. Spencer, MA: Cistercian, 1971.

Berryman, Jerome W. "Children and Mature Spirituality." In *Children's Spirituality: Christian Perspectives, Research and Applications,* edited by Donald Ratcliff, 22–41. Eugene, OR: Cascade, 2004.

Blake, William. *The Complete Writings of William Blake.* London: Oxford University Press, 1966.

Bloch, Ernst. *The Principle of Hope.* Translated by Neville Plaice, Stephen Plaice and David Knight, Cambridge, MA: MIT Press, 1986.

Bochen, Christine M. "Calligraphies." In *The Thomas Merton Encyclopedia,* edited by William H. Shannon et al., 38–40. Maryknoll, NY: Orbis, 2002.

———. "Le Point Vierge." In *The Thomas Merton Encyclopedia,* edited by William H. Shannon et al., 363–64. Maryknoll, NY: Orbis, 2002.

Bollas, Christopher. *Forces of Destiny: Psychoanalysis and Human Idiom.* London: Free Associations, 1989.

Bronte, Charlotte. *Jane Eyre,* London: Penguin, 1966.

Burrows, Ruth. *Love Unknown.* London: Continuum, 2011.

Capra, Fritjof. *The Tao of Physics.* Berkeley, CA: Shambhala, 1975.

Catherine of Siena. *Catherine of Siena: Selected Spiritual Writings*. Edited by Mary O'Driscoll. Hyde Park, NY: New City, 2005.

Cohen, Josh. *The Private Life: Why We Remain in the Dark*. London: Granta, 2013.

Cohen, Kenneth. "Beginner's Mind." *Experience Life*. 2004. Online: https://experiencelife.com/article/beginners-mind/.

Connolly, Cyril. *Enemies of Promise*. London: Andre Deutsch, 1938.

Cunningham, Lawrence. *Thomas Merton and the Monastic Vision*. Grand Rapids: Eerdmans, 1999.

de Trinis, Randall. "A Novice and His Master." *The Merton Seasonal* 34 (2009) 13–27.

Dekar, Paul. "Technology and the Loss of Paradise." In *Thomas Merton: Monk on the Edge*, edited by Ross Labrie and Angus Stuart, 65–78. North Vancouver, BC: Thomas Merton Society of Canada, 2012.

Dillard, Annie. *The Annie Dillard Reader*. New York: HarperPerennial, 1994.

du Boulay, Shirley. *The Cave of the Heart, the Life of Swami Abhishiktananda*. Maryknoll, NY: Orbis, 2005.

Eiland, Howard. "Foreword." In *Berlin Childhood Around 1900* by Walter Benjamin, vii–xvi. Cambridge, MA: Belknap, Harvard University Press, 2006.

Ellwood, Robert. *The Politics of Myth*. Albany, NY: State University of New York Press, 1999.

Finley, James. *Merton's Palace of Nowhere*. Notre Dame, IN: Ave Maria, 1978.

Fowler, James W. *Stages of Faith: The Psychology of Human Development and the Quest for Meaning*. San Francisco: Harper & Row, 1981.

Fox, George. "Journal Extracts 1691." In *Christian Faith and Practice in the Experience of the Society of Friends*, edited by The Society of Friends, 1–14. London: London Yearly Meeting of the Religious Society of Friends, 1960.

Fox, Matthew. *Original Blessings*. Santa Fe, NM: Bear, 1983.

Frank, Mark. *Sermons, Volume 1*. Library of Anglo-Catholic Theology. 2002. Online: http://anglicanhistory.org/lact/frank/v1/christmas2.html.

Friedman, Joseph. "Therpaeia: Play and the Therapeutic Household." In *Thresholds between Philosophy and Psychoanalysis*, edited by Robin Cooper, et al., 56–75. London: Free Associations, 1989.

Frohlich, Mary. "Spiritual Discipline, Discipline of Spirituality: Revisiting Questions of Definition and Method." *Spiritus* 1 (2001) 65–78.

Furlong, Monica. *Thérèse of Lisieux*. London: Darton, Longman and Todd, 1987.

Gadamer, H-G. *Truth and Method*. London: Sheed and Ward, 1979.

Gardner, Fiona. *The Four Steps of Love*. London: Darton, Longman and Todd, 2007.

———. *Journeying Home*. London: Darton, Longman and Todd, 2004.

———. "Thomas Merton and Dr Gregory Zilboorg: Understanding the Dynamics" *The Merton Journal* 11 (2004) 6–12.

Garnett, Angelica. *Deceived with Kindness*. London: Pimlico, 1995.

Gascoyne, David. *Holderlin's Madness*. London: J. M. Dent, 1938. Online: http://archive.org/details/hlderlinsmadneoogasc.

Gheon, Henri. *The Secret of the Little Flower*. New York: Sheed and Ward, 1934. Online: www.ewtn.com/library/MARY/SLF.htm.

Girard, Francois. "Spiritual Childhood—Life in the Spirit: Fr. Marie-Eugene and St Thérèse." *Mount Carmel* 57 (2009) 69–78.

Goergen, Donald J. O. P. "Globalization of Hope." Presented at the Dominican Leadership Conference Annual Meeting. Adrian, MI: October, 2002. Online: http://goergen.domcentral.org/globalization.htm.

Goudge, Elizabeth. *Green Dolphin Country.* London: Hodder and Stoughton, 1956.

———. *The Heart of the Family.* Bungay and Suffolk: Hodder and Stoughton, 1953.

Graham, Dom Aelred. *Zen Catholicism.* New York: Harcourt, Brace and World, 1963.

Griffiths, Bede. *The Golden String.* Glasgow: Collins, 1979.

Guntrip, Harry. "Analysis with Fairbairn and Winnicott." In *Collected Papers,* edited by Jeremy Hazell, 351–70. Northvale: Jason Aronson, 1994.

Hall, Gary. "The Child in the Rain." *The Merton Journal* 19 (2012) 33–41.

Hannah, Barbara. "The Beyond (Death and Renewal in East and West)." In *In the Wake of Jung,* edited by Molly Tuby, 112–28. London: Coventure, 1983.

Haraway, Donna J. *Simians, Cyborgs, and Women: The Reinvention of Nature.* London: Free Associations, 1991.

Hart, Tobin. *The Secret Spiritual World of Children.* Makawao, HI: Inner Ocean, 2003.

Hay, David, and Nye, Rebecca. *The Spirit of the Child.* London: Harper Collins, 1998.

Heaney, Seamus. "The Door Stands Open." In *Czeslaw Milosz, Selected and Last Poems 1931–2004,* edited by Robert Hass and Anthony Milosz, xv–xviii. New York: HarperCollins, 2006.

Heschel, Abraham. *The Insecurity of Freedom.* New York: Schocken, 1972.

Hildegard of Bingen. "Quotations by Hildegardof Bingen. *Spirituality and Practice.* 2012. Online: http://www.spiritualityandpractice.com/books/features.php?id=20274.

Horan, Daniel. *The Franciscan Heart of Thomas Merton.* Notre Dame, IN: Ave Maria, 2014.

Huxley, Aldous. *The Perennial Philosophy.* London: Collins, Fontana, 1963.

Ibsen, Henrik. *John Gabriel Borkman.* In *The Master Builder and Other Plays,* edited by Betty Radice and Robert Baldrick, 285–376. London: Penguin, 1958.

Jarrell, Randall. "On Preparing to Read Kipling." In *Kipling and the Critics,* edited by Elliot L. Gilbert, 133–49. London: Peter Owen, 1965.

John of the Cross. *The Collected Works of St. John of the Cross.* Translated by Kieran Kavanaugh, OCD and Otilio Rodriguez, OCD, Washington, DC: ICS, 1991.

Johnson, Robert A. *Balancing Heaven and Earth.* New York: HarperCollins, 1998.

Johnston, William. *"Arise My Love . . ." Mysticism for a New Era.* Maryknoll, NY: Orbis, 2000.

———. *The Mirror Mind, Spirituality and Transformation.* London: Fount, 1981.

———. *Mystical Journey.* Maryknoll, NY: Orbis, 2006.

Jones, Rufus. "Spiritual Experiences of Friends." In *Christian Faith and Practice in the Experience of the Society of Friends,* 91–93. London: London Yearly Meeting, 1959.

Julian of Norwich. *Revelations of Divine Love.* London: Hodder and Stoughton, 1987.

Jung, C. G. *The Archetypes and the Collective Unconscious, C. G. Jun, The Collected Works Volume Nine.* London: Routledge and Kegan Paul, 1959.

———. *The Development of Personality, C. G. Jung The Collected Works, Volume Seventeen.* London: Routledge and Kegan Paul, 1954.

———. *Memories, Dreams, Reflections.* London: Collins Fount, 1963.

———. *Psychology and Alchemy, C. G. Jung The Collected Works, Volume Twelve.* Princeton, New Jersey: Princeton University Press, 1968.

———. *Psychology and Religion: West and East, C. G. Jung The Collected Works, Volume Eleven.* London: Routledge and Kegan Paul, 1969.

———. *The Structure and Dynamics of the Psyche, C. G. Jung The Collected Works Volume Eight*. London: Routledge and Kegan Paul, 1960.

Kalsched, Donald. *The Inner World of Trauma*. London and New York: Routledge, 1996.

Keats, John. "On Negative Capability: Letter to George and Tom Keats." In "Selections from Keats's Letters (1818)." *Poetry Foundation*. Online: http://www.poetryfoundation.org/learning/essay/237836?page=2.

Kennedy, Robert E. *Zen Spirit, Christian Spirit*. New York and London: Continuum, 2005.

Khan, Pir Vilayat Inayat. *That Which Transpires Behind That Which Appears*. New Lebanon: Omega, 1994.

Kristeva, Julia. "Revolution in Poetic Language." In *The Kristeva Reader*, edited by Toril Moi, 89–136, Oxford: Blackwell, 1986.

Lacan, Jacques. *Ecrits: A Selection*. London: Routledge, 1977.

Laing, R. D. *The Divided Self*. Harmondsworth: Pelican, 1960.

———. *Wisdom, Madness and Folly*. London: Macmillan, 1985.

Lao-tzu. *Tao Te Ching, Sacred Books of the East*. Translated by J. Legge, 1891. Online: http://www.sacred-texts.com/tao/taote.htm.

Lewis, C. S. *Surprised by Joy*. London: Fount Paperbacks, 1998.

Maritain, Raissa. *Raissa's Journal*. Albany, NY: Magi, 1974.

Matthews, Melvyn. *Awake to God: Explorations in the Mystical Way*. London: SPCK, 2006.

———. *Both Alike to Thee: The Retrieval of the Mystical Way*. London: SPCK, 2000.

Merton, Thomas. *The Asian Journal*. London: Sheldon, 1973.

———. "Blake and the New Theology." In *The Literary Essays of Thomas Merton*, edited by Br Patrick Hart, 3–11. New York: New Directions, 1981.

———. *The Collected Poems of Thomas Merton*. New York: New Directions, 1977.

———. *Conjectures of a Guilty Bystander*. Tunbridge Wells: Burns and Oates, 1966.

———. *Contemplation in a World of Action*. London: Unwin, 1980.

———. *Contemplative Prayer*. London: Darton, Longman and Todd, 1973.

———. *The Courage for Truth: The Letters of Thomas Merton to Writers*. Selected and edited by Christine M. Bochen. London: Harcourt Brace, 1993.

———. *Dancing in the Water of Life, The Journals of Thomas Merton, Volume Five, 1963–1965*. Edited by Robert E. Daggy. New York: HarperCollins, 1997.

———. "Day of a Stranger." In *Selected Essays*, edited by Patrick O'Connell, 232–39. Maryknoll, NY: Orbis, 2013.

———. *Entering the Silence. The Journals of Thomas Merton, Volume Two 1941–1952*. Edited by Jonathon Montaldo. New York: HarperCollins, 1996.

———. *Exile Ends in Glory*. Milwaukee, WI: Bruce, 1948.

———. *Faith and Violence*. Notre Dame, IN: University of Notre Dame Press, 1968.

———. "Final Integration: Toward a 'Monastic Therapy.'" In *Selected Essays*, edited by Patrick O'Connell, 452–62. Maryknoll, NY: Orbis 2013.

———. *The Hidden Ground of Love, The Letters of Thomas Merton on Religious Experience and Social Concerns*. Selected and edited by William H. Shannon. London: Collins Flame, 1985.

———. *The Inner Experience*. London: SPCK, 2003.

———. "Introduction." In *The Golden Age of Zen* by John Wu, edited by 1–23. Bloomington, IN: World Wisdom, 2003.

———. *An Introduction to Christian Mysticism: Initiation into the Monastic Tradition 3.* Edited by Patrick F. O'Connell. Kalamazoo, MI: Cistercian, 2008.

———. *Learning to Love, The Journals of Thomas Merton, Volume Six 1966–1967.* Edited by Christine M. Bochen. New York: Harper Collins, 1997.

———. "A Life Free from Care." In *Essential Writings* selected by Christine M. Bochen, 67–71. Maryknoll, NY: Orbis, 2000.

———. *Life and Holiness.* New York, London: Doubleday, 1963.

———. "Louis Zukofsky—The Paradise Ear." In *The Literary Essays of Thomas Merton.* Edited by Br Patrick Hart, 128–33. New York: New Directions, 1981.

———. *Love and Living.* London: Sheldon, 1979.

———. "Message to Poets." In *The Literary Essays of Thomas Merton,* edited by Br Patrick Hart, 371–74. New York: New Directions, 1981.

———. *The Monastic Journey.* Kansas City: Sheed Andrews and McMell, 1977.

———. *My Argument with the Gestapo.* New York: New Directions, 1969.

———. *Mystics and Zen Masters,* New York: Farrar, Straus and Giroux, 1967.

———. "Nature and Art in William Blake." In *The Literary Essays of Thomas Merton,* edited by Br Patrick Hart, 387–453. New York: New Directions, 1981.

———. "A New Birth." In *Essential Writings.* Selected by Christine M. Bochen, 62–67. Maryknoll, NY: Orbis, 2000.

———. *The New Man.* New York: Farrar, Straus and Giroux, 1961.

———. *New Seeds of Contemplation.* London: Burns Oates, 1961.

———. *No Man is an Island.* London: Hollis and Carter, 1955.

———. *The Other Side of the Mountain, The Journals of Thomas Merton, Volume seven 1967–1968.* Edited Patrick Hart, New York: Harper Collins, 1998.

———. "Poetry and Contemplation: A Reappraisal." In *The Literary Essays of Thomas Merton,* edited by Patrick Hart, 338–54. New York: New Directions, 1981.

———. *Raids on the Unspeakable.* New York: New Directions, 1964.

———. "The Recovery of Paradise." In *Selected Essays,* edited by Patrick O'Connell, 52–64. Maryknoll, NY: Orbis, 2013.

———. *The Road to Joy: The Letters of Thomas Merton to New and Old Friends.* Selected and edited by Robert E. Daggy. London: Collins Flame, 1989.

———. *Run to the Mountain, The Journals of Thomas Merton, Volume One 1939–1941.* Edited by Patrick Hart. New York: HarperCollins, 1995.

———. *The School of Charity: The Letters of Thomas Merton on Religious Renewal and Spiritual Direction.* Selected and edited by Br Patrick Hart. London: Harcourt Brace Jovanovich, 1990.

———. *A Search for Solitude: The Journals of Thomas Merton, Volume Three 1952–1960.* Edited by Lawrence S. Cunningham. New York: HarperCollins, 1997.

———. *The Seven Storey Mountain.* New York: Harcourt, Brace, 1948.

———. *The Sign of Jonas.* London: Hollis and Carter, 1953.

———. *Spiritual Direction and Meditation.* Collegeville, MN: Liturgical, 1960.

———. "Theology of Creativity." In *The Literary Essays of Thomas Merton,* edited by Br Patrick Hart, 355–70. New York: New Directions, 1981.

———. *Thomas Merton on Zen.* London: Sheldon, 1976.

———. *Thoughts in Solitude.* Boston: Shambala, 1993.

———. *Turning Towards the World: The Journals of Thomas Merton, Volume Four 1960–1963.* Edited by Victor A. Kramer. New York: HarperCollins, 1996.

———. *The Way of Chuang Tzu.* New York: New Directions, 1965.

————. *The Wisdom of the Desert*. London: Hollis and Carter, 1960.

————. *Witness to Freedom, Letters in Times of Crisis*. Selected and edited by William H. Shannon. New York: Farrar, Straus and Giroux, 1994.

————. *Zen and the Birds of Appetite*. New York: New Directions, 1968.

Meynell, Alice. *Poems and Essays on Children*. Charleston, SC: BiblioBazaar, 2006.

Miller, Alice. *The Drama of Being a Child*. London: Virago, 1988.

————. *Thou Shalt Not Be Aware*. London: Pluto, 1984.

Miller, Jeffrey C. *The Transcendent Function*. New York: State University of New York Press, 2004.

Monnin, Abbé Alfred. *Life of Jean-Baptist Vianney Curé d'Ars*. London: Burns Oates and Washbourne, 1861.

Montaldo, Jonathan. "Thomas Merton and Spiritual Maturity." *The Merton Seasonal* 38 (2013) 17–29.

Moore, Sebastian. "Presence." *Sermon*. Downside Abbey, unpublished, 2012.

————. "The True Terror." *Sermon*. Downside Abbey, unpublished, 2013.

Morson, John. *Christ the Way*. Kalamazoo, MI: Cistercian, 1978.

Moses, John. *Divine Discontent*. London: Bloomsbury Continuum, 2014.

Mott, Michael. *The Seven Mountains of Thomas Merton*. Boston: Houghton Mifflin, 1984.

O'Connell, Patrick. "'The Surest Home Is Pointless': A Pathless Path through Merton's Poetic Corpus." *CrossCurrents* 58.4 (2008) 522–44. Online: www.freepatentsonline.com/article/Cross-Currents/198114915html.

Okri, Ben. *The Famished Road*. London: Jonathon Cape, 1991.

Orsi, Robert A. "A Crisis about the Theology of Children." *Harvard Divinity Bulletin* 30 (2002) 27–29.

Paulsell, Stephanie. "Lost in the Mystery of God: Childhood in the History of Christian Spirituality." *Spiritus* 8 (2008) 83–96.

Pearson, Paul M., ed. "Inseeing and Outgazing: The Shared Vision of Thomas Merton and Rainer Maria Rilke." Online: Merton.org/ITMS/Seasonal/24–2Pearson.pdf. 10–17.

————. *Thomas Merton, Seeking Paradise, The Spirit of the Shakers*. Maryknoll, NY: Orbis, 2003.

Péguy, Charles. "The Mystery of the Holy Innocents." Online: http://www.cin.org/liter/holyinno1.html.

Petisco, Sonia. "Thomas Merton's Antipoetry." *The Merton Journal* 8 (2001) 30–34.

Petitot, H. "A Spiritual Renaissance." In *Christian Simplicity in St Thérèse*, edited by Michael Day, 10–37. London: Burns Oates, 1953.

Phillips, Adam. *Winnicott*. London: Fontana, 1988.

Pickering, Sue. *Spiritual Direction*. Norwich: Canterbury, 2008.

Prater, Donald. *A Ringing Glass: The Life of Rainer Maria Rilke*. Oxford: Clarendon, 1986.

Politella, Joseph. "Meister Eckhart and Eastern Wisdom." In *Philosophy East and West* 15.2 (1965) 117–33.

Pramuk, Christopher. *Sophia: The Hidden Christ of Thomas Merton*. Collegeville, MN: Liturgical, 2009.

Privett, Peter. "I God Am Your Playmate." *Manna* 13 (2013) 16–18.

Pye, Fay. "Transformations of the Persona." In *In the Wake of Jung*, edited by Molly Tuby, 41–47 London: Coventure, 1983.

Rahner, Karl. "Ideas for a Theology of Childhood." In *Theological Investigations: Further Theology of the Spiritual Life Volume 8*, 33–50. London: Darton, Longman and Todd, 1971.

Raine, Kathleen. *Autobiographies*. London: Skoob, 1991.

———. *Defending Ancient Springs*. Suffolk: Golgonooza, 1985.

———. *India Seen Afar*. Devon: Green, 1990.

———. *William Blake*. London: Longmans, Green, 1951.

Reagan, Charles. "Paul, Ricoeur." In *Dictionary of Philosophy*, edited by Thomas Mautner, 534–36. London: Penguin, 2005.

Ricoeur, Paul. *The Symbolism of Evil*. Translated by Emerson Buchanan. Boston: Buchanan, 1969.

Rilke, Rainer Maria. *Letters to a Young Poet*. 1903. http://www.carrothers.com/rilke6.htm

Robinson, Edward. *The Original Vision, Studies in Religious Experience*. Manchester University: The Religious Experience Research Unit, 1977.

Rodman, F. Robert. *Winnicott*. Cambridge, MA: Da Capo, 2003.

Rohr, Richard. *Jesus and Buddha: Paths to Awakening*. 2008. Audio Recording. Online: http://store.cac.org/Jesus-and-Buddha-Paths-to-Awakening_p_97.html.

———. *The Naked Now: Learning to See as the Mystics See*. New York: Crossroad, 2009.

———. "Original Innocence." In *True Self, False Self*. 2014. Online: http://myemail.constantcontact.com/Richard-Rohr-s-Meditation—Original-Innocence.html?soid=1103098668616&aid=nHeDJTjtFJM.

———. *Where You Are is Where I'll Meet You: A Guide for Spiritual Directors*. 2008. Audio Recording. Online: http://store.cac.org/Where-You-Are-is-Where-Ill-Meet-You—A-Guide-for-Spiritual-Directors-CD_p_138.html.

Ross, Hugh McGregor. *Jesus Untouched by the Church: His Teachings in the Gospel of Thomas*. York, England: William Sessions, 1998.

Ross, Maggie. *Writing the Icon of the Heart: In Silence Beholding*. Abingdon: The Bible Reading Fellowship, 2011.

Rupp, Joyce. *The Cosmic Dance, An Invitation to Experience our Oneness*. 2010. Online: http://www.joycerupp.com/CosmicDance.htm.

Rush, Anne Kent. *Getting Clear*. London: Wildwood House, 1973.

Ryan, J. Linus. *Edith Piaf and Thérèse of Lisieux*. Online: http://canticleofchiara.blogspot.co.uk/2007/12/edith-piaf-and-st-therese.html.

Sagar, Keith. "William Blake: Songs of Innocence and Experience." 2002. http://www.keithsagar.co.uk/blake/.

Sahn, Seung. *Zen Master: Child's Mind is Buddha's Mind*. Question-and-Answer Period at the Empty Gate (Berkeley KBC) Zen Center, 1977. Online: http://www.kwanumzen.org/?teaching=childs-mind-is-buddhas-mind.

Sa Nim, Soen. "Child's Mind is Buddha's Mind" The Kwan Um School of Zen and Providence Zen Center, 1977. Online: http://buddhism.org/board/read.cgi?board=KwanumZen&y_number=342

Samuels, Andrew. *Jung and the Post-Jungians*. London: Routledge and Kegan Paul, 1985.

Saward, John. *Perfect Fools*. Oxford: Oxford University Press, 1980.

———. *The Way of the Lamb*. Edinburgh: T. & T. Clark, 1999.

Schiller, Friedrich. "Letters upon the Aesthetic Education of Man." The Harvard Classics 1909–1914. Online: http://www.bartleby.com/32/515.html.

Schloegl, Irmgard (Ven Myokyo-ni). "Introduction." In *Thomas Merton on Zen*. London: Sheldon, 1976.

———. *The Zen Teachings of Rinzai*. Berkeley, CA: Shambhala, 1975.

Schneiders, Sandra M. *Women and the Word: The Gender of God in the New Testament and the Spirituality of Women*. New York: Paulist, 1986.

Shannon, William H. "Mercy." In *The Thomas Merton Encyclopedia*, 292–93. Maryknoll, NY: Orbis, 2002.

———. "Self." In *The Thomas Merton Encyclopedia*. Maryknoll, NY: Orbis, 2002, 417–20.

———. "Tom's Book." In *The Thomas Merton Encyclopedia*. Maryknoll, NY: Orbis, 2002, 489–90.

Shaw, Jeffrey M. *Illusions of Freedom*. Cambridge: Lutterworth, 2014.

Shelley, Percy Bysshe. *Poems of Shelley*. London: Blackie and Son, 1926.

Short, William. "Franciscan Spirituality." In *The New SCM Dictionary of Christian Spirituality*, edited by Philip Sheldrake, 310–12. London: SCM, 2005.

Singer, June. *Seeing Through the Visible World*. London: Hyman, 1990.

Smith, Huston. Preface to *Meister Eckhart: The Essential Sermons, Commentaries, Treatises, and Defense*. Translated and introduction by Edmund Colledge, OSA and Bernard McGinn, xi–xv. New York: Paulist, 1981.

Stapledon, Olaf. *The Opening of the Eyes*. London: Methuen, 1954.

Stevens, Anthony. *On Jung*. London: Routledge, 1990.

Soelle, Dorothee. *The Silent Cry: Mysticism and Resistance*. Minneapolis: Fortress, 2001.

Sulivan, Jean. *Morning Light: The Spiritual Journal of Jean Sulivan*. New York: Paulist, 1988.

Suther, Judith. *Raissa Maritain*. New York: Fordham University Press, 1990.

Suzuki, Shunryu. *Zen Mind, Beginner's Mind: Informal Talks on Zen Meditation and Practice*. 2015. Online: https://www.goodreads.com/author/quotes/62707.Shunryu_Suzuki.

Symington, Neville. *The Spirit of Sanity*. London: Karnac, 2001.

Szondi, Peter. "Hope in the Past: On Walter Benjamin." In *Berlin Childhood around 1900* by Walter Benjamin, 1–33. Cambridge, MA: Belknap, Harvard University Press, 2006.

Tang, Delai. "The Meeting of John Wu with St Therese of Lisieux in the Context of the China Mission." Unpublished thesis for the Master of Religious Study in University of Saint Joseph, Macao. 2011. Online: http://delaitang.blogspot.co.uk/2011/01/meeting-of-john-wu-with-st-therese-of.html.

Taylor, Charles. *A Secular Age*. Cambridge, MA: Belknap of Harvard University Press, 2007.

Teasdale, Wayne. *The Mystic Heart*. Novato, CA: New World Library, 1999.

Thérèse of Lisieux. *Autobiography of a Saint*. London: Collins Fontana, 1958.

Thompson, Phillip M. *Returning to Reality*. Cambridge: Lutterworth, 2012.

Tolle, Eckhart. *The Power of Now*. London: Hodder and Stoughton, 1999.

Toynbee, Philip. *Part of a Journey: An Autobiographical Journal 1977–1979*. London: Collins Fount, 1981.

Traherne, Thomas. *Selected Writings*. Edited by Dick Davis. Manchester: Carcanet, 1988.

Tuby, Molly. *In the Wake of Jung*. London: Coventure, 1983.

Tucci, Giuseppe. *The Theory and Practice of the Mandala*. Mineola, NY: Dover, 1961.

Turkington, Kate. *There's More to Life than Surface*. London: Penguin, 1998.

Ulanov, Ann. *Finding Space: Winnicott, God and Psychic Reality*. Louisville, KY: Westminster John Knox, 2001.

Underhill, Evelyn. *Mysticism*. London: Methuen, 1960.

Vaughan, Henry. "Childe-hood." In *Selected Poems*, selected and introduced by Anne Cluysenaar, 151–52. London: SPCK, 2004.

Walker Bynum, Caroline. *Jesus as Mother: Studies in the Spirituality of the High Middle Ages*. London: University of California Press, 1982.

Weil, Simone. *Gravity and Grace*. London and New York: Routledge, 1999.

Weis, Monica. "The Birds Ask: 'Is it Time to Be?' Thomas Merton's Moments of Spiritual Awakening." In *Beyond the Shadow and the Disguise, Three Essays on Thomas Merton*, 10–27. Stratton-on-the-Fosse: Thomas Merton Society of Great Britain and Ireland, 2006.

———. *The Environmental Vision of Thomas Merton*. Lexington, KY: The University Press of Kentucky, 2011.

———. *Thomas Merton's Gethsemani, Landscapes of Paradise*. Lexington, KY: The University Press of Kentucky, 2005.

Williams, Rowan. *Lost Icons, Reflections of Cultural Bereavement*. Edinburgh: T & T. Clark, 2000.

———. "New Words for God." In *A Silent Action, Engagements with Thomas Merton*, 43–51. Louisville, KY: Fons Vitae, 2011.

———. "Not Being Serious." In *A Silent Action, Engagements with Thomas Merton*, 71–82. Louisville, KY: Fons Vitae, 2011.

Winnicott, D. W. *The Maturational Processes and the Facilitating Environment*. London: Hogarth and the Institute of Psycho-Analysis, 1982.

———. *Playing and Reality*. London: Penguin, 1971.

Woodcock, George. *Thomas Merton, Monk and Poet: A Critical Study*. Edinburgh: Canongate, 1978.

Wordsworth, William. "Ode: Intimations of Immortality from Recollections of Early Childhood." In *Wordsworth*, selected by W. E. Williams, 71–77. London: Penguin, 1950.

Wu, John. *The Golden Age of Zen*. Bloomington, IN: World Wisdom, 2003.

———. *The Science of Love, A Study in the Teachings of Therese of Lisieux*, 1941. Online: http://www.ewtn.com/library/spirit/sci-love.txt.

Zeal, Paul. "Hazards to Desire." In *Thresholds between Philosophy and Psychoanalysis*, edited by Robin Cooper et al., 167–90. London: Free Associations, 1989.

Zentner, Marcel, and Tuomas Eerola. "Rhythmic Engagement with Music in Infancy." *Proceedings of the National Academy of Sciences* 107 (2010) 5768–73.

Index

CPSIA information can be obtained
at www.ICGtesting.com
Printed in the USA
LVHW091324070319
609843LV00001B/145/P